THE SECOND LANGUAGE LEARNING PROCESSES OF STUDENTS WITH SPECIFIC LEARNING DIFFICULTIES

The Second Language Learning Processes of Students with Specific Learning Difficulties is the only recent book available to offer a detailed and in-depth discussion of the second language learning processes of students with specific learning difficulties (SpLDs). It summarizes research advances in the fields of cognitive and educational psychology and integrates them with recent studies in the area of second language acquisition (SLA). Thus the book is relevant not only to readers who are particularly interested in the role of specific learning difficulties in learning additional languages, but also to those who would like to understand how individual differences in cognitive functioning influence SLA. The book focuses on four important areas that are particularly relevant for language learners with SpLDs: the processes of SLA in general and the development of reading skills in particular, the effectiveness of pedagogical programmes, the assessment of the language competence of students with SpLDs and identifying SpLDs in another language. The book also views learners with SpLDs in their social and educational contexts and elaborates how the barriers in these contexts can affect their language learning processes. This is an excellent resource for language teachers, students and researchers in the areas of second language acquisition and applied linguistics.

Judit Kormos is Professor of Second Language Acquisition at Lancaster University, UK. She was a key partner in the award-winning Dyslexia for Teachers of English as a Foreign Language project. She is the lead educator in the Dyslexia and Language Teaching massive open online learning course. She has published widely on the effect of dyslexia on processes of second language learning.

SECOND LANGUAGE ACQUISITION RESEARCH SERIES
Susan M. Gass and Alison Mackey, Series Editors

Recent Monographs on Theoretical Issues:

Philp/Adams/Iwashita
Peer Interaction and Second Language Learning (2013)

VanPatten/Williams
Theories in Second Language Acquisition, Second Edition (2014)

Leow
Explicit Learning in the L2 Classroom (2015)

Dörnyei/Ryan
The Psychology of the Language Learner – Revisited (2015)

Kormos
The Second Language Learning Processes of Students with Specific Learning Difficulties (2017)

Recent Monographs on Research Methodology:

Bowles
The Think-Aloud Controversy in Second Language Research (2010)

Jiang
Conducting Reaction Time Research for Second Language Studies (2011)

Barkhuizen/Benson/Chik
Narrative Inquiry in Language Teaching and Learning Research (2013)

Jegerski/VanPatten
Research Methods in Second Language Psycholinguistics (2013)

Larson-Hall
A Guide to Doing Statistics in Second Language Research Using SPSS and R, Second Edition (2015)

Plonsky
Advancing Quantitative Methods in Second Language Research (2015)

De Costa
Ethics in Applied Linguistics Research: Language Researcher Narratives (2015)

Mackey and Marsden
Advancing Methodology and Practice: The IRIS Repository of Instruments for Research into Second Languages (2015)

Tomlinson
SLA Research and Materials Development for Language Learning (2016)

Gass/Mackey
Stimulated Recall Methodology in Applied Linguistics and L2 Research, Second Edition (2017)

Polio/Friedman
Understanding, Evaluating, and Conducting Second Language Writing Research (2017)

Kormos
The Second Language Learning Processes of Students with Specific Learning Difficulties (2017)

Of Related Interest:

Gass
Input, Interaction, and the Second Language Learner (1997)

Gass/Sorace/Selinker
Second Language Learning Data Analysis, Second Edition (1998)

Mackey/Gass
Second Language Research: Methodology and Design (2005)

Gass/Selinker
Second Language Acquisition: An Introductory Course, Third Edition (2008)

THE SECOND LANGUAGE LEARNING PROCESSES OF STUDENTS WITH SPECIFIC LEARNING DIFFICULTIES

Judit Kormos
LANCASTER UNIVERSITY

Sally
Carpenter

Routledge
Taylor & Francis Group

NEW YORK AND LONDON

First published 2017
by Routledge
711 Third Avenue, New York, NY 10017

and by Routledge
2 Park Square, Milton Park, Abingdon, Oxon, OX14 4RN

Routledge is an imprint of the Taylor & Francis Group, an informa business

© 2017 Taylor & Francis

Library of Congress Cataloging-in-Publication Data
Names: Kormos, Judit, author.
Title: The second language learning processes of students with specific learning difficulties / Judit Kormos.
Description: New York, NY : Routledge, [2017] | Series: Second Language Acquisition Research Series
Identifiers: LCCN 2016018729 (print) | LCCN 2016026885 (ebook) | ISBN 9781138911789 (hardback : alk. paper) | ISBN 9781138911796 (pbk. : alk. paper) | ISBN 9781315692371 (Master) | ISBN 9781317432937 (Web PDF) | ISBN 9781317432920 (ePub) | ISBN 9781317432913 (Mobipocket/Kindle)
Subjects: LCSH: Language and languages—Study and teaching. | Second language acquisition—Study and teaching. | Students with disabilities. | Dyslexia—Education.
Classification: LCC P53.818 .K57 2017 (print) | LCC P53.818 (ebook) | DDC 371.9/0446—dc23
LC record available at https://lccn.loc.gov/2016018729

ISBN: 978-1-138-91178-9 (hbk)
ISBN: 978-1-138-91179-6 (pbk)
ISBN: 978-1-315-69237-1 (ebk)

Typeset in Bembo
by Apex CoVantage, LLC

CONTENTS

FIGURES

TABLES

PREFACE

There is a large proportion of students who find language learning particularly challenging, and within this group of learners are those who have specific learning difficulties (SpLDs). Despite the fact that statistics show that 1 out of 10 students might potentially have some form of learning difficulty, such as dyslexia, language teacher education programmes rarely include any training on how to assist these language learners. When I gained my language teacher qualification 20 years ago, not even the concept of *dyslexia* was well-known to the public, and dealing with dyslexia was often delegated to the realm of medicine and psychology. My interest in researching learning difficulties in second language acquisition was sparked by several of my teacher trainees who came to me to seek advice on how to help their dyslexic students. Together with a growing group of my trainees, postgraduate research students and international colleagues, we embarked on a journey and we researched and learned together about the obstacles and barriers students with SpLDs face in the process of learning an additional language. We also investigated successful educational programmes and designed teacher development courses. Public awareness of SpLDs, in particular of dyslexia, has grown substantially in the past 20 years. I hope that through our work in the field of second language acquisition research and teacher education, language teachers will accumulate sufficient knowledge about SpLDs and will learn how to apply teaching methods and techniques that contribute to the successful inclusion of these learners in the language classroom.

In order to ensure that students with SpLDs have access to education, the job market and sometimes even to relevant daily activities, they need to be supported in acquiring additional languages. Therefore, in an age when equal opportunities for everyone is a fundamental principle of education, conducting research on how students with SpLDs acquire additional languages is our social responsibility. For the design of effective instructional programmes, we need to understand how language learners with SpLDs acquire an additional language, what barriers the educational context presents to them and how these could be overcome. It is also important to investigate how one can reliably identify SpLDs in multilingual speakers and what evidence there is for the success of specific instructional programmes.

This research monograph proposes a comprehensive overview of the second/foreign language (L2) learning processes of students with SpLDs. The book summarizes my research conducted in the field of SpLDs and L2 learning and integrates new findings from other recent studies I have conducted in the area of second language acquisition concerning working memory, language learning aptitude and motivation. The book places SpLDs in the context of the cognitive psychology of learning in general, and of language learning in particular. Thus the book is relevant not only to readers who are particularly interested in the role of SpLDs in learning additional languages, but also to those who would like to learn more about how individual differences in cognitive functioning influence the processes of second language acquisition. It will also integrate recent research in the field of educational psychology on SpLDs with advances in the study of L2 learning processes.

The book focuses on four important aspects of L2 learning: the processes of second language acquisition in general and the development of reading skills in particular, the effectiveness of pedagogical programmes, the assessment of the language competence of students with SpLDs and identifying SpLDs in another language. Although the book primarily considers SpLDs from a cognitive perspective, it also views learners with SpLDs in their social and educational contexts and elaborates how the barriers in these contexts affect language learning processes. An additional innovative feature of the book is that it does not only focus on dyslexia, one of the most well-researched SpLDs in the context of L2 learning, but it also considers a broader range of learning difficulties, such as attention deficit hyperactivity disorder (ADHD) and autistic spectrum disorder (ASD), which may have a significant effect on the process of L2 acquisition.

I hope that by reading this book, researchers, postgraduate students, language and literacy teachers and teacher trainers will find out more about how students with SpLDs learn and can be helped to learn additional languages. The understanding of these learners can then lead to more accepting attitudes, a sense of stronger self-confidence in language teachers and ultimately more inclusive and effective teaching practices. This is my modest contribution to the call of Dyslexia Action:

> Learners of all ages need help and support. They need strategies and tricks to help them get better at what they find hard. They need people who can help them to have confidence when they doubt themselves. They need advice on how to get best out of schools, colleges, night classes and other places of learning.
>
> *Dr. John Rack, Dyslexia Action's Director of*
> *Education and Policy*

1

AN OVERVIEW OF SPECIFIC LEARNING DIFFICULTIES

"In many ways being a dyslexic is a natural way to be. What's unnatural is the way we read and write," says Benjamin Zephaniah, a young poet, writer and musician who is dyslexic (cited in Rooke, 2016). But what exactly is dyslexia, and how does it relate to other types of specific learning difficulties? In order to understand the role of specific learning difficulties such as dyslexia in learning and using another language, in later chapters, we need to define what they are and describe their potential causes and characteristics. This is by no means an easy task. From a cognitive perspective, specific learning difficulties are manifestations of an intricate system of underlying causes and processes that are not directly observable and which can have a variety of effects on cognition, affect and behaviour. From a sociocultural perspective, specific learning difficulties can also be regarded as differences across individuals which, in their interaction with social and educational barriers, hinder full participation in society. I will start this chapter with a discussion of the terminology used to describe specific learning difficulties from these two perspectives. Then, I will give an overview of the concept of specific learning difficulties and discuss the controversy over whether different types of specific learning difficulties can be clearly defined and identified. In the next part of the chapter, I will seek answers to the questions about what cognitive mechanisms are involved in reading and spelling and how children learn to read and write. Helped by an understanding of reading and writing processes as well as their development in children of school age, I will review and evaluate the main theories for the causes of specific learning difficulties and the most recent studies on the cognitive correlates of reading difficulties. In the last part of the chapter, I will acquaint readers with two additional types of learning difficulty: attention deficit hyperactivity disorder (ADHD) and autism spectrum disorders (ASD), both of which can also impact significantly on the processes of the second/foreign language (L2) learning.

1.1 Learning Disabilities, Learning Differences or Learning Difficulties?

In writing this book, I had to face difficult decisions with regard to the terminology I will apply in the discussion of individual differences in cognitive ability and learning. This is because the terms used to describe learning difficulties vary across and even within contexts. For example, the 5th edition of the *Diagnostic and Statistical Manual of Mental Disorders* of the American Psychiatric Association (DSM-5; APA, 2013) uses the term *specific learning disorder*. In the United Kingdom, the term *specific learning differences* is commonly applied in the education sector (see e.g. National Institute of Adult Continuing Education, 2009), whereas the term *learning difficulties* is used interchangeably with *learning disability* in the new Children and Families Act (2014) in the United Kingdom, Australia and many Canadian provinces (Kozey & Siegel, 2008).

The way language is used to describe learning difficulties reflects how society perceives these difficulties and their effect on learning. The terminology used also shapes how teachers and researchers relate to students who display different abilities in learning. This makes it very important to carefully select the terms and labels to be used, not only in this book, but also in academic and public settings. For example, both the Amendments of the Americans with Disabilities Act (2008) and British Equality Act (2010) state that *disability* is a physical or mental impairment which has significant and long-term effects on the normal day-to-day activities of an individual. This definition implies that disability constitutes a series of barriers in one's life and that people with disabilities show deficiencies when compared with others. This view, which exemplifies medical models of learning difficulties, suggests that the source of the problem is the individual and that the responsibility of the scientific community and education is to find the cause of the problem and offer a treatment for it. In this model, which is sometimes also called the deficit model (Thomas & Loxley, 2007), children are seen as having individual needs that have to be met by special education providers, schools and other educational institutions. In contrast, the social model views difficulties as socially constructed barriers and embodies the assumption that disabilities are caused by the environment and social factors (Barnes, 1996; Riddick, 2001) rather than by differences across individuals. The current interactional view of disabilities acknowledges the importance of both the role of the environment and that of individual differences (see e.g. Frederickson & Cline, 2002; Norwich, 2009). This is also expressed by the United Nations Convention on the Rights of Persons with Disabilities (2006), which defines disabilities as "long-term physical, mental, intellectual or sensory impairments which *in interaction* with various barriers may hinder their full and effective participation in society on an equal basis with others" (p. 4, emphasis mine). The interactional view puts the emphasis on the intricate interplay between the educational context and individual strengths and weaknesses (Frederickson & Cline, 2002).

As I explained in the introduction of this book, here I take a primarily cognitive and learner-centred perspective on difficulties in second language acquisition. This cognitive perspective shares common theoretical ground with psychological and psycholinguistic studies of learning difficulties. A biological/psychological conceptualization of learning difficulties is useful in describing the behavioural attributes, cognitive processes and affective characteristics of individuals who have learning difficulties. Nevertheless, in this book, I also contextualize learning difficulties in social and educational settings and discuss issues related to identification, assessment and education. Therefore, where possible, I also consider second language learning difficulties from sociocultural perspectives, explaining how the linguistic, cultural and socioeconomic context shapes the way we define and assess learning difficulties and presents, or removes, barriers to learning additional languages.

Because I incorporate interactionist perspectives on learning difficulties in this book, I want to avoid using a term that is strongly associated with either a biological-medical framework or the environmentalist perspective. The term *learning disability* is used widely in the biological-medical framework, and it often implies that the "problems faced by the individual are part and parcel of their disease" (Norbury & Sparks, 2013, p. 46). *Learning difference*, the terminology favoured by advocates of the social perspective, suggests that if adaptations are made by society, the individual can successfully overcome their difficulties. While *specific learning differences* is an appealing term, so much so that it was included in the title of a previous book that I coauthored on this topic (Kormos & Smith, 2012), I have decided here to use the term *specific learning difficulties,* instead. This is because in addition to being a term that is neutral with regard to the two contrasting theoretical frameworks, the term *learning difficulties* has the advantage of expressing the important assumption that students face problems with certain learning tasks.

1.2 Specific Learning Difficulties: What Are They?

Not only do the terms used to describe specific learning difficulties differ, but there is also considerable variation in how they are defined and what kinds of difficulties are included under this umbrella term. One of the reasons for the often complex and conflicting definitions of and classification systems for specific learning difficulties is that they need to be described in a valid manner from four different perspectives: biological, cognitive, behavioural and environmental (Frith, 1999). There are challenges to definition at all four of these levels. Starting with the *environmental level*, if one sees disability as a barrier to successful participation in society, it is impossible to define it without reference to the educational, social and linguistic contexts of the given society. For example, in a context where lack of literacy skills is not in itself a barrier to becoming a valued member of the community, difficulties with reading and writing might not be perceived as a disability. To illustrate, Norbury and Sparks (2013) review a number of studies that show how the identification of autistic traits in children as well as specific language impairment are influenced by the family structure, educational system and social-value system in various contexts.

At the *behavioural level*, definitions of disabilities aim to describe observable characteristics and behaviours. Learning difficulties are dimensional and are not "either-or" conditions; hence cut-off points in tests of behavioural measures below which children are identified as having learning difficulties are often arbitrary (Frith, 1999). A fundamental question is what type of observable behaviours and characteristics should be considered in the definition of learning difficulties. In the past, learning difficulties were classified into distinct subtypes such as 'dyslexia' or 'reading disability' and 'dyscalculia' or 'mathematics learning disability' (see e.g. the classification system of the American Psychiatric Association [APA] in 1994). These subtypes of learning difficulties represented distinct areas of academic achievement which also impact people's lives outside school. It was found, however, that there is a considerable overlap between these types of learning difficulties. This, taken together with the variations that individuals with learning difficulties show in their behavioural characteristics, makes it very difficult to delineate the various subtypes in a reliable manner (Kirby & Kaplan, 2003; Pennington & Bishop, 2009). As a solution, the APA grouped different learning difficulties under the umbrella term *specific learning disorders* (SLD) in its new *Diagnostic and Statistical Manual* (DSM-5, APA, 2013). These include three subgroups of disorder: specific learning disorder with impairment in reading, written expression and mathematics. SLD in reading can be partially matched with dyslexia and SLD in mathematics to dyscalculia. SLD in writing is concerned with spelling accuracy, grammar and punctuation accuracy and clarity and organization of written expression (see Figure 1.1).

In the category of neurodevelopmental disorders in DSM-5 (APA, 2013), there is an additional group of language-related difficulties that is relevant to consider: language disorder, or in terminology used previously and as it is still commonly called in the United Kingdom, *specific language impairment* (SLI). SLI involves persistent problems with acquiring, comprehending and producing language across modalities (APA, 2013). There seems to be a considerable overlap between reading-related learning difficulties and SLI because a high proportion of children with SLI struggle with literacy-related problems (Tallal, Curtiss & Kaplan, 1988), and there is a strong relationship between language, speech and reading disorders (Pennington & Bishop, 2009; Snowling & Hulme, 2012).

This book takes a broad view of specific learning difficulties and considers the widest range of possible types of difficulties of neurodevelopmental origin that can have a potential effect on the process of learning an additional language. This will primarily include learning difficulties in reading and writing and

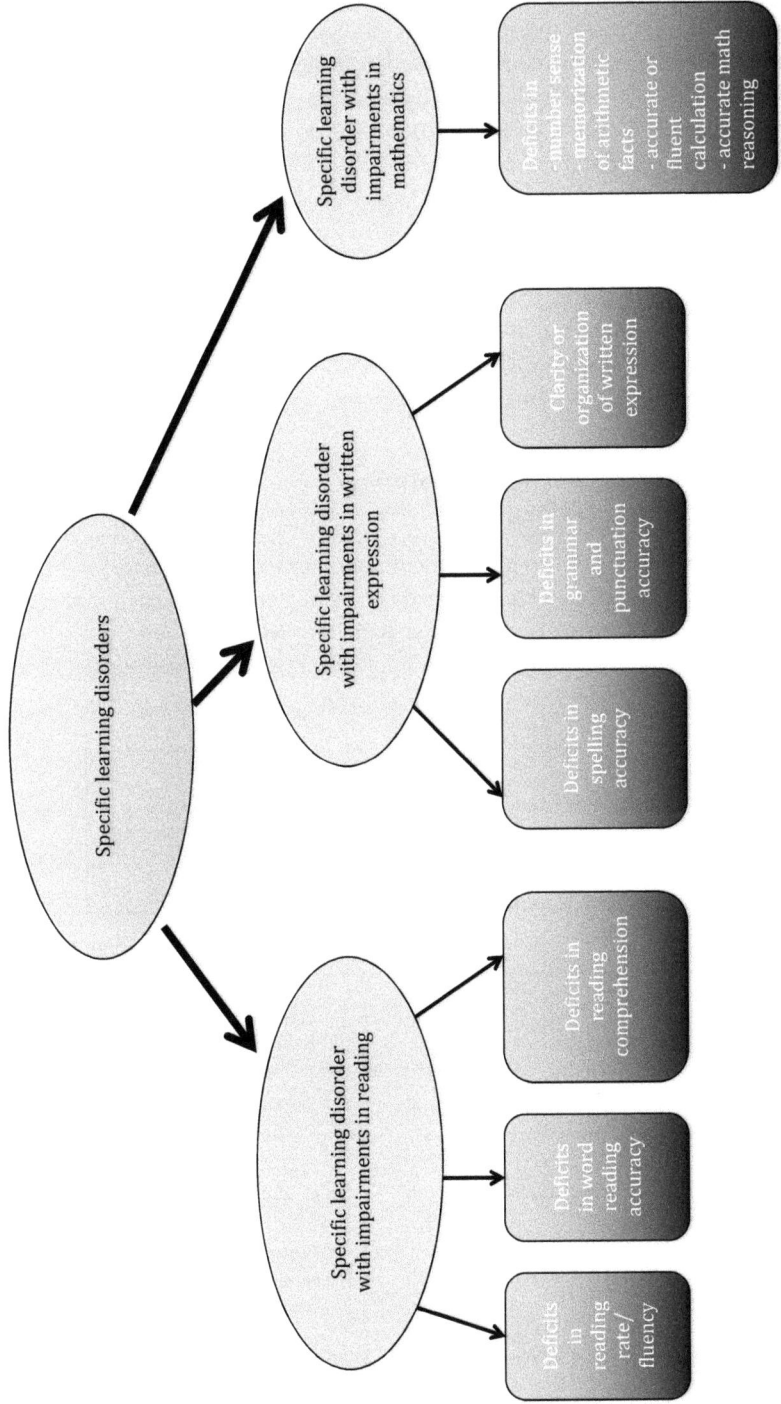

FIGURE 1.1 The Grouping of Learning Difficulties in the *Diagnostic and Statistical Manual* of the American Psychiatric Association (2013)

problems related to attention control such as ADHD. In DSM-5, ADHD is classified separately from specific learning disorders, but its description is immediately followed by specific learning disorders to signal their overlapping features. This is intended to show that ADHD extends "beyond behavior", and LD extends "beyond books" (Tannock, 2013, p. 6). In other words, ADHD can be the cause of learning and literacy-related difficulties, and learning difficulties can affect childrens' lives outside school as well. An additional neurodevelopmental disorder to be included in this book is autistic spectrum disorder because it has a major influence on social communication and reading comprehension. Autistic spectrum disorder also has implications for second language acquisition and bilingual language use, and therefore, it will also be considered in Chapter 3 when I discuss the cognitive effects of specific learning difficulties on the processes of learning an additional language.

1.3 Different Approaches to Defining Specific Learning Difficulties

The definition of specific learning difficulties dominating the international fields of education and psychology until recently was based on the discrepancy between individual's aptitude primarily measured with the help of IQ tests and tests of achievement (see Figure 1.2). An example of this conceptualization is the

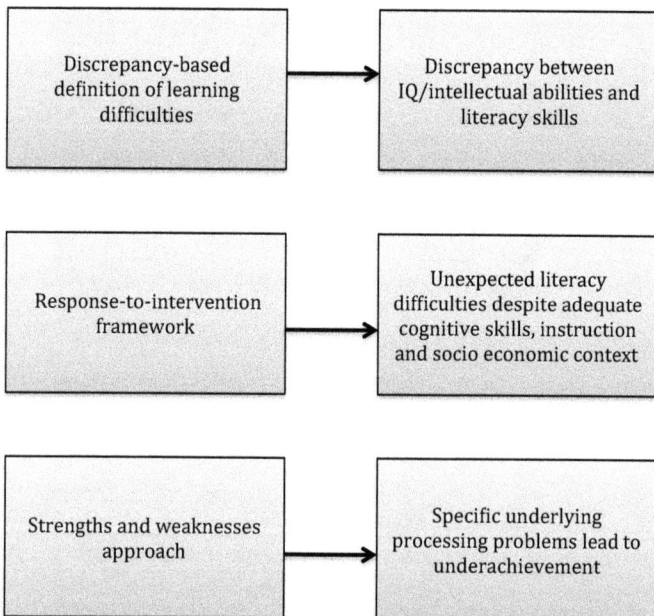

FIGURE 1.2 Different Frameworks of Definitions of Specific Learning Difficulties

definition of dyslexia by the World Federation of Neurology in 1968, which states that "developmental dyslexia is a disorder in children who, despite conventional classroom experience, fail to attain the language skills of reading, writing, and spelling *commensurate with their intellectual abilities*" (p. 26, my emphasis). Definitions based on discrepancies between IQ and academic achievement have, however, come under serious criticism for several reasons. On the one hand, the biased nature of IQ tests towards certain ethnic and social groups can contribute to the overdiagnosis of specific learning difficulties in certain populations (Hale et al., 2010). On the other hand, in order to diagnose specific learning difficulties reliably, the difference between an IQ test score and a test of academic achievement has to be sufficiently large (Miles & Haslum, 1986). Consequently, children whose IQ score is in the lower band of typically developing children often miss being identified. Additional problems with the discrepancy-based definition include the fact that there is large overlap between the underlying cognitive processes that account for both performance on IQ tests and academic tasks (e.g. working memory is both measured as part of IQ tests but also plays an important role in academic performance; for recent overviews see Fletcher, 2012; Tannock, 2013). Furthermore, IQ-based discrepancy definitions often fail to distinguish between learners with specific learning difficulties and low-achieving students (Hale et al., 2010).

The main question that arose after discrepancy-based definitions were discredited was how one might identify learning difficulties without making reference to general intellectual abilities. One possible answer was to introduce the concept of *unexpectedness*, namely that specific learning difficulties might occur despite adequate cognitive skills, appropriate socio-economic circumstances and high-quality instruction (see Figure 1.2). For example, a number of conceptualizations of dyslexia in the 1990s viewed unexpectedness as failure to respond to appropriate high-quality instruction (Fuchs & Fuchs, 1998). An earlier definition of the APA (1994) illustrates this conceptualization: "Developmental dyslexia, or specific reading disability, is defined as an *unexpected*, specific and persistent failure to acquire efficient reading skills despite conventional instruction, adequate intelligence and sociocultural opportunity" (p. 48, my emphasis). The definitions that are based on the notions of 'unexpectedness' and 'failure to respond to instruction' overcome some of the problems associated with discrepancy-based diagnoses, namely that they allow for the early identification of specific learning difficulties and do not involve expensive psychological assessments (Hale et al., 2010; Tannock, 2013). These definitions, however, are not without problems either. Most importantly, there can be many possible reasons in addition to specific learning difficulties why children do not make progress in the academic learning domain despite appropriate intervention. Reliable identification based on this definition is hampered by additional problems, in that there is no consensus on what *appropriate intervention* might mean in a given context or how to establish a cut-off point for failure. Furthermore, there is no empirical evidence that failure to respond to intervention alone is sufficient for the diagnosis of specific learning difficulties (see Hale et al., 2010 for a summary).

In the wide-ranging discussions and thorough analysis of the existing body of research (Hale et al., 2010) that led to the revision of the DSM-5 of APA (2013), consensus was reached that neither discrepancy- nor response-to-intervention-based definitions alone or together provide a solid and reliable basis for the identification of specific learning difficulties. The new framework adapted for the DSM-5 is called the *processing strengths and weaknesses approach* (see Figure 1.2). As its name suggests, in this new framework, the focus is on assessment of the specific underlying processing problems that might lead to underachievement in particular academic domains (Hale et al., 2010). The approach is supported by converging evidence from the meta-analysis of research in this area that has shown that there are significant differences in basic cognitive processing in working memory, executive functioning (planning, organizing, strategizing, paying attention), processing speed and phonological processing between children identified as having specific learning difficulties and their typically developing peers (Johnson, Humphrey, Mellard, Woods & Swanson, 2010). Furthermore, within this approach, valid and reliable measurement tools are available to assess underlying cognitive processing problems. An additional advantage of this assessment framework is that information about the nature and extent of processing weaknesses can greatly assist in intervention which is individually tailored to individuals' needs (Hale et al., 2010).

Based on the processing strengths and weaknesses framework and the available empirical research, DSM-5 (APA, 2013) outlines a novel approach and consequently new diagnostic criteria for the identification of specific learning difficulties. As mentioned before, DSM-5 groups difficulties with word reading, reading comprehension, spelling, written expression, number sense and mathematical reasoning under the diagnostic criterion of 'specific learning disorder' (see Figure 1.1). It specifies that difficulties in these areas need to be present for at least 6 months despite targeted interventions. Another important diagnostic criterion is that "the affected academic skills are substantially and quantifiably below those expected for the individual's chronological age" (APA, 2013, p. 67), and they interfere with academic and occupational performance and daily living. Importantly, it highlights that while in most cases the individual's difficulties arise during the early school years, it is possible that they only have a substantial impact on performance in later years when the academic or occupational demands are higher. Finally, DSM-5 also adds exclusionary criteria such as "intellectual disabilities, uncorrected visual and auditory acuity, other mental or neurological disorders, psychosocial adversity, lack of proficiency in the language of academic instruction, or inadequate educational instruction" (APA, 2013, p. 67).

The strengths and weaknesses framework will be used in further discussion of specific learning difficulties in this book. The framework is useful because it allows us to distinguish various subtypes of literacy-related learning difficulties based on the language-related processing areas affected. At the same time, it also acknowledges the overlaps between various types of learning difficulties by considering the common underlying cognitive processes involved in them. Furthermore, with its explicit focus on cognitive processing, the framework assists in establishing links between second language acquisition and language use processes and the field of specific learning difficulties.

1.4 The Processes of Reading and Learning How to Read

In order to understand reading-related learning difficulties, it is important to consider the processes of reading and how children learn to read in their L1. One of the most influential models used in both the scientific study of reading and the field of specific learning difficulties is Gough and Tunmer's (1986) *Simple View of Reading*. The basic tenets of the original model are that the two most important determinants of successful reading comprehension are general language comprehension skills and accurate and fluent word-level reading skills, and these two components of reading contribute to reading achievement independently of each other (see Figure 1.3).

If we turn our attention to word-level reading skills first, readers in an alphabetic language need to combine different processing mechanisms: *orthographic processing* (recognizing letters), *phonological processing* (phonological activation of word forms, converting letters to sounds, letter combinations to syllables), *accessing semantic and syntactic information* related to the word, and finally *morphological processing* to understand words with suffixes and prefixes (for a discussion of differences in reading in various languages and scripts see Chapter 2). According to the *dual-route model*, there are two ways in which words can be recognized: *the sublexical* and *lexical routes* (Coltheart, 1978). In the sublexical route (indicated by the arrow on the right-hand side in Figure 1.4), the written word is decoded

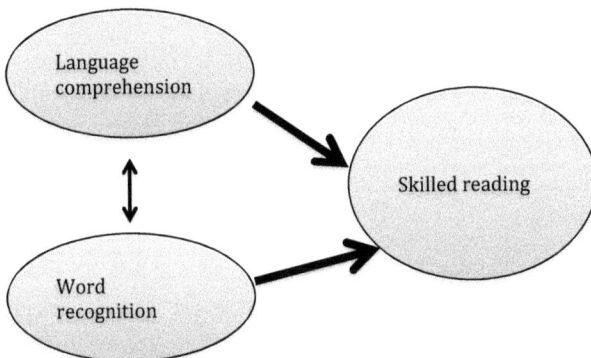

FIGURE 1.3 The Simple View of Reading

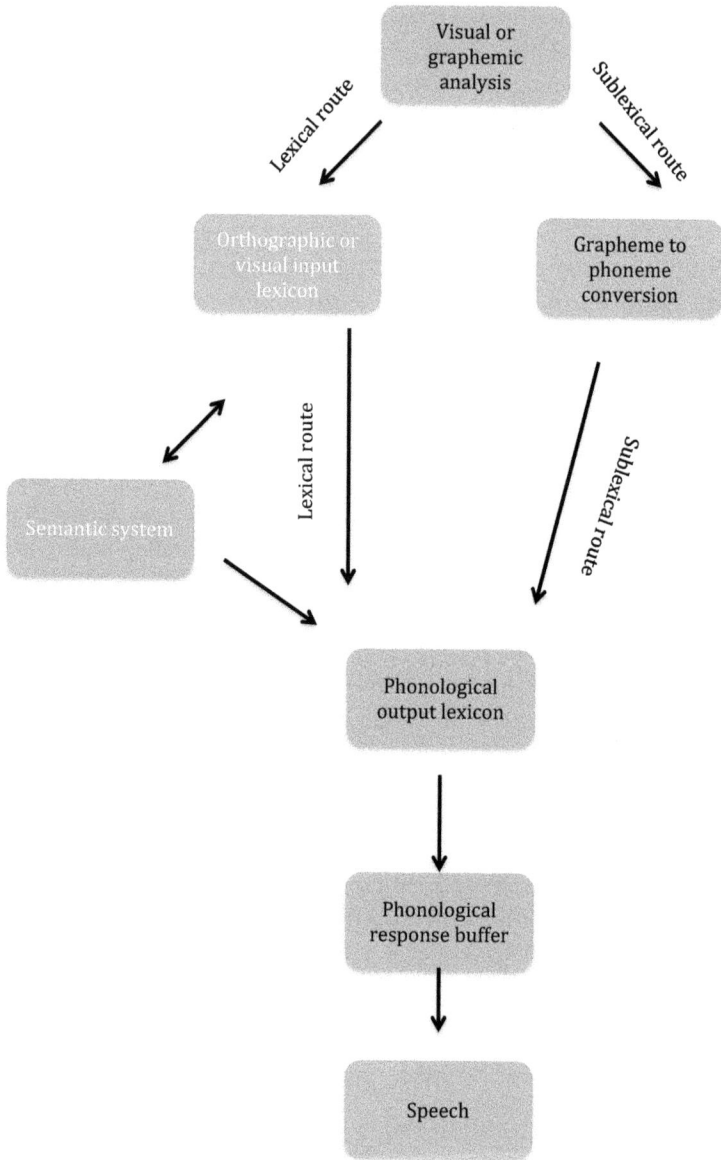

FIGURE 1.4 Illustration of the Dual-Route Word-Reading Model

Source: Coltheart (1978).

by means of the analysis of letter strings. The reader accesses the meaning of a word through the conversion of letters into sounds and assembling the sounds to form the phonological (spoken) form of the word. This orthographic-phonological conversion can take place at the level of letters, *graphemes* (i.e.

combinations of letters denoting a given sound), subsyllabic units (such as rhymes) or syllables. This is the prevalent reading process for familiar regular words and nonwords. There is another route for reading, which bypasses phonological analysis, called the lexical route (indicated by the arrow on the left-hand side of Figure 1.4). In the lexical route, the reader perceives the visual form of a word as a whole unit and recognizes the word-form without having to analyse it into segments. The visually identified word form is retrieved from the visual lexicon and matched with relevant semantic information. Finally, the phonological word form is activated in the phonological output lexicon (see Figure 1.4). This route is typically used for words that have idiosyncratic pronunciations, such as *quay* or *colonel*. Word-level reading not only involves assembling or retrieving the accurate phonological form of the word, but also requires that the appropriate meaning of the word be accessed (Hoover & Gough, 1990).

The above word-level reading processes include the syntactic analysis and assembly of phrasal and clausal constructions, as well as creating a *text model*, i.e. processing the informational content of the text, and a *situation model* which helps the reader to interpret information presented in the text based on relevant background knowledge (Kintsch, 1998). In Gough and Tunmer's (1986) "Simple View of Reading", successful reading comprehension also requires that the reader understands the structure of the text, makes inferences and monitors comprehension. Oral language comprehension hinges on very similar processes to those of reading because the listener also needs to retrieve word meanings, analyse and process the syntactic structure of an utterance, construct a text and situational model and check their own understanding.

In the original formulation of the "Simple View of Reading" (Gough & Tunmer, 1986), word-reading and language comprehension processes were not assumed to be related to each other. Evidence for this assumption came from studies that showed that some children can accurately decode words yet have a limited understanding of text meaning (see e.g. Cain, Oakhill & Bryant, 2004; Nation, 2005). These children often have specific reading comprehension impairments and are labelled 'poor comprehenders' in the literature. Reading comprehension difficulties have also been recognized as a potentially independent type of reading difficulty different from the word-decoding difficulties in the newly revised DSM-5 (APA, 2013).

In other models of reading, such as the lexical quality account (Perfetti, 2007), an interdependent relationship between word decoding and language comprehension is postulated. For example, Perfetti (2007) argues that reading comprehension problems can also be caused by slow and inefficient word recognition. This is because low levels of automaticity in word identification can take away attentional resources from processing a text above the word level. A recent study by Tunmer and Chapman (2012) led to revision of the "Simple View of Reading" by showing that language comprehension can influence word-decoding skills (see Figure 1.5), and therefore language comprehension makes a direct as

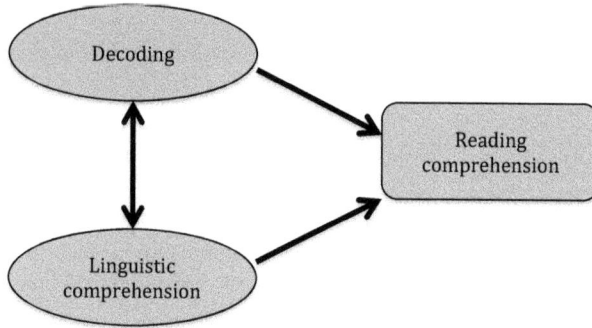

FIGURE 1.5 Tunmer and Chapman's (2012) Modified "Simple View of Reading"

well as an indirect contribution to reading comprehension. The key link between language comprehension and word decoding is oral vocabulary knowledge, which can enhance the efficiency and speed of word decoding (i.e. known words are easier to identify), as well as facilitate text-level comprehension (Tunmer & Hoover, 1993).

An understanding of the processes of how children learn to read is clearly important for the identification of potential sources of reading difficulties. The two most prevalent theories of children's reading development were proposed by Ehri (2005) and Frith (1986). Both of these theories assume that reading develops in different phases or stages. Frith (1986) argues that first children learn to read a few words as a whole unit, which in her model is called the *logographic stage*. In this stage, children do not yet know the alphabet and they process words visually as single units using visual clues (see Figure 1.6). In Ehri's (2005) model, the corresponding stage is called *prealphabetic*. In the next developmental stage, called the *alphabetic stage* in Frith's (1986) model, children learn to segment visually perceived word forms into letters, convert letters into sounds and read words by sounding out letters one by one. The final stage in Frith's (1986) model is the *orthographic stage*, in which children do not process words letter by letter any more, but analyse words into bigger units, such as letter sequences, and convert these into syllables. This is called the orthographic stage because readers have to make use of their knowledge of how written (orthographic) words are constructed from larger chunks, such as morphemes, prefixes and suffixes. In Ehri's (2005) model reading development from the prealphabetic stage proceeds through *partial, full* and *consolidated alphabetic stages*. The consolidated alphabetic stage can be seen as similar to the final stage of fluent word reading described in Frith's (1986) orthographic stage. The two intermediary stages in Ehri's (2005) model make a distinction between children who have partial alphabetic knowledge and cannot yet accurately segment words into phonemes and those who have fully acquired sound–letter correspondence rules and have no difficulties with phonological segmentation (see Figure 1.6).

Frith's (1986)
model

Ehri's (2005)
model

```
┌─────────────────────┐        ┌─────────────────────┐
│  Logographic stage  │        │  Pre-alphabetic stage │
└─────────────────────┘        └─────────────────────┘
          │                               │
          │                               ▼
          │                    ┌─────────────────────────┐
          │                    │ Partial alphabetic stage │
          │                    └─────────────────────────┘
          ▼                               │
┌─────────────────────┐                   ▼
│   Alphabetic stage  │        ┌─────────────────────┐
└─────────────────────┘        │  Full alphabetic stage │
          │                    └─────────────────────┘
          │                               │
          ▼                               ▼
┌─────────────────────┐        ┌─────────────────────────┐
│  Orthographic stage │        │  Consolidated alphabetic │
└─────────────────────┘        │          stage           │
                               └─────────────────────────┘
```

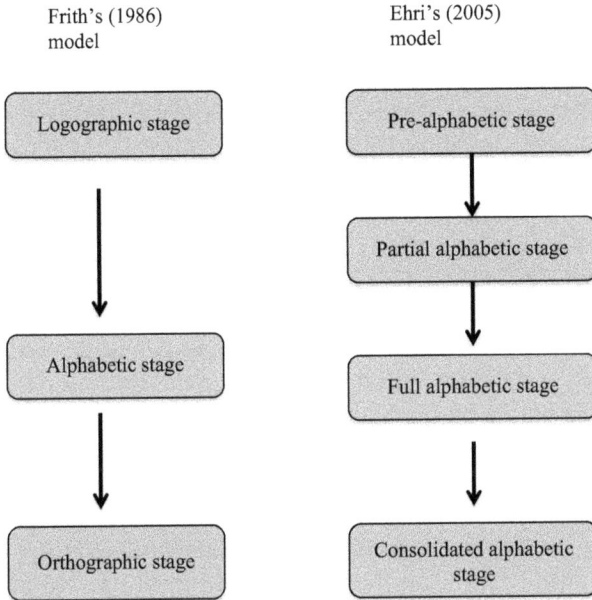

FIGURE 1.6 Models of Learning to Read

As we will see in Section 1.6, the cognitive processing difficulties of children with specific learning difficulties can potentially interfere with their development in phonological segmentation and sound–letter conversion skills, which are both needed to attain fluent word-decoding skills in the models described above. Scarborough and Dobrich (1990) also point out that reading development is often neither linear nor gradual. Development can proceed in spurts, which are then followed by developmental plateaus. They point out that this can explain why, at certain points in time, if individuals with specific learning difficulties are tested on their reading skills, they can perform similarly to their peers and thus show signs of 'illusory recovery'.

1.5 Writing Processes and Learning to Write

Although writing is unique, in that it requires "language use by hand" (Berninger, 2000), it shares some underlying cognitive and linguistic processes with reading, especially in the domain of lower-order processes (Berninger, Abbott, Abbott, Graham & Richards, 2002). Although a comprehensive overview of how writing skills are acquired is beyond the scope of this book, a brief overview of how children learn to write, with a special focus on spelling and what the cognitive determinants of writing are, is needed for the understanding of specific learning difficulties in the writing domain.

Writers express their thoughts on paper, and they usually do it with the mediation of (silent) speech. In order to be able to write, one needs complex motor-coordination skills to form letters. Visual skills are also necessary to help children differentiate and memorize different shapes and forms of the graphic system. Phonemic awareness, that is the ability to segment words into phonemes and convert them into letters, is also a key ability in spelling and word writing (for an overview see Berninger et al., 2006; Treiman & Kessler, 2005). Children also need solid alphabetic knowledge and sound-to-letter conversion skills to acquire spelling in alphabetic languages (Caravolas, Hulme & Snowling, 2001). Additionally, children have to acquire morphological knowledge to help them spell morphological variants of words. Syntactic knowledge is essential for constructing sentences from words and establishing clausal and sentence boundaries in writing. A sufficient level of automaticity in lower-order writing processes is required before children can learn how to construct longer pieces of texts in different genres.

Spelling development is strongly interrelated with children's progress in learning to read, and models of spelling development show great similarities with those of reading development (Ehri, 1997; Frith, 1980) (see Figure 1.7). In the *precommunicative spelling phase*, children draw shapes of letters, but these letter shapes are not systematically linked to corresponding sounds. In the next *phonetic* or *alphabetic phase*, children start to develop consistent phoneme–grapheme mappings, but their word-level spelling is not yet accurate. In the final *orthographic*

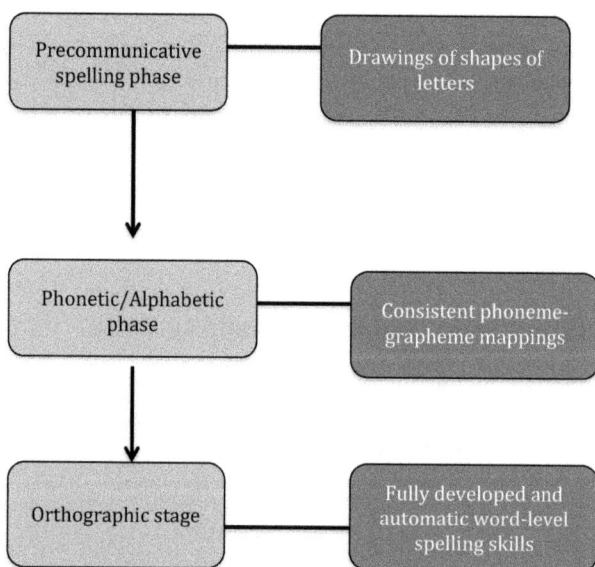

FIGURE 1.7 Stages of Spelling Development

phase, word-level spelling skills are fully developed to the level of automaticity. Just as with models of reading development, we should not consider these stages as clearly distinct because different phases can overlap (Steffler, Varnhagen, Friesen & Treiman, 1998). Learning how to spell is a prolonged process and is also dependent on the specific features of the orthography of a given language (for a review see Caravolas, 2004; Treiman & Kessler, 2005).

As pointed out above, the language-related cognitive skills involved in successful reading and spelling acquisition are assumed to be shared (Caravolas et al., 2001). Word-level reading difficulties are often accompanied by spelling problems. The question is to what extent reading and spelling difficulties co-occur, in other words, whether they are simply two sides of the same underlying learning difficulty. Correlational studies with English-speaking children seem to suggest a very strong relationship between reading and spelling attainment (e.g. Ehri, 1997). Yet DSM-5 (APA, 2013) includes a specific subcategory for a learning difficulty with written expression, which is concerned with spelling accuracy. Empirical evidence suggests that a small proportion of children and adults (approx. 3%–5%) are poor spellers despite apparently accurate and fluent word-level reading skills (Wimmer & Mayringer, 2002). Conversely, in some cases, dysfluent reading has been found to be accompanied by accurate spelling (Lovett, 1987; Wimmer & Mayringer, 2002).

Moll and Landerl (2009) confirm this double dissociation of reading and spelling in the case of German-speaking children. They argue that one possible reason why children might be poor spellers despite adequate word-level reading skills is because phonological deficits are apparent before literacy instruction. These children might have developed their phonological awareness skills in the early school years to such a level that their word-reading skills are not affected, but they might still experience difficulties with spelling. In Moll and Landerl's study, there were also participants who demonstrated accurate spelling skills but were slow and inaccurate at word-level reading. Interestingly, these children showed no impaired phonological awareness, and it was only in rapid automated word naming that they performed below their good reader–good speller peers. Moll and Landerl explain that these children might have reading problems because of slow access to orthographic representations. Since spelling is not as time-constrained as reading, this slower speed of processing does not seem to affect spelling skills. The implications of these types of dissociation between spelling and reading skills will be revisited in Chapter 2 where we will also consider these from a cross-linguistic perspective.

1.6 The Cognitive Determinants and Possible Causes of Specific Learning Difficulties

Just as definitions of specific learning difficulties show large differences and can be underpinned by different theoretical perspectives, there are a number of theories for the possible causes of specific learning difficulties. Similar to the definitions and characterisations of specific learning difficulties, causes can be investigated from biological, cognitive, behavioural and environmental perspectives. There is a burgeoning of studies on biological causal factors, and the evidence gained suggests that heritability is high in specific learning difficulties in general and in reading- and language-related learning difficulties (e.g. SLI) in particular (for a review see Pennington & Bishop, 2009). Related to this, the risk of a child with a family history of learning difficulties having specific learning difficulties is 4–8 times higher than in a family with no such history (Pennington & Olson, 2005). Specific candidate genes and chromosome regions predisposing children to specific learning difficulties have also been identified (again, for a review see Pennington & Bishop, 2009). Brain imaging studies also show that certain regions of the left hemisphere responsible for phonological processing and visual word recognition are underactivated in dyslexic individuals (for a recent overview see Peterson & Pennington, 2015).

Premature birth, low birthweight and bio-environmental risk factors such as prenatal exposure to nicotine and lead poisoning can also pose risks for the development of specific learning difficulties. There are no proven direct socio-environmental causes of specific learning difficulties, but some features and specific elements of the sociocultural context can contribute to specific learning difficulties as well as serve as protection when there is a genetic predisposition or family history of specific learning difficulties. These environmental factors include parental education, home literacy practices and the quality of literacy instruction.

After a discussion of the possible biological causes, it is also important to consider the important questions of whether there is one single cause of specific learning difficulties, whether there is a separate, independent and single cause for a specific type of SpLD such as dyslexia, or whether there are multiple causes of specific learning difficulties and multiple causes for specific subtypes as well. Single-cause models for specific learning difficulties are very few, given the varying although overlapping nature of subtypes of specific learning difficulties such as dyslexia, dyspraxia and dyscalculia (for an illustration, see Figure 1.8). Probably the only such model is the one proposed by Miller, Kail, Leonard and Tomblin (2001), which assumes that specific learning difficulties are caused by a generally slow speed of cognitive processing. Another single-cause model, rapid temporal processing theory, presumes that the reduced processing speed of incoming auditory stimuli accounts for reading difficulties and SLI (Tallal, 2004; Tallal & Piercy, 1973). Gathercole and Baddeley's (1990) phonological short-term memory deficit model aims to explain SLI and reading difficulties with reference to difficulties originating in short-term memory storage and the manipulation of verbal information. Finally, difficulties with procedural learning, in other words abstracting patterns of regularities implicitly from the input, have also been hypothesized as underlying specific learning difficulties (e.g. Nicolson & Fawcett, 1990; Ullman & Pierpont, 2005).

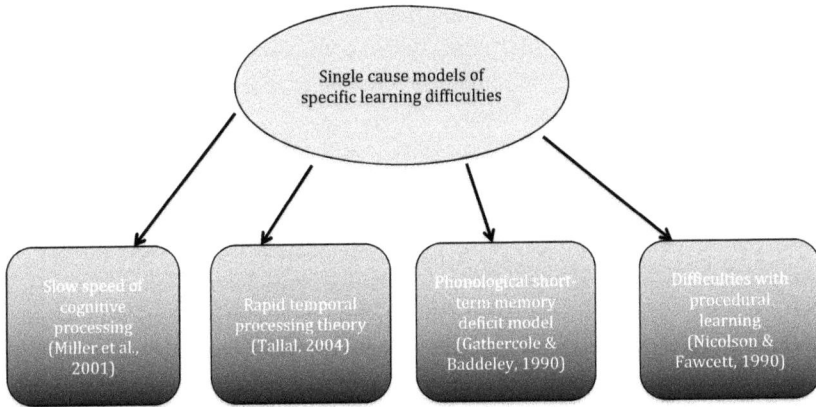

FIGURE 1.8 Single-Cause Models of Specific Learning Difficulties

Single-cause models of specific learning difficulties are problematic for a number of reasons. First of all, while many of the cognitive characteristics of specific learning difficulties overlap, they are also differentiated from each other by certain features. For example, deficits in phonological awareness tend to be associated with dyslexia, but not with dyscalculia or specific reading comprehension difficulties (Johnson et al., 2010). If the underlying cause of specific learning difficulties was a single deficit, then different types of specific learning difficulties would not show such variation in terms of the affected areas of cognitive functioning. It is not only different types of specific learning difficulties that can be dissociated from each other, but individuals who have a specific type of learning difficulty can also vary considerably in their cognitive profiles. Furthermore, the cognitive processing deficits associated with certain types of specific learning difficulties, such as dyslexia and specific reading comprehension difficulties, seem to change from early school years to adolescence (Scarborough, 2001). The implications of such a change in diagnosis and assessment will be discussed in more detail in Chapter 2.

Before discussing the causal theories of specific types of learning difficulties in detail, it is also important to ask the question of whether we can reliably establish causality and differentiate causes from correlates. The finding that children or adults with specific learning difficulties show differences in cognitive functioning in particular areas when compared with a matched population is no evidence for the causal role of a given cognitive factor. Nor does a correlational relationship between certain underlying cognitive factors and learning outcomes prove that these cognitive causes explain achievement or development. Forms of evidence can only be derived from experimental research, that is when intervention targeting one particular cognitive variable results in improvement in attainment. Even then, the effect of intervention can be bidirectional. For example, it has been shown that while training in phonological awareness contributes to the development of word-decoding skills, at the same time, improved word-decoding skills also enhance children's phonological awareness (Ehri & Wilce, 1980; Perfetti, Beck, Bell & Hughes, 1987).

With the above caveats about causality in mind, let us first discuss the various theories that have been proposed for one of the most widely researched specific learning difficulty: dyslexia. The best-known cognitive theory for the causes of dyslexia is the Phonological Deficit Hypothesis (Stanovich, 1988; Vellutino, 1979). As its name suggests, the Phonological Deficit Hypothesis assumes that word-level reading difficulties are caused by an underlying phonological processing difficulty, namely, impaired phonological awareness (see Figure 1.9). Phonological awareness has two levels: syllabic and phonemic knowledge. Syllabic knowledge entails the ability to segment words into syllables and manipulate the syllables in words (e.g. deleting or adding syllables). Phonemic knowledge involves the ability to divide words into sounds, differentiate sounds from each other and manipulate sounds (e.g. deleting, adding and substituting sounds). The Phonological Deficit Hypothesis is based on the observation that dyslexic readers perform significantly worse in tasks requiring phonological awareness, such as nonword reading and nonword repetition, sound differentiation, letter recognition, deleting and adding letters and syllables to words, than their nondyslexic peers. Support for the causal role of decreased phonological awareness, in particular in phonemic knowledge, has been provided by a number of intervention studies, where significant improvement in reading skills was achieved through training in phonemic awareness (for more details see Section 6.3.1). Phonological awareness, however, might not be the ultimate underlying cognitive causal factor for reading difficulties because it is a complex metalinguistic skill that has several subcomponents. Swan and Goswami (1997) argue that children might have reduced phonological awareness because they lack appropriate phonological representations. Whether impairments in phonological representations can be found at segmental (i.e. phoneme), suprasegmental (i.e. syllable) or allophonic (i.e. phonemic variation) levels is still a matter of debate (see Goswami et al., 2002). We will revisit this debate in Chapter 2 as it relates to the diagnosis and identification of specific learning difficulties.

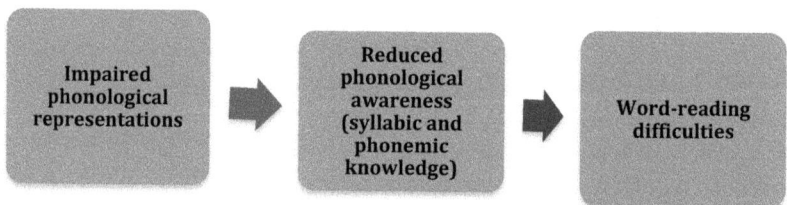

FIGURE 1.9 Illustration of the Phonological Deficit Hypothesis

Although the role of phonological awareness in word-level reading difficulties is evident, the question remains whether phonological deficit is the only cause of dyslexia and indeed what other causes might explain dyslexic reading difficulties. A modified version of the Phonological Deficit Hypothesis is the so-called Double-Deficit Hypothesis, which posits that, in addition to phonological processing problems, naming-speed deficit also plays a role in dyslexia. Research evidence suggests that dyslexic children are significantly slower in word-naming tasks than children with no apparent dyslexia (Denckla & Rudel, 1976), which might point to problems with the speed of processing in the case of dyslexic readers. Wolf and Bowers (1999) argue that differences in naming speed and difficulties with phonological processing are two independent sources of dyslexic reading problems (see Figure 1.10). They support their theory by showing that children who experience reading difficulties can be divided into three groups: those who exhibit speed problems, those with phonological processing problems and finally those most severely impaired whose reading performance is associated with both phonological processing and naming speed. It should be noted that most studies that have tested the Double-Deficit Hypothesis have found that the majority of dyslexic people have difficulties in terms of both speed and phonological processing (e.g. Lovett, Steinbach & Frijters, 2000; Pennington, Cardoso-Martins, Green & Lefly, 2001). These findings seem to suggest that the Double-Deficit Hypothesis is not sufficiently supported with regard to its predictions of different subtypes of dyslexia and the completely dissociated nature of phonological processing and naming speed deficits.

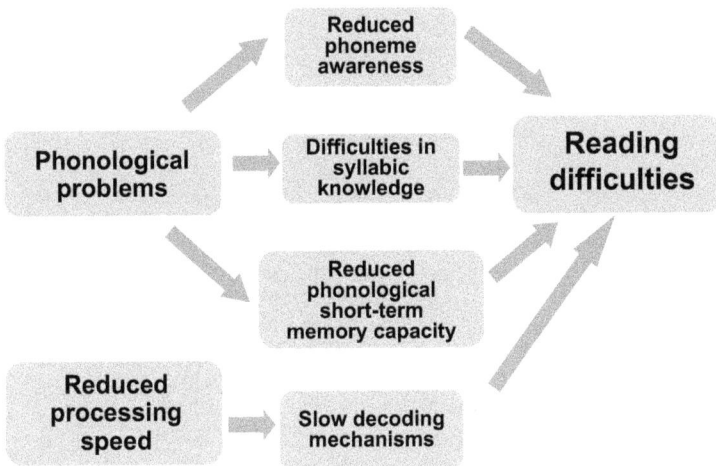

FIGURE 1.10 Illustration of the Double-Deficit Hypothesis

Source: Reproduced from Kormos and Smith (2012), *Teaching Languages to Students with Specific Learning Differences*, p. 35, with permission of Multilingual Matters.

Pennington (2006) proposed a multiple-deficit model of dyslexia, arguing that in addition to deficits in phonological awareness and naming speed, processing speed is also implicated as a possible cause of reading difficulties (see Figure 1.11). Similar to Tallal (2004), he found that perceptual speed proves to be an independent predictor of dyslexic types of reading problems. Most evidence for the multiple-deficit model to date is primarily based on correlational data, and more support is needed for the causal roles of naming speed and processing speed deficits. Nevertheless, the multiple-deficit model is very useful for explaining the overlaps between various types of specific learning difficulties.

Pennington and Bishop (2009) outlined a multiple-deficit account of specific learning difficulties which illuminates the nature of overlaps as well as the distinct features of dyslexia, SLI, speech sound disorders (SSD) and ADHD. They point out that the core deficit in dyslexia, SLI and SSD is an underlying phonological processing problem. Children with SLI and SDD, however, do not develop reading problems at school age if they do not have additional problems with naming speed (see Figure 1.11). Conversely, dyslexia can be differentiated from SLI by the lack of syntactic processing difficulties, and from SSD by the absence of the impaired functioning of articulation motor programmes. Both dyslexic children and those with ADHD seem to be affected by processing speed problems. Pennington and Bishop (2009) claim that the severity of children's language and literacy difficulties is influenced by how many of the underlying cognitive processing deficits they exhibit. They also highlight that the absence of cognitive deficit in particular areas, such as naming speed, can act as a protective factor.

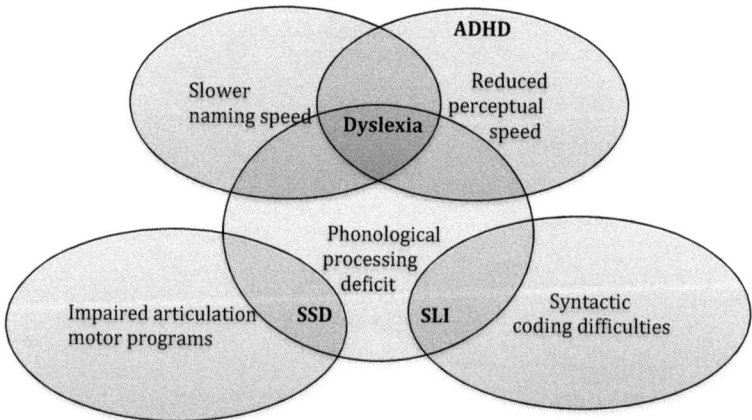

FIGURE 1.11 Overlap of Cognitive Factors in Specific Learning Difficulties in Pennington and Bishop's (2009) Multiple-Deficit Account

Note: SSD = speech sound disorders; SLI = Specific Language Impairment; ADHD = attention deficit hyperactivity disorder

A multiple-deficit account is also useful in considering the potential causes of reading difficulties that manifest themselves above the word level. On the one hand, word-decoding problems can also result in impaired reading comprehension because readers do not have sufficient attentional resources for sentence- and text-level processing (Perfetti, 2007). On the other, reading comprehension can be hampered by additional underlying causes. These include children's reduced skills in making inferences while reading and hence experiencing difficulties with implied meaning and establishing links between ideas and parts of a text (Oakhill, Cain & Bryant, 2003). Impairments in executive functions, namely reduced working memory capacity and weaknesses in inhibition, can also be the cause of reading comprehension problems. Cain et al. (2004) argue that working memory resources are needed to keep already comprehended information active, update it with new information being read and monitor comprehension. If a reader's working memory capacity is reduced, text processing might result in incomplete or inaccurate understanding of the information conveyed. Cain (2006) has also shown that for successful reading comprehension, children need to inhibit irrelevant information or information that is not central to understanding. Finally, impairments in attention control can also result in reading comprehension problems (as is often the case with readers with ADHD—see Section 1.7). The efficient control of attentional resources is needed for monitoring comprehension, focusing on main ideas and ignoring distractions (for a review see Kendeou, van den Broek, Helder & Karlsson, 2014). Causal theories for specific learning difficulties in the nonlinguistic area (e.g. dyscalculia and dyspraxia) are beyond the scope of this book. It is important to note, however, that in a meta-analysis of research studies (Johnson et al., 2010), the cognitive characteristics of students with reading and mathematics difficulties were found to be very similar. The major difference between them was that visual working memory and processing speed seemed to be implicated to a smaller extent in numeracy difficulties than in literacy-related difficulties.

To conclude this discussion of the possible causes of specific learning difficulties, we also need to revisit models of causality. If we look back at Figures 1.10 and 1.11, we can see that all of the models depicted by them are unidirectional causal chains. In order to arrive at a more accurate account of specific learning difficulties, these models should be revised so that they include the possibility of interaction between factors in the causal chain. Such interactivity would be warranted by research findings that demonstrate a reciprocal relationship between phonological awareness and reading skills (e.g. Perfetti et al., 1987). Scarborough (2001) proposes a so-called hybrid model of causation that allows us to view reading difficulties developmentally (see Figure 1.12). This model is based on a single underlying cause that can result in different symptoms, which in turn have a snowball effect on ensuing symptoms. Although it is questionable whether we can establish a single underlying cause for reading difficulties, this model has important implications for diagnosis and pedagogy. Scarborough's model

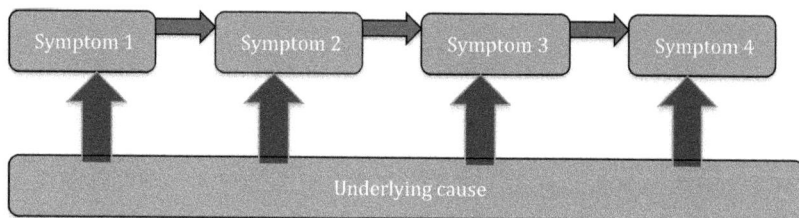

FIGURE 1.12 Scarborough's (2001) Hybrid Model of Causal Relationships in Reading Disabilities

highlights that, at different points in time, various diagnostic criteria might be pertinent, and interventions might need to be targeted at different difficulties that individuals are experiencing.

1.7 Attention Deficit Hyperactivity Disorder

ADHD is classified as a learning difficulty under the umbrella term of specific learning differences in the United Kingdom (DfES Working Group, 2005). In the United States, however, DSM-5 (APA, 2013) categorises it as a neurodevelopmental disorder separate from specific learning disorders. As the name suggests, the two major features of ADHD are inattention and hyperactivity (APA, 2013). These characteristics can be detected in children at a young age, and one of the diagnostic criteria is that they should manifest before the age of 12. Difficulties associated with ADHD persist into adolescence and adulthood, although symptoms of hyperactivity might diminish. The prevalence of ADHD among children varies, between 3% and 7%, depending on the diagnostic criteria and sociocultural attitudes to symptoms (Szatmari, 1992).

Statistics suggest that ADHD seems to be more common in males than in females. The ratio of boys diagnosed with ADHD compared to girls varies between 2:1 and 6:1 (APA, 2013; Barkley, 1997; Ross & Ross, 1976). It is widely acknowledged in the current literature that ADHD is dimensional, that is, it can manifest in different degrees of severity (APA, 2013; Barkley, 2006).

ADHD is identified based on behavioural manifestations reported by teachers and parents, as well as on observations carried out by clinicians. In DSM-5 (APA, 2013) the diagnostic features of ADHD are grouped into two main categories: those relating to inattention and those relating to hyperactivity and impulsivity (see Table 1.1). Six or more of the features in these categories need to persist in children for at least 6 months and need to manifest in two or more settings (e.g. at both school and home). As aforementioned, other diagnostic criteria include that some of the features need to be present before 12 years of age and should have a significant impact on social and academic/occupational activities.

TABLE 1.1 Symptoms of ADHD

Symptoms of inattention

a) Often fails to give close attention to details or makes careless mistakes in schoolwork, work or other activities;
b) Often has difficulty sustaining attention in tasks or play activities;
c) Often does not seem to listen when spoken to directly;
d) Often does not follow through on instructions and fails to finish schoolwork, chores or duties in the workplace (not due to oppositional behaviour or failure to understand instructions);
e) Often has difficulty organizing tasks and activities;
f) Often avoids, dislikes or is reluctant to engage in tasks that require sustained mental effort (such as schoolwork or homework);
g) Often loses things necessary for tasks or activities (e.g. toys, school assignments, pencils, books or tools);
h) Is often easily distracted by extraneous stimuli;
i) Is often forgetful in daily activities.

Symptoms of hyperactivity and impulsivity

Hyperactivity and impulsivity

a) Often fidgets with hands or feet or squirms in seat;
b) Often leaves seat in classroom or in other situations in which remaining seated is expected;
c) Often runs about or climbs excessively in situations in which it is inappropriate (in adolescents or adults, may be limited to subjective feelings of restlessness);
d) Often has difficulty playing or engaging in leisure activities quietly;
e) Is often "on the go" or acts as if "driven by a motor";
f) Often talks excessively
g) Often blurts out answers before questions have been completed;
h) Often has difficulty awaiting turn;
i) Often interrupts or intrudes on others (e.g. butts into conversations or games).

Source: DSM-5; APA (2013), pp. 59–60.

Based on the presence of symptoms shown in the two categories mentioned above, different manifestations of ADHD can be established. Individuals with ADHD might be characterized as predominantly inattentive or predominantly hyperactive and impulsive, or alternatively as a combined type, which are called 'presentations' rather than subtypes to indicate the dimensional nature of ADHD (APA, 2013; Tannock, 2013).

ADHD is hereditary, which indicates that it has a genetic origin. Genetic research has also identified the sections of DNA which seem to be responsible for causing ADHD (for a review see Barkley, 2006). ADHD is also associated with differential brain functioning (reduced activity in the prefrontal regions of the brain; Zametkin et al., 1990). ADHD frequently co-occurs with other specific learning difficulties such as dyslexia and dyscalculia. Depending on the system of diagnosis, the prevalence of dyslexia among children with ADHD is 8%–39% and that of dyscalculia is 12%–30% (Frick et al., 1991).

ADHD has a significant impact on academic performance and the learning of new knowledge and skills with the mediation of working memory and attention control. Research findings suggest that children with ADHD, especially those with primarily inattentive presentations, have a smaller short-term memory span for processing visuo-spatial and verbal information. In terms of storage, only visuo-spatial information is found to be retained less efficiently by children with ADHD, while the storage of verbal material is shown to be unaffected (Alloway, Gathercole & Elliot, 2010; Martinussen & Tannock, 2006). Further cognitive correlates of ADHD that can potentially influence learning processes, including the acquisition of another language, comprise difficulties with inhibiting task-irrelevant responses and planning task execution, as well as reduced alertness to new information and stimuli (Willcutt, Doyle, Nigg, Faraone & Pennington, 2005).

1.8 Autistic Spectrum Disorders

Autistic spectrum disorders are often described as a dyad of persistent difficulties with social interaction and communication on the one hand, and repetitive patterns of behaviour on the other (APA, 2013). The main features of autistic spectrum disorders include difficulties in managing conversations, sharing interests and emotions and establishing and maintaining social relations; inappropriate understanding of figurative and nonliteral language use; pedantic and repetitive speech; poor use of gesture and other means of nonverbal communication; intense absorption in certain subjects (Burgoine & Wing, 1983). Individuals who have autistic spectrum disorder experience difficulties in social communication, take great interest in narrow subjects and engage in repetitive actions (Baron-Cohen, 2008). Autistic spectrum disorders can be accompanied by intellectual and/or language impairment (APA, 2013). DSM-5 differentiates between autistic spectrum disorder and social pragmatic communication disorder), which is characterized by "persistent difficulties in the social use of verbal and nonverbal communication" (APA, 2013, p. 47), but not repetitive patterns of behaviour.

According to the latest statistics, 1 child in every 100 meets the criteria for the diagnosis of autistic spectrum disorders (APA, 2013; Baird et al., 2006), whereas in 1981, this figure was only 1–2 in every 1,000 children (Wing, 1981). This increase in prevalence is due to the reconceptualization of autism as a spectrum, improved diagnostic criteria and raised public and professional awareness. Autistic spectrum disorders occur approximately 4 times more frequently in males than in females (Ehlers & Gillberg, 1993). Autistic spectrum disorders are genetic in origin and hereditary (APA, 2013; Gillberg, 1989). This is attested by both twin and sibling studies, which have shown a high incidence of autistic conditions within specific families. Mutations and systematic variations in the genes and chromosomes of autistic individuals have also been found (for a review see Baron-Cohen, 2008).

1.9 Summary

This chapter aimed to provide definitions of key terms and concepts underlying specific learning difficulties and their effects on literacy skills and academic learning. I explained that use of appropriate terminology is crucial because it affects how we perceive of individuals who experience learning difficulties and the educational approaches we apply. I argued that the disabilities should be viewed in an interactional framework where the strengths and weaknesses of people with learning difficulties are considered in a complex interaction with the social and educational context and the potential barriers they present.

The chapter gave an overview of the various approaches to the definition of specific learning difficulties and the most prevalent theories of the causes of different types of learning difficulties. I explained that in this book, I adapt a definition which is based on the processing strengths and weaknesses approach. This framework provides a detailed description of the specific cognitive processing problems that can potentially lead to literacy- and language-related difficulties. The framework is also compatible with the multiple-deficit account of the causes of learning difficulties, which highlights that there is no single source of specific learning difficulties and that various types of learning difficulties often co-occur and overlap. I called attention to the fact that establishing clear causal relationships between underlying processing problems and specific types of learning difficulties is often difficult. It is likely that as children mature cognitively and develop their literacy skills, different cognitive abilities and processing mechanisms also undergo changes. Therefore, it is very important that practitioners apply developmentally appropriate intervention and instructional techniques. Methods and tools of assessment, which constitute the focus of next chapter, also need to consider the reciprocal relationship between literacy development and cognitive abilities.

2

THE IDENTIFICATION OF SPECIFIC LEARNING DIFFICULTIES IN ANOTHER LANGUAGE

Identifying which students are making slower progress in learning a new language because of a learning difficulty is not always straightforward, and it may seem to be a challenging task to disentangle first language interference and low level of language proficiency from learning difficulties. The aim of this chapter is to give a comprehensive overview of the methods and tools of assessing specific learning difficulties (SpLDs) in monolingual and bilingual settings and to show that reliable and accurate identification of SpLDs is possible even in these contexts. The main focus here will be on identifying word- and text-level reading difficulties among multilingual speakers, but issues related to diagnosing spelling and writing problems will also be covered briefly. After the definition of the constructs of assessment, identification and diagnosis, a detailed description of the process of assessment of literacy skills will be provided. Next, I will discuss the determinants of successful word-decoding and text comprehension across languages, and based on the findings in this field, the consequences for the identification of SpLDs in bi/multilingual speakers will be drawn. The chapter will conclude with a review of current efforts directed at developing new means of assessment of learning difficulties in multilingual settings.

2.1 Assessment, Identification and Diagnosis

In order to identify individuals who encounter difficulties with academic tasks and literacy-related activities, one needs to assess these students' strengths and weaknesses. Assessment is an overarching concept as it refers to the systematic process of collecting a wide range of information about students' behaviour and learning processes. Hence, assessment includes formal testing, screening and diagnosis, as well as informal procedures such as observations or interviews. In the biomedical paradigm of SpLDs, the major aim of assessment is diagnosis, which establishes the source of difficulties as it relates to the individual, whereas in the interactional view of SpLDs (Frederickson & Cline, 2002), the assessment of the learning context and the students' sociocultural environment also forms an important part of the process.

Assessment can have a number of purposes including most importantly the observation and description of the individual's characteristics and level of attainment at a particular point in time and over a given period. On the basis of assessment reports, decisions and recommendations can be made concerning referral for further assessment, placement in a specific class or school, additional support, accommodations in teaching and tests, and targets for attainment (Phillips et al., 2013). The outcomes of assessment can also inform stakeholders such as schools, local authorities and educational policy makers with regard to potential changes required in legislation, the educational context and methods, and the allocation of resources. Finally, the process of assessment and its consequences should be informative for the assessed students and help them understand their difficulties and learn about possible coping strategies and ways of development (Kormos & Smith, 2012). In sum, assessment should not only focus on the individual in question, but it also needs to carefully examine how the environment might potentially contribute to or even cause the difficulties of the student. Accordingly, the outcomes of assessment have implications not only for the student, but also for their educational contexts.

Under the broader construct of assessment, it is important to differentiate identification from diagnosis. Identification is usually carried out at school level and can be a process initiated by classroom teachers and consequently taken further by qualified specialist teachers or a team of school-based experts. The aim here is to detect as early as possible that a child's progress is below the expected level in a particular academic domain and to generate a plan of action to meet the needs of the student and make changes in the learning environment. Identification does not necessarily have to establish the cause of the difficulties, but should provide a detailed description of the students' learning processes and difficulties. Identification can initially be carried out by classroom teachers using informal data collection methods such as observations and interviews, and following the evaluation of the data collected through these means, more formal approaches such as screening tests can be applied. Screening procedures, which are more structured than the initial assessment steps, aim to provide a more formal and standardized evaluation of students' skills, abilities and attainment. For example, there exist standardized screening tests of dyslexia such as Dyslexia Portfolio (Turner, 2008) or the Bangor Dyslexia Test (Miles, 1997) that can be used by specialist teachers, special educational needs coordinators and psychologists.

The final stage of diagnosis is usually carried out by a psychologist. The main goal of diagnosis is not only to identify and classify the students' learning difficulty but also to offer an explanation for the cause of the students' problems (Johnson et al., 2010). Just as in the case of identification, diagnosis should not simply involve the statement of the learners' difficulty and its potential reasons, but should outline ways in which students can be assisted in their learning and should give suggestions for modifications in the teaching methods and the learning environment (for a detailed description of diagnostic procedures, see Alderson, Brunfaut & Harding, 2014). In fact, the 5th edition of the *Diagnostic and Statistical Manual of Mental Disorders* of the American Psychiatric Association (DSM-5; APA, 2013) relates the severity of SpLDs to the level and intensity of support required, and defines mild manifestations as cases when "individuals may be able to compensate and function when well when provided with appropriate accommodations and support services" (p. 67). Students with moderate SpLDs need "some intervals of intensive and specialised teaching", whereas those with severe SpLDs would demand "ongoing intensive individualized and specialized teaching" (APA, 2013, p. 68).

Overall, it is important to remember that identification is a chain of actions and not a single event (Alderson, Haapakangas, Huhta, Nieminen & Ullakonoja, 2014). Classroom teachers play a crucial role in initiating the process, and therefore their assessment competence is key to the success of identification. Alderson, Brunfaut and Harding (2014) highlight that teaching experience, understanding the process of reading and the procedures of diagnostic testing are essential for the valid and reliable identification of struggling L2 readers. They also recommend that teachers use a variety of sources of information and assessment techniques and regularly consult with other colleagues, specialist teachers and experts.

2.2 The Process and Tools of Assessment

The process of assessment starts with the phase of observation, during which teachers collect information about the students' performance as well as their strengths and weaknesses (see Figure 2.1). In addition to the use of checklists, observations and screening tests, this phase also needs to involve the students' self-assessment (Harding et al., 2014). Based on the outcomes of the initial assessment, teachers have to take steps for addressing the students' difficulty by means of accommodations in the classroom and additional support. If these lead to no improvement in the learners' progress, further assessment procedures are recommended. Information from other teachers and parents might be collected and formal, standardized tests can be administered to ascertain whether the students' difficulties are due to some type of SpLD or other factors such as hearing impairment or home language status. This is the point where school-based assessment can be complemented or followed up by diagnosis made by a specialist.

The assessment report and the diagnosis should be made available to the student, parents and the teachers and should be used to implement changes in the teaching environment and the pedagogical programme. The assessment process, however, does not stop at this stage because it is essential that the student's response to the implemented programme is monitored carefully. If the interventions and modifications in the educational environment lead to no progress, further assessment might be needed (see Figure 2.1). This time, the

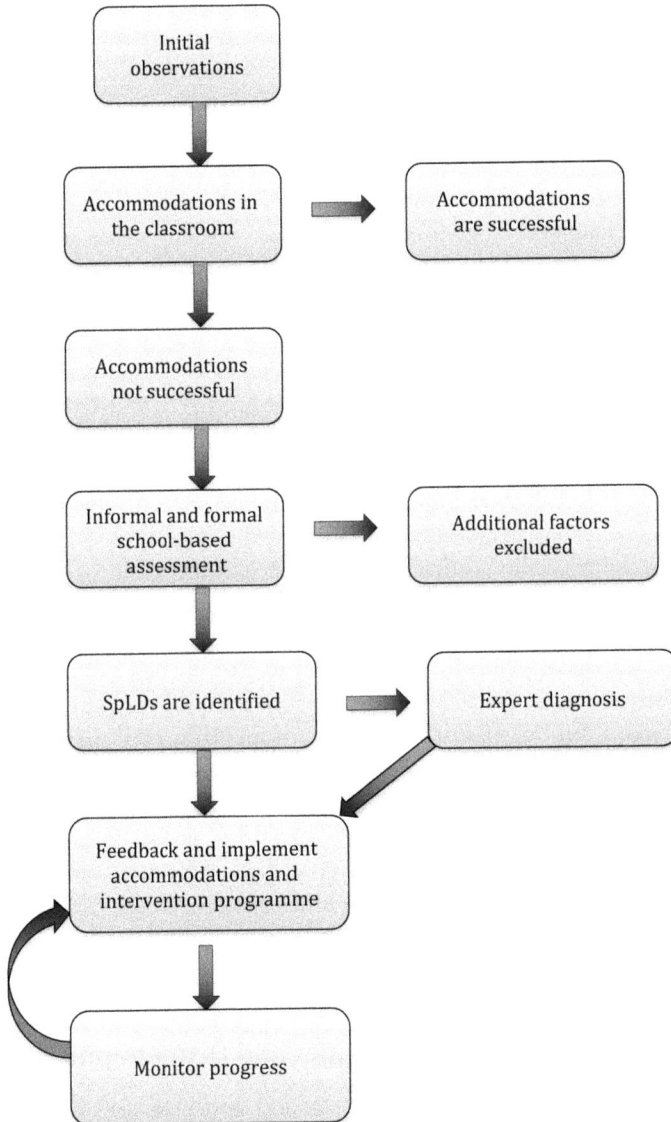

FIGURE 2.1 The Process of Assessment of SpLDs

Source: Based on Phillips, Kelly and Symes (2013).

major focus has to be on the effectiveness of the initially proposed programme and the potential barriers in the classroom and the curriculum, but in some cases, the accuracy of the diagnosis might also need to be queried.

The detailed description of the various tools that can be used to collect information for assessment is beyond the scope of this book. Interested readers can refer to Phillips et al.'s (2013) practical handbook on the use of various instruments. For our purposes, it is important to highlight that standardized and formal tests are not the only means by which teachers and experts can gain knowledge about students' difficulties. As already mentioned, unstructured observations of classroom behaviour, students' work patterns and study processes as well as structured observation schedules that require consistent sampling of events at time intervals can be applied in the initial stages of assessment. Collection of students' work in a portfolio and interviews with students, teachers and parents can provide additional useful insights. Published screening tests as well as teacher-prepared instruments such as reading passages and short pieces of writing can be highly informative before more formal assessment procedures are initiated. Even formal diagnostic assessment needs to be based on multiple sources of information and not just on standardized tests of academic achievement and cognitive functioning. For example, the DSM-5 (APA, 2013) lists portfolios, school reports and curriculum-based assessment as additional data sources. DSM-5 also stresses the importance of documenting students' difficulties in the context of their lives (e.g. family and academic learning history and impact on functioning in home, school and work contexts), as well as over time.

Finally, the possibilities offered by dynamic assessment also need to be mentioned. Dynamic assessment, as its name suggests, aims to establish what students can achieve if they are given feedback on their performance as they complete the test (Feuerstein, 1980; Lantolf & Poehner, 2011). This type of assessment allows for gauging students' learning potential and provides information about what students can do when they are given support as they work on the test. Assistance given can involve modifying the presentation format of the information (i.e. from visual to oral) and allowing more trials. The administrator of the test can also observe students' strategies and offer feedback on how effective these are; alternatively explicit instruction, hints and clues can be provided (Swanson & Lussier, 2001). The score on dynamic assessment tests is not determined as the achievement on the specific test, but as the difference between the assisted and unassisted performance.

2.3 Reading in Different Languages and Orthographies

Before we discuss the wide range of issues and questions related to identifying literacy-related learning difficulties in multiple languages, it is important to consider how languages differ with regard to their orthographic systems and how these differences affect the processes of reading and learning how to read.

Cross-linguistic variation in orthographic systems is also relevant from the perspective of literacy-related learning difficulties, especially dyslexia, because it might be possible that dyslexia affects reading development and reading processes differently across languages.

Writing systems of the world can be classified either as logographic or as phonographic (Treiman & Kessler, 2005). A typical example of the logographic system is Chinese where writing symbols (graphemes) denote words and morphemes. In phonographic systems graphemes can represent syllables, parts of syllables or sound segments (phonemes). Writing systems where a grapheme stands for a specific phoneme are called alphabetic. In order to understand the effects of orthography on learning to read and reading difficulties, it is important to remember that no writing system is purely and consistently alphabetic because phonological and morphological features, historical factors, dialectic variation and loan words often influence orthographic representation (Treiman & Kessler, 2005). It is also to be noted that while there are huge advantages of alphabetic systems in terms of the relatively small number of letters used to represent sounds (i.e. compare the 26 letters used in English with 3000 logograms that need to be learned by Chinese children), there are also disadvantages that affect spelling processes and the acquisition of literacy skills.

One of the disadvantages of alphabetic systems is that basic literacy skills depend on children's ability to segment the sound stream into phonemes and matching graphemes to corresponding phonemes. I will return to this problem when I present the psycholinguistic grain size theory (Ziegler & Goswami, 2005, 2006) below. Another drawback of alphabetic systems concerns the fact that it is difficult to implement a fully alphabetic system in which there is a consistent one-to-one correspondence between sounds and written symbols. It is along this line that languages using alphabetic scripts differ. Inconsistencies in orthographic systems can be the result of the fact that languages vary in how transparent their spelling system is, in other words, how consistent grapheme–phoneme associations are. In languages such as Finnish and Turkish, the majority of sounds systematically map on to letters, and these orthographic systems are called transparent. In nontransparent, or in other words, deep orthographies phoneme–grapheme mappings are inconsistent in that there are many-to-one sound–letter correspondences or many-to-one letter correspondences. The difficulty with learning to read and spell in English is that there are many-to-many sound–letter correspondences. For example the sound /ɔ/ can be spelled as *o, a, oa, augh, aw* (just to mention a few), and the letter 'i' can be pronounced as /ɪ/ or /aɪ/. In addition to being nontransparent, English, similarly to French, is an opaque language because it has silent letters. English spelling is also influenced by morphology as the morphological relationships are signaled in spelling despite differing pronunciation (e.g. heal and health; Caravolas, 2004).

The question is then whether the transparency of the orthography in different alphabetic languages influences reading processes and the manifestations of reading difficulties. One hypothetical answer to this question was offered by the *orthographic depth hypothesis*, which assumed that in transparent languages different reading processes are applied than in nontransparent ones. This hypothesis is built on Coltheart's (1978) dual-route model of reading, which was described in Section 1.4. In this model, readers can decode the written word through the *sublexical route*, that is, by means of converting the letters of the word into sounds and assembling the sounds to form the phonological (spoken) form of the word. Alternatively, readers can also follow the *lexical route* by recognizing the visual form of a word as a whole unit and without having to analyse it into phonological segments. The strong version of the orthographic depth hypothesis (Turvey, Feldman & Lukatela, 1984) claimed that readers in transparent languages predominantly decode written words via the sublexical route, whereas the lexical route is favoured by readers in nontransparent orthographies. Empirical evidence, however, did not provide support for the strong version of the orthographic depth hypothesis (Besner & Smith, 1992). The weaker version of the hypothesis postulated that children at the initial stages of learning to read might prefer different processing strategies depending on the transparency of the orthography. For example, Wimmer and Goswami (1994) demonstrated that children learning to read in German, which has more transparent orthography than English tended to be more accurate in reading pseudowords, that is, nonexistent words that require processing through the sublexical route, than their English peers. Wimmer and Goswami highlight that while it is likely that children learning to read in a transparent orthography might initially develop a preference for the sublexical route and use phonemes as the smallest unit of analysis and decoding, other factors such as the type of instruction might also influence reading development. To illustrate, the predominant approach to teaching reading in German is the phonics approach which lays emphasis on the explicit teaching of phoneme–grapheme correspondences, whereas in English, the whole word approach is still often applied in teaching reading (for more detail see Chapter 6).

Another difference between orthographies concerns the size of the unit within a word that can reliably predict sound–spelling associations. In transparent languages, the smallest size of such a unit is the phoneme, but as Ziegler and Goswami (2005, 2006) in their psycholinguistic grain size theory argue, languages also differ with regard to the size of these units and the contributions these various grain sized units make to reading and reading development. In the case of English, for instance, the vowel–consonant cluster at the end of syllables, which is called rime, often maps more consistently on pronunciation than the individual graphemes do (e.g. compare b*and*, h*and*, l*and* with c*all*, b*ark*, b*and*). Therefore, in order to become a successful reader in nontransparent languages such as English, one does not only need phoneme awareness, but also the ability to manipulate larger units such as rimes (see Figure 2.2 for the illustration of various grain size units). Furthermore, as there are many more combinations possible when grain sizes are larger compared to small-size units such as phonemes, developing readers

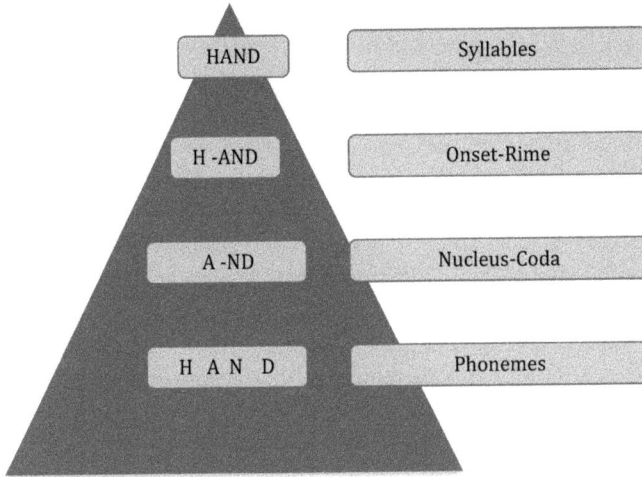

FIGURE 2.2 An Illustration of Different Psycholinguistic Grain Sizes

Source: Based on Ziegler and Goswami (2005).

in languages have a more difficult task because they also need to learn a larger number of these units. Notwithstanding the larger number of units to be acquired, larger grain size units might not always map consistently onto pronunciation either, such as in the case of b*ead* and h*ead*.

Based on the orthographic differences across languages, it is no surprise to find that the rate of reading and spelling development differs across alphabetic languages. In a comparative study which investigated the word-level reading attainment of children and the end of Grade 1 in 13 languages, Seymour, Aro and Erskine (2003) found that German, Finnish, Greek and Spanish children had close to 100% accuracy, participants from Portugal, France and Denmark scored around 80%, but English children achieved only a 34% accuracy rate. The study also concluded that the children's differential alphabetic knowledge or the age when formal schooling starts did not account for the differences across languages. Similar advantages for children acquiring literacy skills in transparent orthographies were observed with regard to spelling development (see e.g. Caravolas, 2004).

So far the discussion has centred around alphabetic and European languages, but one can justifiably ask whether reading processes are universal in logographic scripts such as Chinese or syllabic orthographies such as Japanese. One might hypothesize that in these languages, the lexical processes of reading dominate and phonological analysis might not be carried out during the word-reading process. It has been argued, however, that phonological processing is an essential and universal element of reading regardless of the type of orthography (Perfetti, Zhang & Berent, 1992). To illustrate, in Chinese, there are only a small set of possible syllable combinations and words are monosyllabic. This gives rise to the fact that one syllable might stand for 20 different words, which are either completely identical in pronunciation or are differentiated by tones (Chao, 1968). Chinese characters represent a semantic radical on the left side and phonetic radical on the right side, and as a consequence readers first activate semantic information and phonological information next (Wang, Georgiou, Das & Li, 2012). Perfetti, Liu and Tan (2005) summarize empirical evidence that phonological processing is an integral part of word reading in Chinese. In sum, it seems plausible that there are certain universal features of reading across languages such as reliance on phonological processing (Perfetti & Harris, 2013). Nonetheless, it is important to acknowledge that the characteristics of writing systems, which are interrelated with the language they represent, also influence reading processes and how children learn to read.

2.4 Cognitive and Linguistic Predictors of Reading Outcomes and Reading Difficulties in Different Languages

Based on the *Universal Phonological Principle* (Perfetti et al., 1992), which posits that phonology plays an important role in reading in every language of the world, the first issue to consider is what contribution individual variations in phonological skills make to attainment in reading and the rate of reading development across various languages. One key construct that has been identified to predict reading skills and also word-level reading difficulties (i.e. dyslexia) is phonological awareness (see Chapter 1 for more detail). Phonological awareness refers to the ability to manipulate phonological units of various grain size (Ziegler & Goswami, 2005, 2006) such as syllables, onsets, rimes and phonemes (see Figure 2.2). Phonemic awareness, which is a subcomponent of phonological awareness, is a skill of manipulating sounds such as segmenting words into sounds, deleting sounds from the beginning or end of the words, blending sounds and adding sounds to words. The distinction between phonological awareness and phonemic awareness is important because research evidence suggests that phonological awareness at the word and syllable level develops before reading instruction, whereas neither children before they go to school nor illiterate adults demonstrate substantial levels of phonemic awareness (for a review see Ziegler & Goswami, 2005, 2006). Phonological awareness at the level of syllable, onset and rime has been shown to be a good early predictor of word-level reading skills in Dutch and Finnish, and consequently of dyslexia, before schooling starts (de Jong & van der Leij, 2003; Puolakanaho et al., 2007). Longitudinal studies have shown that as children learn to read, and concomitantly as their phonemic awareness starts to develop, phonological awareness at the level of syllables and rimes becomes a less reliable indicator of dyslexia in Dutch and German (de Jong & van der Leij, 2003).

Phonemic awareness seems to be a relevant construct in predicting the development of word-level reading skills and dyslexia in a number of languages, not only including Chinese (for a recent study see Wang et al., 2012), but also other non-Indo-European languages such as Arabic and Hebrew (Abu-Rabia, Share, & Mansour, 2003; Share, 1995; Share & Levin, 1999). The question is whether the role of phoneme awareness in word-level reading is central across all languages or whether its impact varies. One might hypothesize that in more transparent orthographies such as in German or Finnish beginning readers are assisted in developing their phonemic awareness because there is a near one-to-one relationship between phonemes and graphemes (de Jong & van der Leij, 2003; Wimmer, Mayringer & Landerl, 2000). Phonemic awareness of children from these backgrounds also increases because the prevalent instructional method of teaching reading is based on phonics (Ziegler, Perry, Jacobs & Braun, 2001). Therefore, it is conceivable that phonemic awareness plays a less important role in learning to read and is a less reliable predictor of dyslexia in transparent orthographies than in opaque ones. A number of studies investigating this question have found that in German and Greek, which both have transparent orthographies, phonemic awareness played a secondary role compared to rapid automated naming (RAN) (Georgiou, Parrila & Papadopoulos, 2008; Mann & Wimmer, 2002). Other large scale cross-linguistic comparisons which used similar batteries of tests, however, brought different results. In a study comparing the predictors of word-level reading skills of Grade 2 children in five different languages (Finnish, Hungarian, Portuguese, Dutch and French), Ziegler et al. (2010) demonstrated that except for Finnish, which was the most transparent of the languages involved, phonemic awareness was the most important predictive factor. Rapid automated naming (RAN) also played a substantial role in most languages except for Finnish and French, whereas vocabulary knowledge and phonological short-term memory capacity varied greatly in their predictive power across contexts. Landerl et al. (2013) conducted a similar cross-linguistic study on predictors of dyslexia, where the findings of the earlier study by Ziegler et al. (2010) with a nondyslexic sample were replicated. The results confirmed that for all the six languages involved (Hungarian, Dutch, English, French, Finnish, German), phonemic awareness was the strongest indicator of dyslexia, followed by RAN. Phonological short-term memory capacity was significantly but weakly associated with dyslexic difficulties. An additional noteworthy finding of Landerl et al.'s (2013) study was that the relative contribution of phonemic awareness and RAN to word-reading difficulties varied in different languages. Children learning to read in less transparent languages such as English were more accurately classified as dyslexic based on their phonemic awareness and RAN scores than those whose first language used transparent orthography. Recent longitudinal research also underscores the importance of phonemic awareness in reading and spelling development regardless of the transparency of orthography. Caravolas et al. (2012) and Caravolas, Lervåg, Defior, Seidlová

Málková and Hulme (2013) conducted a series of studies involving young Czech, Slovak, English and Spanish children whose reading development was followed longitudinally. They found that phonemic awareness assessed before or shortly after formal reading instruction started, was a significant predictor of both reading accuracy and reading speed, as well as the rate of development in word-level reading skills.

It has been shown that in transparent orthographies, children reach a high level of word-reading accuracy relatively quickly, and therefore in these languages, reading speed is assumed to be a better measure of word-reading abilities (e.g. Seymour et al., 2003). Even children with dyslexia are more accurate in word reading in more transparent orthographies such as German compared to less transparent languages (Landerl, Wimmer & Frith, 1997). While phonemic awareness makes a significant contribution to both reading accuracy and reading speed at word-level, RAN, due to its timed nature, has been hypothesized to be an important predictor of reading speed, especially in transparent orthographies (Wimmer et al., 2000). Indeed RAN, which is usually measured as the speed of object, colour or digit naming, was found to be a good indicator of both dyslexic-type word-reading problems and word-level reading speed and accuracy (for a review see Kirby, Georgiou, Martinussen & Parrila, 2010). There is, however, some variation in the role of RAN based on how it is measured. For example when RAN was assessed by object naming in Ziegler et al.'s (2010) study, it was found to be weakly associated with word-level reading abilities in most of the languages they investigated. When RAN was operationalized as digit-naming speed in a follow-up study by Landerl et al. (2013), it was a strong predictor of dyslexia and its statistical effect was even larger than that of phonemic awareness in German and Dutch. The role of RAN was found to be similar to phonemic awareness in forecasting reading and spelling ability in English, Czech and Spanish, but when it came to predicting how quickly reading skills develop in the first 2 years of schooling, it was only RAN that played a significant role. It also needs to be noted that RAN seems to be an important marker of reading problems for a longer period, even after initial years of reading instruction when phoneme awareness often fails to differentiate among good and poor readers (Landerl & Wimmer, 2008; Lervåg, Bråten & Hulme, 2009).

The third important predictor of word-level reading and spelling abilities at early stages of literacy acquisition in alphabetic languages is letter knowledge (e.g. Caravolas et al., 2012). Letter knowledge is part of the larger construct of orthographic processing, which comprises not only children's ability to match sounds with corresponding letters, but also the efficiency with which they are able to do this in real time. Orthographic processing skills have been found to differentiate dyslexic readers of Chinese from their nondyslexic peers (Wang et al., 2012) and predict reading comprehension ability in Arabic (Elbeheri et al., 2011). While it is certainly important to assess students' orthographic processing skills when identifying reading difficulties across a wide range of languages, it is useful to note that there might be overlaps between RAN and orthographic processing (Georgiou, Parrila & Kirby, 2009; Wang et al., 2012).

In nonalphabetic languages, an additional important contributor to word-level reading difficulties is morphological awareness. In the case of Chinese, a number of studies demonstrated that morphological awareness is a key predictor of dyslexia (e.g. Chung & Ho, 2009). Morphological awareness was also found to be related to word-reading skills (e.g. Mahony, Singson & Mann, 2000) and comprehension in English (Carlisle, 2000), Arabic (Saeigh-Haddad & Geva, 2008) and Hebrew (Ravid & Malenky, 2001).

Other predictors of word-reading abilities and dyslexia include phonological short-term memory and working memory capacity (Jeffries & Everatt, 2004). Phonological short-term memory is responsible for the temporary storage and manipulation of verbal information (Baddeley & Hitch, 1974), and it assists in keeping phonological information active while one is processing words (see Section 3.1 for more detail). Figure 2.3 gives an overview of the constructs that need to be considered in the assessment of word-reading difficulties. It is important to remember, however, that reduced skills and abilities in any of the areas listed above and shown in Figure 2.3 might not be the direct causes of dyslexia.

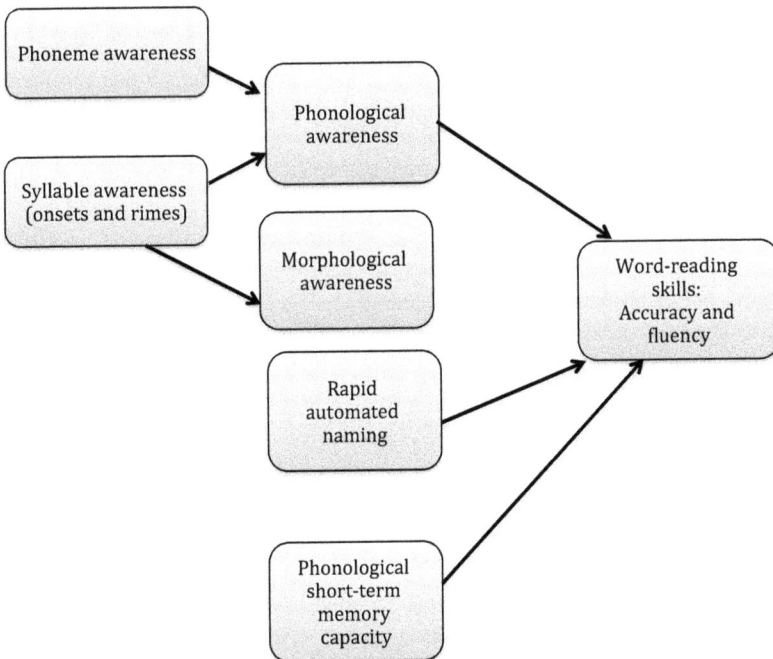

FIGURE 2.3 Predictors of Word-Level Reading Skills

Causal theories of dyslexia are discussed in Section 1.6, and here the focus is on what underlying skills and abilities identification can be based on.

So far the discussion has concentrated on word-reading and dyslexia, but as I explained in Chapter 1, children and adults can also have reading difficulties above word level. If we revisit Gough and Tunmer's (1986) "Simple View of Reading" described in Chapter 1, it becomes apparent that word-level reading problems are only one of the potential causes of reading comprehension difficulties. A number of linguistic and cognitive measures can be used to identify readers who demonstrate difficulties with text comprehension despite adequate word-reading skills. One predictor of specific reading comprehension difficulties has been found to be problems related to the function of working memory (Cain, 2006; Cain et al., 2004). As already explained in Chapter 1, working memory has an important function in keeping processed bits of information active, updating the understanding with new information, and orchestrating all the comprehension processes. An additional related key cognitive component required for efficient text processing is attention-allocating abilities (Oakhill, Hartt & Samols, 2005), which helps readers to maintain focus while reading and inhibit irrelevant information.

The linguistic predictors of reading comprehension difficulties are reduced syntactic, morphological and phonological awareness. Syntactic awareness is "the ability to reason consciously about the syntactic aspects of language, and to exercise intentional control over the application of grammatical rules" (Gombert, 1992, p. 39). Syntactic awareness helps readers to understand the syntactic structure of clauses and sentences and to predict upcoming parts of the text. Syntactic awareness was found to play an important role in the development of early reading comprehension skills in children (Willows & Ryan, 1986) and to be a significant contributor to reading comprehension difficulties (Tunmer, Nesdale & Wright, 1987). Morphological awareness is necessary for successful reading comprehension (Elbro & Arnbak, 1996), and phonological awareness albeit with a smaller effect, also predicts problems with reading comprehension (Siegel, 2008). Finally, one of the key elements of accurate text comprehension involves appropriate level of vocabulary knowledge including well-developed phonological, orthographic and semantic representations of words in the mental lexicon (Perfetti, 2007).

At the textual level, inference-making ability is also an important skill to assess when identifying reading comprehension difficulties (Oakhill et al., 2003). Without generating inferences, it is almost impossible to create an appropriate mental representation of the text. Inference making is needed when connecting information presented in sentences, resolving nonexplicit references within the text, decoding implied meaning and relating background knowledge to the information conveyed by the text (for a recent review see Kendeou et al., 2014). Figure 2.4 gives an overview of the predictors of reading comprehension difficulties.

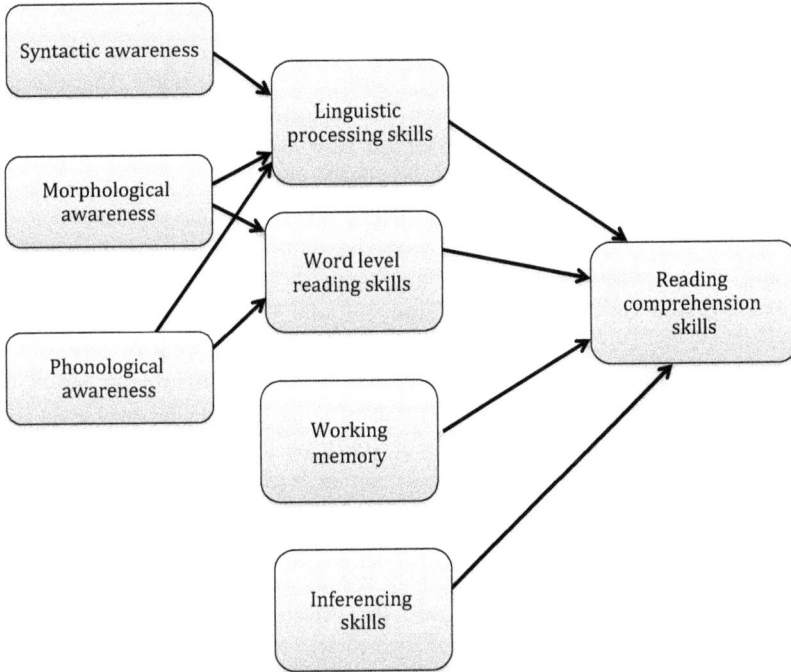

FIGURE 2.4 Predictors of Reading Comprehension Skills

2.5 The Role of Social, Educational and Contextual Factors in Reading Difficulties

Cognitive factors play a key role in word- and text-level reading comprehension, yet the importance of other social, instructional and psychological factors should not be underestimated. In the *component model of reading,* Aaron, Joshi, Gooden and Bentum (2008) argue that the psychological and ecological components of reading should also be considered in both the identification and remediation of reading difficulties. Among the psychological determinants of reading, they list motivation and attitudes to reading, self-regulation and self-related beliefs, learning styles, gender differences and teacher expectations. Indeed Chiu and Chow (2010) found that interest in reading, extrinsic motivation and effort and persistence were positively related to reading outcomes in a large-scale international study conducted in 41 countries. Girls were also found to be more highly skilled readers, which they explained with reference to different socialization practices (for more detail see Chiu & McBride-Chang, 2006).

The socioeconomic and instructional factors in Aaron et al.'s (2008) component model of reading are subsumed under the heading of ecological components of reading. The factors in the close proximity of the individual include a number of social characteristics of the family such as socioeconomic status and parents' education, as well as the attitudes of the family to education and reading and the frequency of literacy-related activities. Closely related to this is an often used variable in questionnaire research, the number of books at home. Outside the home environment, a key factor is the educational context. School-based factors are comprised of resources of the school, specialist support available, communication between school and parents, peer achievement and peer attitudes to literacy (Chiu & McBride-Chang, 2006). Teachers' level of qualification, expertise in literacy teaching and job satisfaction were also found to play a role in students' reading achievement (Podhajski, Mather, Nathan & Sammons, 2009).

The findings of the large scale study on the factors influencing reading achievement in 45 countries involving over 180,000 participants are worth considering in the diagnosis and identification of reading difficulties (Chiu et al., 2012). Although the measures for cognitive variables were retrospective, and consequently they might not be very accurate, it was found that cognitive factors accounted for only a very small proportion of reading difficulties (1%). The explanatory power of variables at the level of the individual was also very low, a mere 8%. The most important contributor to overall reading achievement was the GDP per capita variable (83%), which was found to have a direct influence on the number of books at home and the overarching socioeconomic status factor (see Figure 2.5). Socioeconomic status was strongly associated not only with the resources available to students, but also with reading attitudes and reading self-concept. Parents' attitudes to reading turned out to be a factor that made an important contribution to reading skills independent of socioeconomic status. Somewhat counter-intuitively, Chiu et al.'s (2012) results indicate that teachers played a limited role in reading achievement and rather it was school climate, the literacy-level of peers, school resources and home-school involvement that were related to reading outcomes.

Based on these findings, Chiu et al. (2012) conclude that "low reading achievement is largely a societal phenomenon, rather than an individual one" (p. 402). Their conclusion calls attention to the social and psychological factors that need to be carefully examined when one wants to identify the sources of reading problems in addition to or above the cognitive causes of reading difficulties. If identification and diagnosis takes place in an environment where the family and socioeconomic background of children is similar and where the school-based resources are comparable, it is likely that cognitive causes of reading difficulties will be in the primary focus of assessment. Considering the students' home and educational context, however, is particularly important if students' socioeconomic status and instructional context is heterogeneous. Pertaining to the very high contribution GDP per capita makes to reading success (Chiu et al., 2012), it is essential to obtain information about previous literacy-learning contexts, resources and family background in the case of immigrant children and adults (see Geva & Wiener, 2014 for details on specific interview questions and case studies).

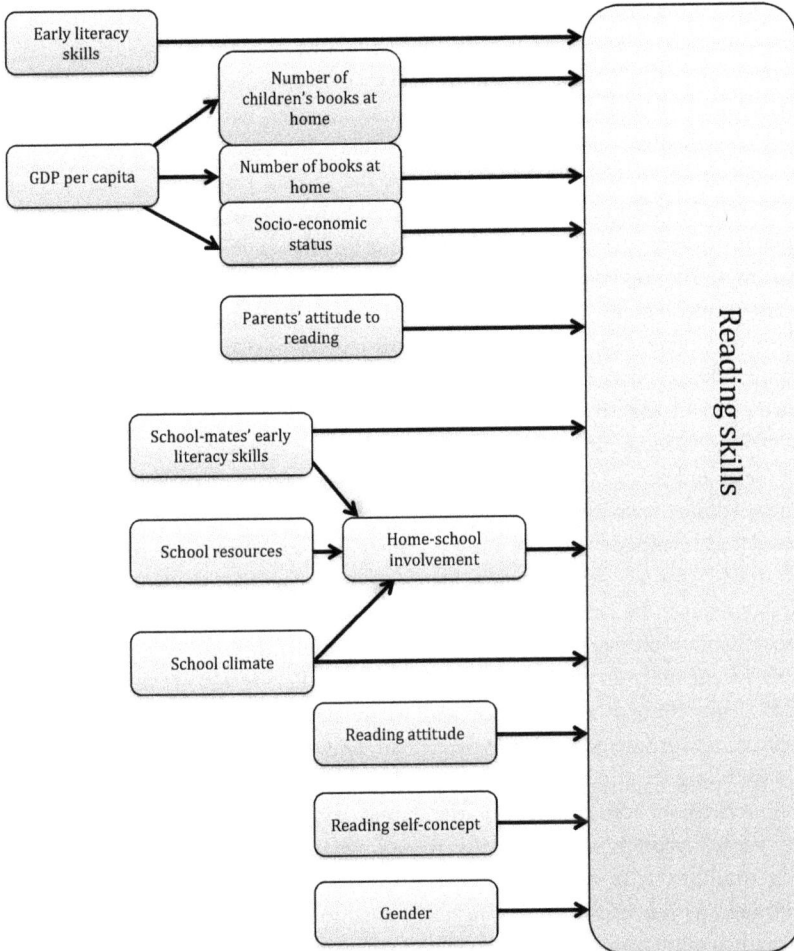

FIGURE 2.5 The Contributors of Reading Achievement in Chiu, McBride-Chang and Lin's (2012) Study

2.6 Identifying Reading and Learning Difficulties in Multilingual Students

The analysis of the predictors of word- and text-level reading difficulties in Section 2.4 reveals that there are cross-linguistic variations with regard to the relative role of cognitive and linguistic abilities needed for successful literacy outcomes. Yet the fundamental factors that can contribute to difficulties are highly similar. In their *common underlying cognitive processes framework,* Geva and Ryan (1993) argue that there is a core set of individual difference variables such as working memory, phonological short-term memory, phoneme awareness, RAN and self-regulatory functions that explain differences among students in reading outcomes across languages and in multilingual learners. Geva and Ryan's (1993) framework complements Cummins' (2000) *interdependence hypothesis*, which postulates that "academic language proficiency transfers across languages such that students who have developed literacy in their first language, will tend to make stronger progress in acquiring literacy in the second language" (p. 173). Cummins' (1981, 2000) argument about the facilitative role of well-developed literacy skills in students' L1 is particularly relevant for higher-order text comprehension processes. For lower-order word-reading processes and spelling development, it is also important to consider typological and orthographic differences and the effect of *positive and negative transfer* across languages (Genesee, Geva, Dressler & Kamil, 2006; Geva & Lafrance, 2011). A series of studies conducted with bilingual learners in a large variety of settings including both alphabetic and nonalphabetic as well as transparent and nontransparent orthographies have provided support for Geva and Ryan's (1993) common underlying cognitive processes framework. These studies have consistently shown that phoneme awareness and RAN are key determinants of word-reading accuracy and speed in both the participants' L1 and L2 (for a recent overview see Geva & Wiener, 2014). Not only do these factors seem to be the key determinants of word-decoding abilities, but they are also reliable indicators of spelling skills in L1 and L2 (Geva & Lafrance, 2011).

A recent meta-analysis by Melby-Lervåg and Lervåg (2014) has revealed that with some contextual variations and partly depending on the socioeconomic context, first language readers perform substantially better than second language and/or bilingual students on tests of reading comprehension and general language comprehension administered in the target language. Although differences in word-level decoding showed smaller monolingual advantage, monolingual students were found to score slightly higher in word-reading tests too. If these tests, which are generally normed for monolingual populations, are used for the identification of reading difficulties, both dyslexia and reading comprehension problems might be overidentified in multilingual students, in other words inaccurately attributed to an underlying learning difficulty (Samson & Lesaux, 2009). The differences between monolingual and multilingual readers in word- and text-reading scores can also give rise to a situation when timely assessment is missed. For example, Limbos and Geva (2001) found that while teachers were accurate in identifying struggling monolingual readers, they often incorrectly assumed that the word-reading difficulties of multilingual children were due to underdeveloped language proficiency.

One of the most important questions in assessing dyslexia and the cause of literacy-related learning difficulties is what language should be used in the identification and diagnostic process in the case of bi- or multilingual students. Based on Cummins' (1981, 2000) interdependence hypothesis, one possibility is to administer cognitive and literacy-tests in the students' first language because it can be assumed that reading abilities transfer from one language to the other (e.g. Lindsey, Manis, & Bailey, 2003; Sparks, Patton, Ganschow, Humbach & Javorsky, 2006, 2008). This might, however, not be practical due to the fact that comparable and standardized assessment of reading difficulties and relevant cognitive tests do not exist in all languages, and assessors proficient in the given language might not be available. Nevertheless, if appropriate tests exist and well-trained experts are at hand, assessment in the children's first language certainly contributes useful insights into the nature of reading difficulties.

Based on Geva and Ryan's (1993) common underlying cognitive processes framework, another possibility is to apply cognitive assessment tools that provide information about the predictors of reading outcomes. The large scale research programme led by Geva (2006) in Canada has convincingly shown that in the case of bi/multilingual children who have more than 2 years of schooling in the target language, tests of phonological awareness, phonological short-term memory capacity and RAN administered in the target language can be used as reliable predictors of dyslexia. Geva and Yaghoub Zadeh (2006) and Lesaux and Siegel (2003) have also demonstrated that these tests are good diagnostic tools even when children's oral language comprehension in the L2 is significantly below their monolingual peers. Similar results were obtained in the United Kingdom context with younger bilingual children aged 7–8 (Everatt, Smythe, Adams & Ocampo, 2000) and older children aged 10–12 (Frederickson & Frith, 1998). In these studies, the phonological awareness, RAN and working memory components of dyslexia screening tests were found to differentiate between students who had word-reading difficulties regardless of L1 status.

While it has been shown that word-level reading and spelling problems might be reliably identified in bilingual children with at least 2 years of schooling in the target language environment or with a similar period of exposure outside school (home, or preschool environment) using cognitive assessment tools, the question is whether reading comprehension problems can also be diagnosed using measures in the children's L2. Geva and Massey-Garrison's (2013) recent study with Canadian monolingual and bilingual children seems to indicate that the cognitive profile of poor comprehenders is quite similar. Both language groups are characterized by a smaller range of vocabulary, lower level of syntactic processing skills, difficulties with oral language comprehension and making inferences. The children with reading comprehension difficulties could also be reliably distinguished from those who had word-level decoding difficulties because they did not display phonological awareness, phonological short-term memory and rapid-naming problems. The results also indicate that monolingual and bilingual children in Canada only differed from each other in RAN speed and the range of receptive vocabulary, but not in other components of the administered tests. Geva and Massey-Garrison conclude that in contexts where children have sufficient exposure to the language of schooling, tests in the L2 can be used to assess both word- and text-level reading difficulties "provided that cultural and contextual issues are taken into account" (p. 398).

Although this chapter has mainly focused on reading-related learning difficulties so far, it is also important to consider what contributes to writing problems in bi- and multilingual children. It was already pointed out above that the determinants of spelling and word-decoding skills are highly similar in both L1 and L2 (Geva & Lafrance, 2011). This is due to the fact that both writing and word-reading draw on phonological processing and orthographic knowledge (Berninger, Abbott, Abbott, Graham & Richards, 2002). Reading comprehension difficulties and problems with text-level writing skills have also been found to be strongly related in L1 speakers (Berninger et al., 2002). Ndlovu and Geva's (2008) research confirmed the existence of a strong relationship between phonological awareness, word-decoding abilities and narrative composing skills in mono- and bilingual Canadian children. Their study also suggests that in the case of learners who had approximately 4 years of exposure to the language of schooling tests of phonological awareness, RAN and word reading are good predictors of both lower-level writing problems (spelling and punctuation) and higher level composing skills (constructing syntactically and lexically accurate and appropriate sentences, maintaining cohesion, logical ordering of events, creating an interesting storyline).

The case of children with learning difficulties who have not had enough contact with the target language and adult immigrants might be different though. Unfortunately to date, there is very little research conducted with these populations. Elbro, Daugaard and Gellert (2012) in a study of adult Danish immigrants and L1 Danish speakers found that, if the same components of the dyslexia screening test are administered to these groups by using the same cut-off point, dyslexic L2 readers are almost 8 times more likely to be overidentified. They suggest that for these populations dynamic assessment (see Section 2.2) might provide more accurate information about dyslexic difficulties. They devised a test in which participants had to learn new sound-symbol correspondences (e.g. ᖴ = /s/, ◊ = /m/, ▪ = /a/) and then use this knowledge for reading two and three-letter words (e.g. ᖴ▪ ◊= /sam/). The participants were given corrective feedback, but they were not told the correct answer. Elbro et al. (2012) found that this test had appropriate psychometric properties and good predictive power. Importantly, their analyses also showed that performance on this test was independent of proficiency in the societal language and years of schooling. This promising language-independent way of assessing dyslexia in multilingual populations is also used in a new test under development by Smith (2013).

In a different foreign language learning context in classroom settings, Pižorn and Erbeli (2013) report that for 12-year old Slovenian children, the structure of predictors for L2 reading outcomes among dyslexic children is somewhat different from those who do not have an official diagnosis of dyslexia. The nondyslexic group's reading comprehension scores in L2 English were most strongly predicted by word-level reading fluency and orthographic knowledge, whereas the dyslexic group's performance was primarily associated with the auditory comprehension of morphemes and words, vocabulary knowledge and orthographic skills. Word-reading fluency was only a second-order factor among the investigated dyslexic learners. Despite the difference in the relative importance of predictors of L2 reading comprehension scores, Pižorn and Erbeli's (2013) results suggest that even for students whose exposure to the target language was mostly through classroom instruction, cognitive tests administered in the L2 yield reliable information. Similar conclusions can be drawn from Alderson, Haapakangas, Huhta, Nieminen and Ullakonoja (2014) research conducted in Finland where working memory, RAN, phonological awareness and tests of word-reading speed conducted in L2 English differentiated better between competent and less competent L2 readers than tests in the students' L1.

2.7 An Overview of Assessment of Specific Learning Difficulties for Multilingual Learners

The timely assessment of specific learning difficulties among multilingual learners is just as important as in the case of monolingual children. Geva's work in the past 20 years (for an overview, see Geva & Wiener, 2014) provides a compelling argument that lack or low level of oral language proficiency in the target language should be no reason for delaying identification. The overview of studies in this chapter has shown that even for students who have primarily classroom exposure to the L2 only, tests administered in the L2 can be good predictors of literacy difficulties. There are also promising new developments in the field of dynamic assessment (Elbro et al., 2012) and in tools devised specifically for multilingual students (Smith, 2013).

As explained in Section 2.1, the assessment process needs to start with a thorough analysis of the students' strengths and weaknesses as observed in the classroom and/or while performing literacy-related activities. A detailed understanding of the socioeconomic and educational context and psychological factors described in Section 2.5 has to be gained, for which one of the most suitable tools is an interview with the student, family members and teachers. It is also important to assess students' reading and writing abilities. This can be done both in their first and second language, and standardized word- and text-reading, spelling and writing assessment can be used for this purpose. Reading texts selected by teachers also yield useful information in terms of the accuracy of reading, speed of decoding and higher level discourse comprehension.

Key elements of the assessment of SpLDs in the literacy domain are the tests of phonological awareness. Tasks that provide information about phoneme awareness require participants to segment words into sounds, blend sounds to form words and delete, add, reorder or replace sounds of words (see for example the Comprehensive Test of Phonological Processing (CTPP) by Wagner, Torgesen & Raschotte, 1999, for ages 5–24 and Phonological Assessment Battery (PhAB) for ages 6–14 by Frederickson, Frith & Reason, 1997). In order to avoid the confounding effect of lexical knowledge, which is particularly relevant in multilingual contexts, it is suggested that nonwords be used in these tasks. Phonological awareness at the level of syllable can be assessed by tasks tapping into the perception of rhyme and the ability to segment and blend syllables (e.g. PhAB, 1997). Some tests have an additional auditory discrimination component where test-takers have to decide whether the two words they hear are the same or different (e.g. the Test of Auditory Processing Skills for ages 4–18 by Gardner (2005)). Smith's (2013) Cognitive Assessments for Multilingual Learners also includes a sound discrimination task in the participants' L1.

Furthermore, the assessment battery needs to include tests of phonological short-term memory and working memory capacity. Phonological short-term memory tests are usually comprised of tasks that ask students to repeat nonexisting words in increasing length or an increasing number of digits, while working memory capacity is often assessed by a backward digit span task (Wechsler & Stone, 2009). These give more reliable information if they are administered in the students' L1, but if adjustments are made in terms of cut-off scores and if nonwords are compiled so that they have a simple syllable structure, tools available in L2 can also be used. Tests of visual memory that require students to recall an increasingly complex sequence of shapes are also components of SpLD assessment tests (see e.g. Smith, 2013).

Tests of rapid automated naming are additional key elements of most existing identification tools. As mentioned in Section 2.4, students can be asked to name objects, colours, numbers, letters or even months of the year as quickly as they can (see e.g. The Comprehensive Test of Phonological Processing by Wagner et al., 1999). Smith (2013) proposes that this test can be administered in students' L1 using photos of well-known objects.

As pointed out earlier in this chapter, teachers, including those teaching additional languages, have great responsibility in identifying students with SpLDs in the classroom. Early identification is paramount if we want to ensure that students become successful language learners and they do not lose their motivation and self-esteem. Therefore, appropriate level of teacher awareness of the relevant characteristics of SpLDs across languages and writing systems described in this chapter is essential. Teachers also need to be familiar with the available screening and identification methods and tools so that their judgements about whether a student's difficulty is due to SpLDs is not based on intuition alone. In the next chapter, we will turn our attention to how SpLDs affect the learning of additional languages. Understanding the learning processes and challenges of language learners with SpLDs is another important foundation for effective inclusive language teaching practices and pedagogical interventions.

3

THE COGNITIVE EFFECTS OF SPECIFIC LEARNING DIFFICULTIES ON THE PROCESSES OF LEARNING AN ADDITIONAL LANGUAGE

Specific learning difficulties not only have an effect on the acquisition of oral and literacy skills in the first language, but also influence the processes of second language learning. This chapter starts with a detailed discussion of how the cognitive correlates of specific learning difficulties (SpLDs), such as reduced phonological awareness, working and phonological short-term memory capacity, difficulties with attention control and implicit learning, can affect the processes of second language acquisition. Particular consideration will be given to how learners with SpLDs attend to, process and integrate new language input, as well as produce and learn from output. The cognitive effects of SpLDs on explicit and implicit learning processes will also be elaborated. This will be followed by a critical summary of previous research on how SpLDs affect the learning of second language skills such as reading and writing. While most of the discussion in this chapter will be centred on the cognitive correlates of SpLDs and additional difficulties with attention control, at the end of this chapter, I will also consider the language learning processes and outcomes of learners with autistic spectrum disorders (ASD) from a cognitive perspective.

The cognitive factors that are held to be important predictors of success in language learning for any learner population are intelligence (Skehan, 1986), language learning aptitude (Carroll, 1981; Carroll & Sapon, 1959), working memory capacity and phonological short-term memory capacity (for an overview, see Juffs & Harrington, 2011). As language learners with SpLDs show significant differences in their working memory and phonological short-term memory capacity and some of the fundamental components of aptitude compared to their peers who do not have SpLDs, this chapter will only consider the role of these cognitive factors. Attention control, which in some models is part of working memory (i.e. Baddeley, 2003), but in others is regulated by the central executive (e.g. Miyake et al., 2000), will also be discussed with regard to the language learning processes of learners with SpLDs.

As I highlighted in Chapter 1, various subtypes of SpLDs show substantial overlap. The difficulties involved in separating manifestations and correlates of dyslexia, dyspraxia and dyscalculia as well as ADHD make it almost impossible to distinguish the unique cognitive and emotional effects of these learning differences on the acquisition of additional languages. Therefore in this chapter, we will mainly consider the impact of the particular cognitive characteristics of SpLDs on second language learning, rather than the distinctive role played by each subtype of SpLD separately. Specific subtypes of SpLDs such as dyslexia will only be mentioned when the research findings reviewed explicitly refer to a particular group of learners. As identification and inclusion criteria for research participants varied across studies as well as over time, I will always use the original terms that the authors of the studies in question use to describe the participating sample.

3.1 The Construct of Working Memory

In order to explain how working memory affects the processes of language learning in the case of individuals with SpLDs, it is important to describe the construct of working memory and its constituents. The first important issue to consider with regard to the conceptualization of working memory is the relationship between working memory and long-term memory. According to Baddeley and Logie (1999), working memory is a processing module which is separate from, but interacts with, long-term memory, whereas other researchers perceive working memory as the relevant activated component of long-term memory (e.g., Cowan, 1995, 1999; Engle, Laughlin, Tuholski, & Conway, 1999). Although these two standpoints differ greatly, they both agree that long-term memory representations, in other words, previous knowledge and expertise, play an important role in the mental operations carried out in working memory (see Section 3.4 for a more detailed discussion).

The most widely accepted conceptualization of short-term memory today is the working memory model developed by Baddeley (1986); Baddeley and Hitch (1974). The working memory model proposed by Baddeley (2003) is a multi-component memory system with a central executive which coordinates two modality-specific subsystems, the phonological loop and the visuo-spatial sketchpad. Later, a fourth component was added to the model—the episodic buffer; this uses multidimensional coding, integrates information to form episodes, and is in communication with long-term memory (Baddeley & Logie, 1999). The visuo-spatial sketchpad works with visual and spatial information, while the phonological loop is specialized for the manipulation and retention of speech.

The central executive has several functions, including attentional control, directing the flow of information through the system, and planning (Gathercole,

1999). The architecture of the central executive in cognitive operations has been further elaborated and is now seen to play an important role in three processes of attention control (for a review see Miyake et al., 2000). First, the central executive is assumed to assist individuals shift between tasks they need to carry out in parallel or consecutively (Monsell, 1996), which is called the "task-switching" function of attention. Second, the updating and monitoring function of attention control helps people select, revise and review information which is relevant to successful completion of a task (Morris & Jones, 1990). Finally, the central executive also has an inhibitory function that hinders automatic responses when they are not relevant or useful to a particular task.

Another widely researched component of working memory is the phonological loop. This subsystem consists of a phonological store, which holds information for a few seconds, and an articulatory rehearsal process, which refreshes decaying information, amongst other functions. The rehearsal process is analogous to sub-vocal speech and takes place in real time, resulting in a limited span of immediate memory.

As described in Chapter 1, learners with SpLDs, especially those with dyslexia, often have smaller phonological short-term memory capacity than their peers with no SpLD, and their working memory span is also shorter (Jeffries & Everatt, 2004). Problems with sustained attention and attention control, the locus of which is the central executive, are also frequent in the case of individuals with SpLDs, even in the absence of a formal identification of ADHD (e.g. Fletcher, Morris & Lyon, 2004; Snowling, 2008). For people with ADHD, research findings consistently indicate reduced working memory capacity and less efficient control of the central executive processes (see Willcutt, Pennington, Chhabildas, Olson & Hulslander, 2005) compared to children with no ADHD.

3.2 The Construct of Language Learning Aptitude and Its Interrelationship With Working Memory

In the field of second language acquisition, Carroll, who developed the first language aptitude test, defined language learning aptitude as "some characteristic of an individual which controls, at a given point of time the rate of progress that he will make subsequently in learning a foreign language" (1974, quoted by Sawyer & Ranta, 2001, p. 310). In Carroll's original conceptualization of aptitude, this cognitive factor was assumed to predict the rate of learning and not the actual success in second language acquisition. Recent research on the role of language learning aptitude has, however, proposed a reconceptualization of aptitude (see Kormos, 2013). As Snow (1992) points out, aptitude has several meanings, including readiness, suitability, susceptibility and proneness for learning in particular situations. He also highlights that aptitude is not a constant and innate intellectual capacity, rather it is a conglomerate of individual characteristics that dynamically interact with the situation in which learning takes place. From this view of aptitude, it follows that different sets of abilities can enhance learning under various learning conditions, which I will discuss later in Section 3.5.1.

One of the longstanding issues in the field of SLA is the lack of a clear definition of what one means by language learning aptitude, and this stems from the fact that most developers of language aptitude tests have followed an empirically based psychometric approach to test development. For example, Carroll and Sapon (1959) administered a great variety of tests that seemed likely to predict language learning success on about 5,000 students. Based on the results, they selected the tasks which best differentiated between successful and unsuccessful language learners but did not correlate strongly with each other (Carroll & Sapon, 1959). These components of language learning aptitude included: (1) phonetic coding ability, that is, the "ability to identify distinct sounds, to form associations between those sounds and symbols representing them, and to retain these associations"; (2) grammatical sensitivity, that is the ability "to recognize the grammatical functions of words (or other linguistic entities) in sentence structures"; (3) rote learning ability, defined as "the ability to learn associations between sounds and meanings rapidly and efficiently, and to retain these associations"; and (4) inductive learning ability, which is "the ability to infer or induce the rules governing a set of language materials, given sample language materials that permit such inferences [to be made]" (Carroll, 1981, p. 105).

In response to criticisms of the traditional construct of aptitude, Robinson (2001) proposed a theoretically motivated model of aptitude, in which cognitive resources and abilities are combined into aptitude complexes. In Robinson's model, primary abilities include pattern recognition, speed of processing in phonological working memory and grammatical sensitivity. These general cognitive abilities, which, with the exception of phonological memory, are based on the traditional construct of aptitude, help the so-called second-order abilities. These latter abilities are specific to language learning and include noticing a gap, memory for contingent speech, deep semantic processing, memory for contingent text and metalinguistic rule rehearsal.

Robinson (2005a) argues that general working memory and phonological short-term capacity can be seen as important components of aptitude complexes, in addition to some other traditional components of aptitude such as inductive ability. Robinson (2002) also tested the link between working memory and language learning aptitude and found that working memory, as measured with a reading span test, had a moderately strong correlation with aptitude scores. In another research project, Sáfár and Kormos (2008) reported a moderately strong relationship between a backward digit span test, which is a test of complex working memory, and total aptitude scores, with the two tests sharing approximately 13% of the variance. This finding shows that these two constructs are related but only partially overlap. With regard to the correlation between the different components of aptitude and working memory capacity, the only significant relationship that emerged in Sáfár and Kormos' (2008) research was between working memory scores and the inductive ability test. This indicates that the ability to maintain and manipulate verbal information in working memory might be related to the efficiency with which learners can induce linguistic rules from the input in a language unknown to them, as measured by this component of the aptitude test. Sáfár and Kormos (2008) also examined the link between aptitude test scores and phonological short-term memory capacity, which was assessed using a nonword repetition task. They found no significant correlation between phonological short-term memory capacity, aptitude components and total aptitude test score. This might suggest that the storage capacity for verbal material is, in itself, without a processing and attention regulating function, a cognitive ability distinct from traditional aptitude constructs. This assumption may also be supported by findings from educational psychology showing that short-term memory exhibits weaker links with aptitude complexes than working memory capacity (Daneman & Carpenter, 1980; Engle, Laughlin, Tuholski, & Conway, 1999).

As mentioned in Chapters 1 and 2, in the phonological deficit account, dyslexia is a type of learning difficulty which is caused by impairments in pho-nological processing and representations (Frith, 1985; Snowling, 2000; Stanovich, 1988; Vellutino, 1979). Consequently, a number of studies have found that individuals with dyslexia show reduced phonological awareness (e.g. Fletcher et al., 2006; Snowling, 2000), which is strongly associated with the phonetic coding ability component of language learning aptitude. It was also pointed out above that language learners with SpLDs usually have a smaller working memory capacity and a shorter phonological short-term memory span, both of which are implicated in various components of language learning aptitude, such as rote learning ability and inductive learning ability (see the results of Sáfár and Kormos (2008) on the interrelationship of working memory capacity and inductive learning ability).

3.3 Language Learning Aptitude and SpLDs

Based on the above description of the interrelationship of phonological short-term memory, working memory and aptitude, it can be assumed that learners with SpLDs will score lower on tests of language learning aptitude than those with no SpLDs. Indeed, empirical research on the language learning aptitude of language learners with dyslexia shows that they tend to achieve consistently lower scores on all the components of tests of language learning aptitude than those with no appar-ent signs of dyslexia (e.g. Downey, Snyder & Hill, 2000) (see Figure 3.1). Sparks and Javorsky (1999) found that American college students classified as 'learning disabled'[1] scored below average on the long form of the Modern Language Aptitude Test (MLAT). They also noted, however, that the norms against which these students were scored might have been outdated. Importantly, Sparks, Philips, Ganschow and Javorksy (1999) found that college students who were labelled learning disabled

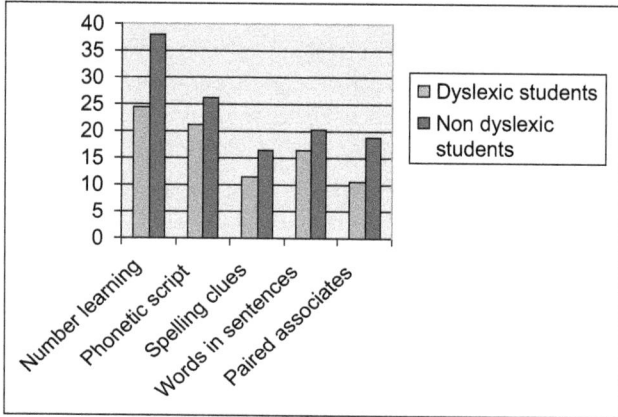

FIGURE 3.1 Differences Between Dyslexic and Nondyslexic Students in Components of the Modern Language Aptitude Test in Downey, Snyder and Hill's Research (2000)

Source: Reproduced from Kormos and Smith (2012), *Teaching Languages to Students with Specific Learning Differences*, p. 63, with permission of Multilingual Matters.

and exempted from foreign language study in their American context showed no significant differences in aptitude components from those learning-disabled students who received course exemption and who were not identified as having a learning disability but were low-achievers in foreign language courses (for a review see Sparks, 2001).

The findings concerning language learning aptitude with regard to exemptions and the lack of significant differences between low-achieving students and students identified with a learning difficulty have a number of important consequences. First of all, as Sparks et al. (1999) highlight, many of the American college students in their context had official certification of their learning disability because of their foreign language problems. They also report that, in many cases, the sole basis of a decision for exemption, and sometimes even for identification, was substandard performance on the MLAT test. The MLAT test, however, was never intended for the diagnosis of learning difficulties. Although it has been found to be an important predictor of L2 learning outcomes (for a recent collection of articles see Granena & Long, 2013), it is only one of the many factors that can, potentially, affect the success of L2 learning. Second, the results highlight that in terms of the cognitive profile of students who have formal identification versus those who do not but exhibit L2 learning difficulties, there are no major differences in aptitude that would warrant exemption from foreign language study (Sparks, 2001). These findings also constitute a strong argument for a pressing need to create a learning environment and establish curricula that can ensure the full inclusion of students with SpLDs wishing or needing to learn an additional language (see Chapter 6 for more details).

Although, as Sparks' (2001) review suggests, there might not be major differences between the aptitude profiles of students with SpLDs and low-achieving L2 learners, Borodkin and Faust (2014) identify important variations in certain underlying phonological skills between these two groups of learners. These phonological skills have not been previously considered as components of language learning aptitude, nonetheless they provide an important foundation for L2 learning and are related to the phonetic coding component of aptitude. In their Linguistic Coding Differences Hypothesis, Sparks and Ganschow (1993) claim that the major difference between low-achieving students and those with learning difficulties lies in the degree of difficulty they experience with phonological processing. In Chapter 1, we reviewed the multiple-deficit models of SpLDs that argue that learning differences might be present in different combinations in different types of SpLDs and in each individual (Bishop & Snowling, 2004; Pennington, 2006). In this account, the differences between low-achieving and students with SpLDs might not lie in the degree of their phonological processing difficulties, but rather in which components of phonological processing they have impairments. In fact, Borodkin and Faust's results (2014) seem to provide support for this latter account. Their findings reveal that in the domain of L1 phonological awareness and rapid automated word naming in L1, there are significant differences between low-achieving students and language learners who held a formal diagnosis of dyslexia. These two groups, however, were significantly different from the high-achieving group in terms of phonological short-term memory and retrieving phonological word forms in L1 in an artificially induced tip-of-the-tongue task.

Borodkin and Faust's (2014) conclusions are important because they highlight that "L2 learning might be more vulnerable than L1 reading acquisition to subtle L1 phonological difficulties, as it involves a unique constellation of factors that create an additional burden on the phonological system" (p. 136). Their findings may offer an explanation for the phenomenon described by Sparks et al. (1999) that a considerable number of students showing low achievement in FL learning with no previously reported L1 difficulties seek and receive identification of their learning difficulties. Borodkin and Faust's findings also suggest that highly specific tests of phonological processing are needed, rather than a language aptitude test targeting general linguistic domains, to differentiate low-achieving language learners and students with SpLDs.

Research conducted by Sparks and his colleagues has also examined the foreign language learning aptitude of students with attention deficit hyperactivity disorder (ADHD; Sparks, Humbach & Javorsky, 2008). When the overall aptitude scores of students with ADHD were compared to those students who were classified as 'learning disabled' in the American public high school context investigated, the results showed that students with ADHD were similar to students identified to have a 'learning disability'. In another study, Sparks, Ganschow and Patton (2008) report subscores for different aptitude components of a short version of the

MLAT for students with no 'learning disabilities', students with 'learning disability' and those with ADHD. An inspection of the mean values for these groups shows that students with ADHD performed very similarly to high achievers in L2 learning in a paired-associates task, which assesses rote learning ability. The scores of the students with ADHD were also superior to both the low-achieving and learning-disabled groups in the grammatical sensitivity component of the aptitude test. In the spelling clues task, however, their performance was below both the low-achieving and the learning-disabled group (see Figure 3.2). Although no tests of statistical significance for these comparisons were reported in Sparks, Humbach, et al.'s (2008) study, the findings are informative as they show that learners with ADHD might not be significantly different in terms of memory ability and grammatical sensitivity from their peers who have no SpLDs. It is more in areas of aptitude that require efficient attention control and attention to detail, where their abilities might be different from their peers. The results of Sparks, Ganschow and Patton (2008) also reveal that the ADHD group had a very diverse cognitive and linguistic profile. When an attempt was made to predict group membership based on cognitive characteristics, only 40.9% of the students with ADHD were correctly classified in their groups. Interestingly, 36.4% of the students shared cognitive and linguistic characteristics with high achievers, but no student with ADHD was misclassified as having a learning disability.

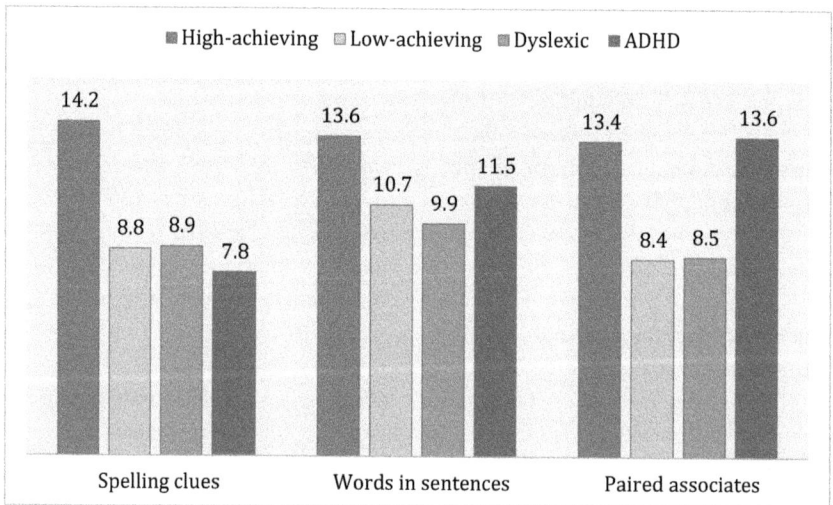

FIGURE 3.2 Differences Between High-Achieving, Low-Achieving, Dyslexic and ADHD Students in Components of the Modern Language Aptitude Test

Source: Sparks, Ganschow and Patton (2008).

3.4 The Interrelationship of Cognitive Abilities, L1 Skills and L2 Learning

Before we discuss the cognitive effects of SpLDs on specific L2 learning processes and outcomes, it is important to consider how cognitive factors and L1 skills jointly and separately influence SLA. In other words, we need to ask whether difficulties in L2 learning are caused by the transfer of underdeveloped L1 skills or by cognitive abilities that underlie both L1 and L2 learning.

At the core of individual difference factors that can, potentially, influence the success of second language acquisition, we find basic cognitive abilities that are also necessary in order to acquire one's mother tongue and literacy skills in L1. Phonological short-term memory assists in learning new words in both L1 and L2. It also plays an important role in the decoding of sequences of sounds and associating them with words and their meanings, which is essential when learning to read and spell in both L1 and L2. Verbal reasoning skills can be matched to two components of language learning aptitude: grammatical sensitivity and inductive language learning ability, both of which play an important role in the acquisition of syntax and morphology by helping language learners to discover patterns and regularities in the L1 and L2. Central executive processes assist in regulating attention to relevant linguistic features, maintaining chunks of language in memory for further processing and inhibiting irrelevant stimuli and automatic response patterns, such as L1 words and phrases when speaking in L2. As shown in Chapter 1, phonological awareness and naming speed are important predictors of success in learning to read and write in both L1 and L2. These similarities between the cognitive skills necessary for the acquisition of one's L1 and literacy skills in L1 on the one hand, and outcomes in learning an L2 on the other, led Geva and Ryan (1993) to the construction of their *common underlying cognitive processes* framework. They argued that the same basic cognitive processes account for the strong link between similar L1 and L2 skills and learning outcomes (see also Section 2.6). Sparks and Ganschow's (1993) Linguistic Coding Differences Hypothesis also reinstates this by claiming that the underlying reasons for lack of success in L2 acquisition are very similar to the causes of learning difficulties in L1.

If we consider that L1 skills provide an important foundation for L2 learning (Cummins, 1981, 1991; Dufva & Voeten, 1999; Skehan, 1986; Spolsky, 1989), it can be seen that, in addition to a direct effect, the cognitive components of language learning aptitude also influence ultimate L2 attainment indirectly through the mediation of L1 skills (see Figure 3.3). It is also worth referring to Ackerman's (2007) argument that crystallized intelligence, which mainly comprises previous subject-matter knowledge, is a more important predeterminant of learning outcomes in formal learning situations than fluid intelligence (i.e. working memory capacity and verbal reasoning skills). This shows that there is an additive effect of cognitive abilities as they contribute to initial states of

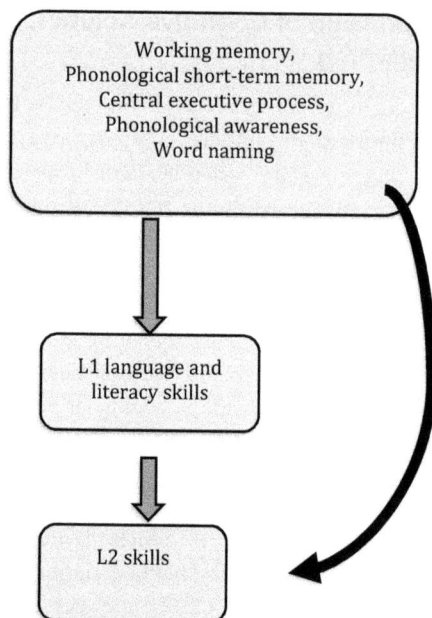

```
┌─────────────────────────────┐
│     Working memory,         │
│ Phonological short-term     │
│        memory,              │
│ Central executive process,  │
│  Phonological awareness,    │
│     Word naming             │
└─────────────────────────────┘
              │
              ▼
   ┌──────────────────┐
   │  L1 language and │
   │  literacy skills │
   └──────────────────┘
              │
              ▼
   ┌──────────────────┐
   │    L2 skills     │
   └──────────────────┘
```

FIGURE 3.3 The Role of Cognitive Abilities in Ultimate L2 Attainment

knowledge, in our case to L1 skills and the initial level of L2 competence from which development should proceed. This additive effect might explain the second language learning difficulties experienced by individuals with SpLDs, which are often proportionately more serious than the challenges they face in L1 literacy skills (see Section 3.3).

In addition to the work of Sparks and his colleagues (see a recent review by Sparks, 2012), there is considerable evidence for a strong relationship between L1 skills and L2 learning outcomes in the field of SLA that is worth considering as they provide an indication of areas of L2 learning difficulties for individuals with SpLDs. For example, Dufva and Voeten (1999) found that L1 word-decoding skills and phonological short-term memory accounted for considerable variance in the L2 vocabulary, writing and listening comprehension skills of Finnish elementary schoolchildren. Van Gelderen et al. (2004) also observed a strong link between L1 and L2 reading comprehension ability. As also seen in Sparks' (2012) recent overview, the strongest associations between underlying cognitive ability and L1 skills and L2 learning can be detected in the area of L2 vocabulary size and reading, with weaker yet significant links in the area of listening.

It is important to note, however, that the interrelationship between cognitive abilities, L1 language and literacy skills and L2 learning outcomes is also mediated by typological, orthographic and phonological differences between the learners' L1 and L2 (for more detail see Section 2.4). Contextual factors can also interact with cognitive processes and either enhance or diminish the effect of cognitive impairments on learning outcomes. These factors include among others the learners' socioeconomic and educational context (Organization for Economic Cooperation and Development, 2009), literacy experiences at home (Heath, 1983; Teale & Sulzby, 1986) and at school (Cummins, 2012), attitudes to reading and literacy (Spolsky, 2004) and age of arrival in the target language country (Jean & Geva, 2012).

3.5 The Effect of SpLDs on the Processes of Second Language Learning

3.5.1 The Effect of SpLDs on Explicit and Implicit Learning

There are a number of reasons why it is almost impossible to describe the general effect of SpLDs on L2 learning processes. First of all, SpLDs comprise a wide spectrum of learning difficulties (see Chapter 1), which have a large variety of cognitive and behavioural correlates. Second, specific types of SpLDs, such as dyslexia, can be present in individuals to varying degrees and can co-occur with other types of SpLDs. Therefore, rather than describing the overall effects of SpLDs, I will elaborate how the underlying cognitive characteristics of SpLDs, reviewed above, might influence the processes of SLA. This is a potentially more useful approach as it does not take the hypothetical and typi-cal learner with an SpLD as the basis of analysis but allows for the assessment of potential learning difficulties of specific learners given knowledge of their cognitive characteristics.

There are two fundamental ways in which learning can take place, which are described by N. Ellis (1994) as follows:

> Implicit learning is acquisition of knowledge about the underlying structure of a complex stimulus environment by a process which takes place naturally, simply, and without conscious operations. Explicit learning is a more conscious operation where the individual attends to particular aspects of the stimulus array and volunteers and tests hypotheses in a search for structure.
>
> *(p. 1)*

Second language learning, in most contexts, involves a combination of explicit and implicit learning processes. For a long time the mainstream position in educational and cognitive psychology was that explicit learning mechanisms were greatly influenced by individual learner differences, such as crystallized and fluid intelligence, the latter including executive functioning and working memory (e.g. Reber, 1993). In contrast, as implicit learning was seen to be an automatic associative process, individual learner factors were assumed to play a minimal role in it (e.g. Feldman, Kerr & Streissguth, 1995; Reber, Walkenfeld & Hernstadt, 1991). These assumptions have, however, recently been challenged by explorations into the role of attention in implicit learning. A number of studies have found that in order for implicit learning to take place, selective attention to the relevant aspect of the input stimulus is necessary, and only after the input stimulus is selectively attended to will automatic and unintentional learning mechanisms be triggered (Jiang & Chun, 2001; Jiménez & Méndez, 1999). Therefore, individual learner characteristics that cause variation in selective attention can be assumed to influence the outcomes of implicit learning processes. In a study examining the factors accounting for differential outcomes in an implicit learning task, Kaufman et al. (2010) found that, among cognitive variables, processing speed and scores on a verbal reasoning test were the best predictors of performance. In the field of second language acquisition research, De Graaff (1997), Robinson (1997, 2002), and Williams (1999) have established that language learning aptitude and working memory capacity correlate with learning outcomes under both explicit and implicit learning conditions.

From the above research findings, it is apparent that as reduced working memory capacity and lower language aptitude often characterize language learners with SpLDs, they might be less efficient in learning under both explicit and implicit learning conditions. In fact, in interviews, participants with SpLDs often recount experiences when they found it very challenging to extract patterns and regularities of grammar in implicit learning conditions and preferred explicit explanations of syntax, morphology and spelling (Kormos & Mikó, 2010). This preference of individuals with SpLDs for more explicit teaching and metalinguistic explanation may also be supported by the findings of Robinson (1997) that showed stronger links between aptitude and learning outcomes under implicit conditions than under explicit conditions. Research in the field of educational psychology also shows that low-aptitude learners tend to benefit more from explicit and structured learning activities (for a review, see Kyllonen & Lajoie, 2003) as opposed to high-aptitude learners who show considerable learning gains in less structured learning environments as well.

3.5.2 The Effect of SpLDs on Input Processing

Input plays a crucial role in language development and is a necessary condition for learning to take place (Gass, 1997). Nevertheless, now, ample evidence has been accumulated that indicates that not everything L2 learners are exposed to will be acquired and input in itself is an insufficient condition for linguistic development (see e.g. Sharwood Smith, 1993; White, Spada, Lightbown & Ranta, 1991). In this section, I will discuss the effect of SpLDs on how L2 learners comprehend input and process it for further learning.

Input can be defined as "the potentially processable language data which are made available by chance or by design, to the language learner" (Sharwood

Smith, 1993, p. 167). This definition of input regards nearly all the stimuli a learner is exposed to as a potential source of learning. Other views of input restrict the construct to information that might be in the attentional focus of learners and which, consequently, might be processed further and incorporated into the learner's knowledge system (see e.g. Sato & Jacobs, 1992). Here I will adapt the former broader meaning of input as it allows me to discuss input processing in a more general sense. From this perspective, almost any verbal material that learners are exposed to can be considered input, including the various texts learners read, watch or listen to, and written and oral interactions they engage in.

SpLDs that are associated with reduced phonological awareness, smaller pho-nological short-term memory and impairment in the functioning of working memory exert a significant effect on how L2 learners process written and spoken input for comprehension and subsequent learning. One way of accessing input for learning is through reading. In Section 1.4, I provided a detailed description of the reading processes of individuals with SpLDs. With regard to reading in L2, reduced phonological awareness and difficulties with rapid automated word naming lead to word-decoding problems. Reading comprehension difficulties can either result from word-level reading problems or from global language compre-hension deficit (Geva & Massey-Garrison, 2013). The working memory problems of individuals with SpLDs might also hinder comprehension by limiting the number of verbal units (L2 phonemes, morphemes, words, clauses) the learner can hold in memory while reading the text (see e.g. Abu-Rabia & Siegel, 2002).

In a recent study, Geva and Massey-Garrison (2013) investigated the deter-minants of reading comprehension of L1 and L2 speaking children in Canada. They analysed the role of working memory, rapid automated word naming, phonological awareness, vocabulary knowledge, syntactic skills and listening comprehension ability in reading across three groups of children: poor decoders (i.e. children with low word-decoding ability), poor comprehenders (children with low reading comprehension scores) and normal readers. Overall, their results suggested that the same cognitive abilities proved important in predicting word- and text-level comprehension among L1 and L2 children. They found differences in the role of rapid automated word naming in L1 and L2 poor decoders, but the two language groups were similar with regard to the contribution of phonological awareness and working memory to decoding problems. They also argued that the phonological processing difficulties of the poor comprehender group "lead, in a cascading fashion, to more limited language skills, including vocabulary and syn-tactic skills and listening comprehension" (p. 397). Children who demonstrated poor reading comprehension skills in the absence of phonological processing dif-ficulties and reduced working memory capacity were found to have smaller recep-tive vocabulary size and tended to produce syntactically less complex sentences. Additionally, they were less successful not only in drawing inferences but also in answering questions about factual information in a listening comprehension test. These results show the pervasive effect of two subtypes of SpLDs, namely word-level decoding problems, traditionally considered as dyslexic-type reading difficulties, and reading comprehension difficulties on written and oral input processing in L2 contexts.

The difficulties of individuals with SpLDs in L2 reading have also been well documented in other studies in both foreign and second language contexts. For example, in the cases of both Norwegian children (Helland & Kaasa, 2005) and Hungarian children learning English as an additional language (Kormos & Mikó, 2010), it was found that children with an official diagnosis of dyslexia scored significantly lower on a test of L2 word reading than their nondyslexic peers (see Table 3.1). Hungarian dyslexic children also performed significantly worse on a test of sentence comprehension than their peers matched for age (Kormos & Mikó, 2010). Geva, Wade-Woolley and Shany (1993) obtained similar findings in a Canadian English as an additional language context and Crombie (1997) came to the same conclusion in the case of Scottish primary and secondary schoolchildren learning French. Sparks and Ganschow (2001) summarize evidence from their studies showing that L2 word-decoding skills were frequent correlates of L2 learning difficulties in Spanish as a foreign language in both high school and college contexts in the United States. Kormos and Mikó (2010) also reported that Hungarian schoolchildren with a formal diagnosis of dyslexia perceived that they had significantly more difficulties with reading comprehension in either German or English as an L2 than did their nondyslexic peers (see Table 3.2). This finding shows that even reading in German with its relatively more transparent orthography causes considerable challenges for language learners with SpLDs. In another study conducted with bilingual Swedish and Finish university students, Lindgrén and Laine (2011) showed that while dyslexia had only a small effect on reading speed in Swedish, an orthographically less transparent language than Finnish, the accuracy of reading was affected to a similar extent in both languages (for a more detailed discussion of the effects of SpLDs on reading in different languages see Section 2.3). In contrast, the bilingual students who were identified as being at risk of dyslexia in Lindgrén and Laine's study did not score lower on global reading comprehension in any of the languages. This indicates that for older populations who participate in university education and who are highly proficient in both languages, SpLDs might not necessarily result in difficulties with higher-order comprehension processes.

With regard to students with ADHD, L2 reading difficulties did not seem to surface in the case of high school and college students in Sparks, Ganschow and Patton's (2008) study. This finding might be due to the sample of students investigated in this study. Recent research in the field of L1 reading shows that students who were identified as having the characteristics of the inattentive or combined inattentive and hyperactive subtype of ADHD demonstrated both word-level decoding and reading comprehension problems (Cain & Bignell, 2014). Working memory and central executive functions, both of which tend to be

TABLE 3.1 Dyslexic and Nondyslexic Hungarian Schoolchildren's Perceptions of Their Language Learning Difficulties

Item	Sample	Mean	SD	F Dysl	F Language	F Interaction
I find spelling easy.	Dysl-English	2.83	1.38	99.40**	0.81	0.28
	Dysl-German	2.69	1.35			
	Ndysl-English	3.75	1.11			
	Ndysl-German	3.72	1.17			
	Total	3.59	1.22			
I find it easy to read texts.	Dysl-English	2.89	1.23	78.93**	0.18	0.22
	Dysl-German	2.92	1.21			
	Ndysl-English	3.65	0.99			
	Ndysl-German	3.70	1.04			
	Total	3.55	1.08			
I can pronounce words easily.	Dysl-English	2.82	1.38	23.97**	5.14*	1.22
	Dysl-German	2.94	1.24			
	Ndysl-English	3.21	1.21			
	Ndysl-German	3.56	1.25			
	Total	3.25	1.26			
I can easily understand listening texts in class.	Dysl-English	3.13	1.18	3.47	4.44	0.01
	Dysl-German	2.94	1.08			
	Ndysl-English	3.31	1.21			
	Ndysl-German	3.11	1.03			
	Total	3.22	1.11			
I find it easy to understand the rules of grammar.	Dysl-English	2.90	1.18	24.98**	0.46	0.09
	Dysl-German	2.86	1.22			
	Ndysl-English	3.40	1.11			
	Ndysl-German	3.31	1.12			
	Total	3.30	1.14			
I find it easy to express myself orally in another language.	Dysl-English	2.94	1.08	40.61**	2.51	0.23
	Dysl-German	2.76	1.14			
	Ndysl-English	3.45	1.02			
	Ndysl-German	3.36	1.02			
	Total	3.34	1.05			
I find it easy to learn new words.	Dysl-English	2.98	1.21	85.68**	0.57	0.27
	Dysl-German	2.96	1.28			
	Ndysl-English	3.86	1.03			
	Ndysl-German	3.75	1.08			
	Total	3.69	1.12			

Source: Based on Kormos and Mikó (2010).

TABLE 3.2 The Performance of Hungarian and Norwegian Dyslexic and Nondyslexic Students in an English L2 Test Developed by Helland and Kaasa (2005)

	Group	Mean	SD	T	Facility Value	Norwegian Data From Helland and Kaasa (2005)
Sentence comprehension	D	8.4	2.50	1.89	0.56	9.95
(listening)	ND	10.9	3.34		0.73	13.60
Sentence production (oral)	D	3.6	4.08	3.78**	0.24	4.35
	ND	10.2	3.70		0.68	9.45
Oral communication	D	6.1	1.52	2.27*	0.76	n.d.a.
	ND	7.3	0.67		0.91	
Spelling	D	12.6	4.46	4.14**	0.57	5.75
	ND	19.5	2.75		0.88	13.90
Sentence reading	D	9.2	1.31	1.63	0.92	n.d.a.
	ND	9.9	0.31		0.99	
Sentence translation	D	4.2	2.25	4.80**	0.42	n.d.a.
	ND	8.5	1.71		0.85	
Pronunciation of words	D	20.1	2.02	2.96*	0.91	11.8
	ND	22.0	0.00		1	19.9
Vocabulary knowledge	D	13.4	5.62	3.01*	0.60	12.25
	ND	19.1	2.17		0.86	19.10

D = Dyslexic
ND = Nondyslexic
n.d.a. = No data available
*p < 0.05
**p < 0.01

impaired in students with ADHD (Barkley, 1997; Gathercole et al., 2008), play an important role in reading comprehension in L1 (Cain, 2006). Consequently, we can assume that language learners with ADHD, especially those with primarily inattentive symptoms, will experience reading comprehension problems in L2.

Understanding speech is a complex interactive process; consequently, it shares a number of similarities with reading in terms of psycholinguistic processing. In Anderson's (1995) framework of language comprehension, individuals attend to the sounds of the incoming stream of speech in the perceptual processing stage. During parsing, the speech signal is segmented into words, and then word recognition and syntactic analysis of the utterance takes place. In the utilization stage the processed meaning of the message is related to existing background knowledge and the context of the discourse. These processing mechanisms can, in part, run in parallel and interact with each other, although, similar to reading, a certain level of automaticity and efficiency in lower-order processing at the perceptual and parsing level is necessary for successful comprehension of the intended meaning of the utterance in the utilization stage. L2 comprehension, however, is often effortful, and Goh (2000) gives a detailed account of the difficulties L2 learners can experience while listening, partly due to problems in identifying phonemes and word boundaries in the incoming string of sounds. L2 learners may also have problems associating phoneme sequences with words; and as a consequence of a potential lack of syntactic and textual knowledge of the L2, they might not be able to decode the meaning of the text they have heard. L2 listening ability is also strongly influenced by working memory ability, as comprehending spoken texts requires storing and manipulating longer stretches of verbal information in phonological short-term memory and the efficient control of attentional resources (for a recent meta-analysis of research in this area see Linck, Osthus, Koeth & Bunting (2014)). As already mentioned, SpLDs are often associated with impairments in phonemic awareness and phonological processing skills. These difficulties are also apparent in the global speech comprehension rate of children identified as dyslexic in their L1 (Bowers & Swanson, 1991; Wolf, 1991). Furthermore, oral comprehension problems are frequent accompanying characteristics of reading comprehension difficulties (for a recent overview see Oakhill, Cain & Elbro, 2014). These comprehension problems might present additional challenges in listening to L2 input when learners have to identify phonemes in another language and associate a string of phonemes with an L2 word and its meaning. They also have to process grammatical constructions in another language, assemble the meaning of sentences and consider sentence meaning in a discourse context that they might not have sufficient cultural and linguistic understanding of.

The nature of problems that learners with SpLDs experience in understanding spoken L2 texts depends on their phonological processing skills, phonological short-term memory and oral language comprehension ability in their L1. Geva and Massey-Garrison's (2013) study showed that poor comprehenders regardless of whether they were L1 or L2 speakers performed significantly worse on a listening comprehension test than both poor decoders and normal readers. In other words, the extent of listening comprehension difficulties depended on whether the participants had phonological processing deficits or global oral language comprehension problems. Other research findings also suggest that learners with SpLDs have varying degrees of difficulty in understanding L2 speech. Within the learners with a diagnosis of dyslexia, who can be compared to the poor decoder group in Geva and Massey-Garrison's (2013) study, those who showed less serious phonological processing problems and no associated oral language processing difficulties did not seem to exhibit problems in the listening task of the English 2 Dyslexia test in a Norwegian context (Helland & Kaasa, 2005). The findings obtained by Kormos and Mikó (2010) using the same test in the case of Hungarian schoolchildren did not indicate significant differences in terms of sentence-level listening comprehension between formally diagnosed dyslexic and nondyslexic children either. Also, in their study, children with dyslexia did not perceive that they had significantly more difficulties with processing L2 input through the auditive channel (see Tables 3.1 and 3.2). Among

Scottish schoolchildren learning French, however, Crombie (1997) found significant differences in the mean grade scores for a listening test between children identified as dyslexic and those who did not exhibit any SpLDs.

A certain level of comprehension and automaticity in decoding processes is a necessary condition for learning, as in cases where understanding breaks down completely, there is little to assist in discovering new linguistic knowledge. In the area of vocabulary acquisition, Laufer (1989) originally suggested that 95% of the words in a text need to be known to L2 learners for sufficient comprehension and possible vocabulary acquisition, whereas Hu and Nation (2000) later argued that the coverage needs to be as high as 98%. There are no comparable data available with regard to what percentage of the syntactic and morphologic aspects of the input needs to be comprehensible for L2 learners to promote learning, but we can expect a similarly high percentage in this area as well. The process that bridges this difference between input comprehended and not comprehended is traditionally called 'noticing the gap' (Schmidt, 1990) in the field of second language acquisition. Although the concept of noticing the gap has been criticised by Truscott and Sharwood Smith (2011) for being imprecise, there seems to be consensus that noticing is a conscious process that requires attention (for a recent discussion see Godfroid, Boers & Housen, 2013). The availability of attention for noticing while processing input is partly dependent on how automatic L2 learners' decoding processes are, because automaticity frees up attentional resources. From this line of argumentation, it follows that if phonological processing problems and weaknesses in phonological short-term memory result in effortful decoding of either written or spoken input, L2 learners with SpLDs might find it difficult to both acquire new words and notice grammatical constructions in the input under incidental learning conditions. This was evidenced by the interviews Kormos and Mikó (2010) conducted with language learners who gave accounts of their difficulties in learning from written input outside classroom contexts and also in language teachers' experiences (unpublished data from the interview study conducted by Kormos & Kontra, 2008).

Psycholinguistically, Robinson's (2002) conceptualization of noticing helps us explain the mechanisms responsible for converting detected input into memory traces. He claims that noticing involves rehearsal in working memory, and indeed subvocal rehearsal in phonological short-term memory plays a key role in a number of the processes of second language acquisition, such as learning vocabulary. It helps learners to keep verbal material active in phonological short-term memory before it can be encoded in long-term memory, just like repeating the digits of telephone numbers for oneself before one can either write them down or commit them to memory (Baddeley, 2003). Robinson (2002) also explains that rehearsal can simply involve the maintenance of traces in working memory, as in our example of remembering telephone numbers, which leads to item-based learning. This process can account for how L2 learners acquire, among other things, form-meaning associations for L2 words. Additionally, rehearsal might entail elaboration of the material in working memory, which can result in the emergence of analysed knowledge and the recognition of systematic features in the input, such as syntactic or morphological regularities or collocation patterns (Robinson, 2002). Key factors in both types of noticing processes are working memory and central executive functions, and hence impairments in these cognitive functions frequently associated with SpLDs might cause further difficulties for L2 learning.

3.5.3 The Effects of SpLDs on Encoding New Knowledge in Long-Term Memory and Automatization

The creation of memory traces in long-term memory and the development of associations between new and existing knowledge require frequent encounters with the items to be learned (for a review of frequency-based learning, see N. Ellis, 2002). To illustrate, Nation (1990) suggests that 5 to 16 repetitions might be necessary for learners to acquire a new word fully, but Webb's (2007) study showed that even 10 encounters were not sufficient for learners to develop all the different types of word knowledge of the items targeted. These repetitions also need to be phased so that forgetting does not occur before a new encounter (Baddeley, 1999). Both language learners with SpLDs and their teachers report that a very high number of encounters and many practice activities are necessary for the successful memorizations of new words (see Tables 3.1 and 3.2 for data and Sarkadi (2008) for a case study of the vocabulary learning difficulties of a dyslexic language learner).

The difficulties of learners with SpLDs to commit L2 words to long-term memory are in all likelihood caused by their reduced phonological short-term memory capacity. The link between phonological short-term memory and L2 word-learning was first shown by Service and her colleagues (Service, 1992; Service & Kohonen, 1995), who found that the ability to repeat English-sounding pseudowords was a good predictor of English language learning success (as expressed by children's grades in English) among Finnish primary school pupils during the first 3 years of instruction. Cheung's study (1996), conducted with 12-year-old Chinese high school students, also indicated that nonword repetition score was the best predictor of second language vocabulary learning among those participants whose vocabulary level was below the group average, while in the case of a subgroup with a wide range of vocabulary, no such relationship was detected between the two variables. According to Cheung, this suggests that there is interaction between phonological short-term memory and long-term phonological knowledge about the L2, which explains how, in the case of participants with higher levels of lexical competence, their long-term knowledge supports the learning of new words. Papagno and Vallar (1995) showed that phonological short-term memory and word-learning abilities are related in adults as well. In a study with university students, Speciale, Ellis and Bywater (2004) found that both phonological sequence learning and phonological short-term memory capacity contribute to vocabulary learning. When beginning to learn a language, these two cognitive abilities contributed to vocabulary learning independently of each other. As students progressed in language learning, they began to recognize the phonological regularities of the language, and vocabulary knowledge enhanced the efficiency of short-term phonological storage as well as the learning of further sequences. These results indicate that the reciprocal relationship between phonological sequence learning and the development of vocabulary knowledge. Martin and Ellis' (2012) study also demonstrates the link between phonological short-term memory capacity and the learning of form-meaning associations in an artificial language. They conclude that phonological short-term memory is important in "forming stable long-term representations of novel phonological material" (p. 383), which provides an explanation for the L2 word-learning difficulties of individuals with SpLDs who have reduced pho-nological short-term capacity.

In the previous paragraphs, I discussed item-based learning, but learning another language also involves inducing regularities and frequencies of co-occurrences from the input and applying these in new contexts and with the purpose of creating new constructions. This has been traditionally called grammar learning, but it applies to wider areas of second language acquisition than syntax and morphology and might also be relevant for the acquisition of collocational and pragmatic knowledge. Phonological short-term memory and working mem-ory capacity have been found to be important predictors of success in grammar learning. In a recent study, Martin and Ellis (2012) found that "both phonological short term memory and working memory have strong relationships with par-ticipants' ability to generalize and apply grammar rules in both production and comprehension" (p. 394). As shown in the case of committing words to long-term memory, those language learners with SpLDs who have reduced working memory and phonological short-term memory capacity also experience difficul-ties with the acquisition of L2 grammar.

Kormos and Mikó (2010) investigated the differences between dyslexic and nondyslexic children concerning their knowledge of grammatical structures. They found that, after 4 years of study in primary school, Hungarian learners of English with an official diagnosis of dyslexia lagged behind their nondyslexic peers in terms of grammatical knowledge. None of the dyslexic children could construct a passive sentence. Making positive statements (declaratives) was less problematic for dyslexic children than forming questions and using negation (see Figure 3.4). These findings indicate that as syntactic structures become more complex, children with SpLDs experience more difficulties in acquiring them. These difficulties in the area of grammar were also perceived by the learners themselves in a questionnaire survey conducted by Kormos and Mikó (2010).

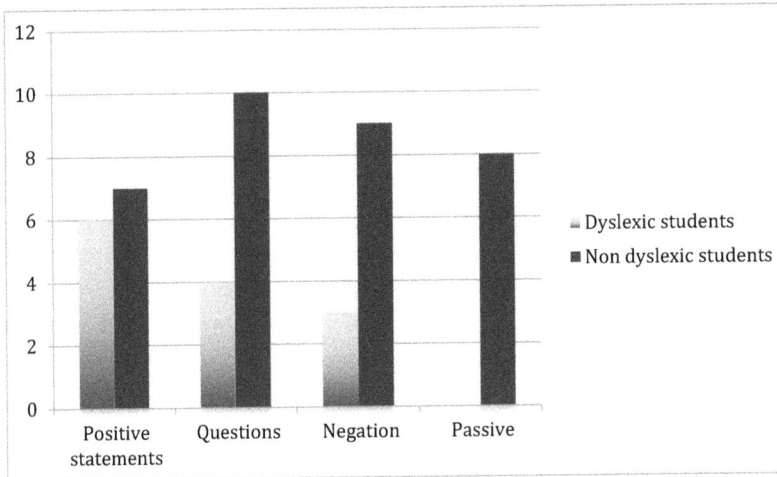

FIGURE 3.4 Comparison of the Grammatical Knowledge of Dyslexic and Nondyslexic Children in Kormos and Mikó's (2010) Study

Source: Reproduced from Kormos and Smith (2012), *Teaching Languages to Students with Specific Learning Differences*, p. 72, with permission of Multilingual Matters.

Another important phase in L2 learning is the process of automatization, in the course of which acquired knowledge becomes proceduralized and, as a next step, automatic processes develop (see e.g. Anderson's (1995) ACT* theory). Studies in the field of educational psychology demonstrate that working memory resources might play an important role in the automatization of knowledge (e.g. Ruthruff, Van Selst, Johnston & Remington, 2006). As reviewed in Chapter 1, SpLDs are often associated with slower and less successful automatization processes (Nicolson & Fawcett, 2008), which can carry over into the field of L2 learning. Currently, experimental evidence is lacking with regard to how SpLDs affect automatization processes when acquiring an additional language. Indirect support for automatization difficulties with regard to grammar learning is found in Kormos and Mikó's (2010) interview study where one of the participants explained that although she found it relatively easy to understand the formal features and meaning of grammatical constructions, when it came to applying them and using them in the course of communication, she faced challenges. This might indicate that difficulties arise not only at the stage of automatization, but also when L2 learners try to convert explicit knowledge into procedural knowledge.

3.5.4 The Effect of SpLDs on Output Production

Output has been shown to play an important role in promoting linguistic development in the field of second language acquisition. Swain's (1995) *Output Hypothesis* outlines three major ways in which output facilitates learning: by producing written and spoken texts and engaging in communication learners can test hypotheses about the L2, notice gaps in their knowledge and expand their existing linguistic resources. Before considering how the learning opportunities of individuals with SpLDs might differ from those who do not have SpLDs, we will first describe how SpLDs affect learners' production of written and spoken output in an additional language.

Writing, both in one's L1 and in L2, is one of the most complex literacy activities. L2 writers usually bring their L1 writing experience and skills to the task of constructing L2 texts, but L1 writing skills cannot be transferred to L2 automatically. L2 writers might need to acquire a new script system and previously unfamiliar motor-coordination skills. They also have to learn novel sound–letter correspondences and phonological and morphological rules to be able to write L2 words. Sufficient L2 vocabulary and syntactic knowledge are also prerequisites for constructing texts at and above the sentence level (for a review of the cognitive mechanisms involved in L2 writing see Schoonen, Snellings, Stevenson & van Gelderen, 2009).

Working memory capacity, phonological short-term capacity and phonological awareness play a key role in influencing L2 writing processes, and hence SpLDs associated with weaknesses in these areas can have an important impact on both the quality of writing learners produce and the way they compose their texts. For example, whereas L1 writers with no SpLDs might automatically encode syntactic and morphological structures, retrieve syntactic information related to words and associate orthographic form with lexical entries, for L2 writers all these encoding procedures require conscious attention and the suppression of competing L1 clues, both of which are reliant on working memory resources. The reading processes involved in the editing, revision and proofreading stages of writing also tend to be less automatic in L2 than in L1; and as shown above, reading skills are greatly affected by cognitive impairments associated with SpLDs. Indeed, Lindgrén and Laine (2010) found that bilingual Finnish and Swedish students who were identified to have dyslexia detected significantly fewer errors in a text, in either of their languages, than their peers with no dyslexia. Moreover, transcribing processes (i.e. handwriting or typing), which are the most highly automatized mechanisms of L1 writing, might demand attention in L2 if the orthographic and spelling system of a student's L1 is very different from that of the L2. Transcribing processes can also be affected by potential problems with fine motor skills, such as those often found in dyspraxia. As a consequence, it can be assumed that each stage of L2 writing might be influenced by SpLDs.

Additionally, it is important to consider that even though writing is generally not constrained by time and does not necessitate parallel processing similar to speech, it is still important that writers orchestrate their writing processes, and certain mechanisms of writing often run in parallel. Therefore, working memory is also involved in coordinating parallel writing processes, such as planning while typing. Central executive functions, which are responsible for the allocation of attention, might determine how much attention L2 learners can pay to various stages of the composing process and how they coordinate their attention to accuracy, content and organization. To illustrate, during editing, writers need to read their output and attend to specific aspects of writing, such as coherence, cohesion, accuracy and appropriateness, at the same time. The central executive processes responsible for regulating attention in these phases of writing can also be affected by SpLDs and might cause difficulties for L2 learners with SpLDs.

In the field of second language acquisition research, there is a scarcity of research on the role of working memory and phonological short-term memory capacity in L2 writing. Kormos and Sáfár (2008) found that scores awarded in the writing component of a proficiency test showed moderate correlation with phonological short-term memory span, but not with a backward digit span test, which was used to assess complex working memory capacity. Although this study offers support for the role of phonological short-term memory in L2 writing, it does not seem to provide evidence for the importance of complex working memory capacity in the L2 writing process. Somewhat similar findings were obtained by Adams and Guillot (2008), whose study shows links between spelling performance among bilingual writers and phonological short-term memory capacity, but no significant relationship between text composition and working memory capacity.

Research conducted with learners with SpLDs has shown significant differences between the written production of children with SpLDs and their peers with no SpLDs. Ndlovu and Geva (2008) compared the writing skills of L1 and L2 speaking children in Canada, who were assessed as being 'reading disabled' or 'nonreading disabled'. They found that regardless of language background, the children identified as being reading disabled had difficulty with spelling, punctuation and the monitoring of syntax. The results also indicated that these children struggled "with higher level aspects of writing such as sentence structure constraints and the generation and coordination of vocabulary, as well as with aspects of the overall structure of their compositions including the ability to compose stories with interesting plots and story lines" (p. 55). Crombie (1997) also observed significant differences between Scottish students who held an official diagnosis of dyslexia and their peers in terms of their performance in a test of writing in French. With regard to fluency in a free writing task, however, the bilingual dyslexic students in Lindgrén and Laine's (2011) study did not show differences from their peers in either of their languages. It needs to be noted though that these students were studying at university and were highly proficient in two languages, while in other populations with SpLDs, differences in writing speed might emerge.

With regard to lower-level writing skills such as spelling, Kormos and Mikó (2010) found that the spelling scores of formally diagnosed dyslexic children and nondyslexic Hungarian learners of English were significantly different (see Table 3.2). Helland and Kaasa's (2005) study, using the same instrument, also produced similar results. In a case study of a dyslexic language learner, Sarkadi (2008) asked her participant to list some features in English which make spelling difficult for her. The learner mentioned the presence of vowel and consonant clusters in words and explained that in words containing such clusters she often leaves out or reverses letters. Interestingly, however, when Hungarian dyslexic children studying German and English were asked to report their difficulties with spelling, learners of German perceived spelling to be just as difficult as those children who studied English (Kormos & Mikó, 2010). Likewise, the bilingual Swedish and Finish students with dyslexia in Lindgrén and Laine's (2010) study spelled significantly fewer words correctly in a dictation task and made significantly more spelling errors in dictation and free writing, both in Finnish, which is an orthographically transparent language, and Swedish. Taken together with the results of Sparks, Ganschow and Patton (2008) who found significant differences in Spanish L2 spelling between learning-disabled and non–learning-disabled students, these findings indicate that regardless of the transparency of the spelling system of the L2, students with SpLDs experience difficulties at this level of writing.

SpLDs can have varying effects on L2 speech production mechanisms. L2 speech production involves the complex process of planning what one wants to say, encoding it linguistically, articulating it and monitoring the accuracy of output. For an L2 speaker, not only do conceptual planning and monitoring require attentional control but, depending on the level of proficiency, L2 users display varying degrees of automaticity in linguistic encoding. The orchestration of speech production processes also needs attentional control. Therefore, it can be assumed that impairments to central executive processes and working memory limitations can impact on L2 speech production mechanisms. Crombie (1997) and Kormos and Mikó (2010) found significant differences between formally diagnosed dyslexic and nondyslexic language learners in their oral performance scores, whereas no such differences were detected in a Norwegian context by Helland and Kaasa (2005). In the field of second language acquisition, the majority of studies also indicate a limited impact of working memory resources on oral performance (for a review see Kormos, 2015). Nevertheless, the associations between phonological short-term memory capacity and various speech production measures have been found to be stronger (see e.g. Kormos and Sáfár, 2008; O'Brien, Segalowitz, Collentine & Freed, 2007). One can therefore assume that reduced phonological short-term memory capacity might have a greater impact on L2 speech production processes than impairment to working memory capacity.

As I argued at the beginning of this section, output can play a potentially important role in promoting linguistic development. For language learners to be able to learn through output, however, some level of automaticity and efficiency in the output production processes are necessary so that attentional resources become freed up for noticing and processing new linguistic information. It was shown above that in the case of learners with SpLDs, even lower-order output processes, that are often automatic or require less conscious attentional control for other learners, might be effortful. Taken together with possible limitations in working memory and difficulties with the regulation of attention, L2 learners might be restricted in their opportunities to learn through output tasks. Indirect evidence for this assumption can be obtained by considering the results of recent research by Mackey and Sachs (2012) who showed that students with high working memory scores benefitted more from feedback in the context of oral communication tasks than students with a shorter working memory span (for similar research findings see also Mackey, Philp, Egi, Fujii and Tatsumi, 2002).

3.6 The Second Language Learning Processes of Individuals With Autism Spectrum Disorders

As described in Chapter 1, children and adults with ASD can be characterized by varying degrees of verbal communication problems. Some of the children show minimal speech delays and, grammatically, can express themselves accurately and use a wide range of vocabulary, only experiencing difficulties at the sociopragmatic level of language. Other children and adults might face challenges with verbal communication in all linguistic areas. Therefore, it can be expected that this group of individuals will bring a wide range of L1 skills and verbal abilities to the task of L2 learning. Unfortunately, as Jegatheesan (2011) reports, it is common practice that parents receive professional advice that children with ASD should only be exposed to one language. This suggestion can mean that, in multilingual contexts, parents are advised to use only the language of the country, or the language of mainstream education, at home and to avoid communication in any other language. The advice is based on the assumption that exposure to multiple languages will cause further delays in linguistic development and might result in enhanced difficulties for a child with ASD understanding and using the sociopragmatic conventions of different languages. The recommendations of professionals are often made regardless of the verbal developmental difficulties of children with ASD.

Notwithstanding the emotional consequences when children with ASD are excluded from communication in the home, with relatives or in religious contexts (see Jegatheesan (2011) for a vivid and detailed description), the lack of opportunities for learning an additional language can have serious consequences for children with ASD. In the past few years, a number of studies have been conducted in bilingual contexts that have shown that exposure to two or even more languages in childhood does not result in delayed linguistic development for children with ASD when they are compared to children who grow up monolingually. Petersen, Marinova-Todd and Mirenda (2012) administered a number of receptive and expressive language measures to 14 Chinese-English bilingual and 14 English monolingual children with ASD and found no significant differences between the bilingual and monolingual groups. Similar findings were obtained by Ohashi et al. (2012), in a follow-up study with a larger population and involving children from a number of different linguistic backgrounds in Canada. Hambly and Fombonne (2012) examined whether the timing of exposure to multiple languages affected the language development of children with ASD. Their results indicated that children who were bilingual by birth as well as those who were introduced to an additional language after 12 months of age did not show delayed language development in comparison with monolingual children with ASD.

The discussion so far has centred on bilingual language acquisition contexts, but individuals with ASD also frequently study additional languages at school. Unfortunately, there is a scarcity of studies on the foreign language learning processes of people with ASD. Anecdotal accounts of individuals with high-functioning autism (HFA) suggest that these learners can attain high levels of competence in a foreign language (see e.g. the case study by Kanner, 1971). In an unpublished MA dissertation, Prainsson (2012) found that three language learners with HFA who displayed impaired development in their L1 (Icelandic) demonstrated significantly higher L2 (English) proficiency than their peers. In another context, McMullen (2013) conducted a case study with five children with HFA in a Hong Kong primary school. Teacher and student interviews as well as the analysis of children's marks in English and Putonghoa (Mandarin Chinese) revealed that 4 out of 5 students performed above average in English, but their literacy skills in Putonghoa were either average or below average. On the one hand, McMullen explained these differences by making reference to the different types of orthography and instructional methods in the two languages. On the other hand, her interviews brought to light the different motivational thinking that students with HFA displayed towards to the two languages (for more detail on the motivational aspects of this study see Section 4.2.2).

Wire (2005) gives an account of her experience of teaching French to learners with ASD which shows that many of them enjoy learning an additional language and achieve considerable success in doing so. She mentions particular strengths of students with ASD that are beneficial for second language learning, such as rote learning ability that aids the memorization of new words, tolerance of monotony that can assist with automatization and learners' often remarkable ability to imitate various foreign accents. Taken together with the initial findings from case studies of individuals with ASD learning additional languages, this suggests that, despite potential difficulties with the sociopragmatic components of language, children and adults with ASD can achieve considerable success in L2 learning.

3.7 The Cognitive Benefits of Learning Additional Languages

So far this chapter has focused on how cognitive factors affect the processes of language learning, but it is also important to consider whether the underlying cognitive characteristics of students with SpLDs are amenable to change and whether subsequent improvement in various areas of cognitive functioning can enhance their success in L2 learning. Furthermore, the question of whether there might be cognitive benefits from learning additional languages for individuals with SpLDs also needs to be raised.

In the field of second language acquisition, a number of researchers have argued that "language aptitude is a form of developing expertise rather than an entity fixed at birth" (Grigorenko, Sternberg & Ehrman, 2000, p. 401). This would then suggest that improvements in learners' aptitude profiles can be made, which in turn might have beneficial effects for L2 learning. In support of this, Sparks, Ganschow, Fluharty and Little (1995) reported that instruction in Latin resulted in an increase in language aptitude scores in the case of both learning-disabled and non–learning-disabled high school students, although their study did not measure concomitant gains in language proficiency. Sáfár and Kormos (2008) also conducted a quasi-experimental study in which they administered a standardized Hungarian language aptitude test to two groups of learners, at both the beginning and the end of an academic year. One of the groups participated in an intensive language learning programme with fifteen hours of English language instruction per week, whereas the control group only received four hours of instruction per week. They found that the change in overall aptitude scores between the two testing occasions was significantly higher among the students participating in the intensive language learning programme than among the control group. The results also showed that students in the intensive language learning programme improved in tests of phonological sensitivity and metalinguistic awareness to a significantly greater extent than participants in the control group. They drew attention to the fact that research in the field of SpLDs has shown that phonological awareness can be developed with the help of phonological awareness-raising programmes (for more details, see Section 6.3.1). It seems that intensive language learning without considerable explicit training in phonological awareness, as in the intensive language learning context in their study, can also contribute to the enhancement of students' ability to recognize and memorize different sounds. They also pointed out that because, in instructed SLA, it is very important to understand the grammatical function of lexical items, it is understandable that metalinguistic awareness develops as a result of intensive second language instruction. The findings of these studies point to the potential gains that students with SpLDs might also make in their underlying aptitude components from learning one or more additional languages.

Recent research has also investigated whether working memory performance can be improved through training and whether such training has any additional beneficial effects on language processing. Novick, Hussey, Teubner-Rhodes, Harbison and Bunting's (2014) study suggests that systematic training in central executive processes did indeed result in better performance, not only in similar working memory tasks, but also in language processing tasks requiring executive control. Taken together with findings on the cognitive advantages of bi- and multilingualism (e.g. Bialystok & Majumder, 1998; Gold, Kim, Johnson, Kryscio &

Smith, 2013), this provides evidence for the positive effects that learning additional languages can have on the cognitive system. These potential benefits for cognitive functioning gained from L2 learning experience may further underscore the value of learning additional languages for individuals with SpLDs.

3.8 Conclusion and Implications

In this chapter, I have discussed the cognitive correlates of SpLDs and how they can affect the processes of second language learning, comprehension and production of students with SpLDs. As this part of the book is concerned with the cognitive functioning of language learners with SpLDs, it is inevitable that the discussion followed the biological-medical model of SpLDs (see Chapter 1). This chapter highlighted the differential functioning of language learning processes of students with SpLDs and sought to identify the causes of language learning difficulties. Nevertheless, the consideration of these difficulties and the findings of previous research presented in this chapter have important implications for the interactional model of disability (see Chapter 1) and may contribute to demolishing some of the socially constructed barriers in the field of teaching additional languages to students with SpLDs.

First of all, all the results presented in this chapter underscore that there are no well-founded reasons in the cognitive domain that justify students with any type of SpLD, including ASD, being exempted from learning additional languages. Second, the findings with regard to the similarity of low-achieving students in second language learning and those learners with diagnoses of SpLDs suggest that there is a group of L2 learners who do not perceive the existence of socially constructed barriers in acquiring literacy in L1 and academic achievement when the language of instruction is their L1. For this group, the first major obstacle in the educational context they have to face is the learning of an additional language. As shown in this chapter, subtle differences in cognitive functioning can differentiate those students who face no barriers in L1 academic domains and yet experience difficulties in L2 learning, and those for whom literacy instruction in L1 already presents challenges and who also underachieve in L2 learning. It is possible though that it is not only cognitive differences that explain the difficulties of these learners in learning an additional language, but the nature of the instructional context in which the L2 is taught and the aspects in which this context is different from the one in which they acquired their L1 literacy skills (for a detailed discussion of the educational context for language learners with SpLDs, see Chapter 6).

Third, previous studies also reveal that while students might show differential outcomes in areas of L2 learning that are based on written literacy, they might achieve similar levels of L2 competence in the oral domain of L2. There are a number of contexts in which written literacy in additional languages is essential for career and academic purposes, and therefore adjustments to the curriculum and teaching methods that would reduce the priority of those areas might not be possible. Nevertheless, in a number of contexts, competence in an additional language in the oral domain might be sufficient, and changes in the educational goals and targets could be made.

Note

1 I retained the original terminology used in the series of studies conducted by Sparks and his colleagues.

4

SPECIFIC LEARNING DIFFICULTIES AND AFFECTIVE FACTORS IN LANGUAGE LEARNING

Individual differences that can, potentially, influence second language learning outcomes were traditionally divided into cognitive, affective and personality-related factors (Gardner, 1985). Recent conceptualizations of individual differences in second language acquisition (SLA) research, however, consider these three dimensions of students' characteristics to be strongly interrelated. Dörnyei (2010) has outlined a tripartite system of individual differences, consisting of cognition, emotion and motivation, and has demonstrated how cognition and motivation dynamically interact, both in the appraisal of language learning tasks (Dörnyei & Tseng, 2009) and in the formation of the learner's self-concept (Dörnyei, 2010). In an earlier paper, Schumann (1998) argued that "emotional reactions influence the attention and effort devoted to learning, and . . . patterns of appraisal may underlie what has been considered motivation in SLA" (p. 8). He proposed that emotional reactions play an important role in explaining why students repeatedly engage with learning activities or avoid them. The affective appraisal of learning tasks, the instructional environment and social relations within the classroom, and emotional responses are also interrelated, and they add an additional social dimension to affective factors (Garrett & Young, 2009).

In Chapter 3, I discussed the cognitive correlates of specific learning difficulties (SpLDs), and in this chapter, I describe the role of affective factors in influencing the language learning processes and second language self-concept of students with SpLDs. Relevant links between cognition and affect will be made with a special emphasis on how the cognitive appraisal of learners' difficulties impacts on their emotions, including enjoyment and anxiety, and how affective reactions can reciprocally influence the cognitive processes of language learning. Among the affective factors relevant to the study of SLA and SpLDs, the chapter will also consider language learning motivation, self-concept and self-esteem. Although the focus of the chapter is the individual student, and their affective reactions and dispositions, I will also briefly examine how the social and educational context interacts with the affective correlates of SpLDs.

4.1 Language Learning Anxiety and Students With SpLDs

4.1.1 The Construct of Foreign Language Anxiety

Anxiety is an emotion which is intricately linked to working memory and cognition and which has an important effect on the L2 learning processes of students with SpLDs. Anxiety can be defined as "the subjective feeling of tension, apprehension, nervousness, and worry associated with an arousal of the autonomic nervous system" (Spielberger, 1983, p. 1). It is one of the most important affective factors than can influence learning processes and performance in any cognitive domain. Anxiety can be both a general personality trait and a feeling aroused in response to particular situations. The role of anxiety in second and foreign language learning is particularly relevant, because communicating in another language might often invoke feelings of uncertainty and perceptions of a threat to one's self-esteem and self-concept (Horwitz, Horwitz and Cope, 1986). It is this feature of second language communication that led Horwitz et al. (1986) to argue for the existence of a type of situation-specific anxiety, which they termed foreign language anxiety (FLA). FLA was shown to be distinct from general trait anxiety and other situation-specific anxieties such as test anxiety (for a summary see Horwitz, 2000).

FLA was found to be negatively related to achievement in second language learning, although the strength of association between scales measuring FLA and grades and test scores has been found to vary from weak to moderate in most studies (Horwitz, 2001). A negative relationship between FLA and attainment in other language skills, including speaking, writing and tests of grammatical ability, was also found (see e.g. Gardner & MacIntyre, 1993). Correlational studies, however, cannot provide evidence for causation, which made Sparks and Ganschow (1991) reverse the question of whether FLA impacts on achievement negatively. They argued that FLA is the result of foreign language learning difficulties caused by underlying L1 processing problems. In a subsequent study, Ganschow et al. (1994) showed that students scoring highly for FLA differed significantly from their less anxious peers in terms of their L1 skills and aptitude scores. Sparks and Ganschow's (1991) hypothesis has, however, been widely debated, and both Horwitz (2000) and MacIntyre (1995) have highlighted the fact that it is not only L2 learners with learning difficulties who experience anxiety in foreign language learning. Nevertheless, as we will see below, it has been demonstrated that students with SpLDs tend to demonstrate higher levels of FLA than their peers with no SpLDs.

In order to understand the interrelationship of SpLDs and anxiety, it is important to refer to Eysenck's (1992) *cognitive interference theory*, which argues that anxiety exerts a negative effect on performance by interfering with cognitive processes. Eysenck (1992) claimed that worry, which is the cognitive component of anxiety, induces a fear of negative evaluation and failure as well as excessive concern about one's own ability. These self-related thoughts draw attention away from task-related cognitive activities and result in interference during task performance. In the field of SLA, MacIntyre and Gardner (1994) also drew on Tobias' (1986) model of anxiety when they argued that anxiety affects second language learning processes at three points: processing input, carrying out the cognitive operations involved in turning input into knowledge representations, and producing L2 output. They termed these three types of anxiety input, processing and output anxiety, respectively.

In a more recent version of this theory called Processing Efficiency Theory, Eysenck and Calvo (1992) point out that increased anxiety does not always result in diminished performance because anxious individuals may put more effort into completing the task due to a fear of failure or negative evaluation. Therefore, one needs to consider processing efficiency (hence the name of the theory), which consists of the effort and time spent on performing the task, and not just effectiveness, i.e. the accuracy of performance. The inclusion of this motivational component in their model of anxiety might explain why a number of studies have found only weak correlation between L2 performance measures and FLA. It also highlights that other individual difference variables, such as motivation, goals and intended effort and investment in language learning, interact with FLA.

Eysenck and Calvo's (1992) Processing Efficiency Theory also elucidates how anxiety affects attentional processes and imposes demands on working memory resources, which in turn impacts on L2 learning and production and comprehension processes. This theory makes specific predictions about what components of working memory will be affected by anxiety. They argue that because self-related cognition, in other words worry, interferes mostly with the phonological loop and the functioning of the central executive, tasks that require keeping verbal material in short-term memory, and sustained and focused attention will be most prone to anxiety effects. Empirical evidence largely supports these predictions (e.g. Calvo & Eysenck, 1996). In a later extension of the theory, they further specify that it is the inhibition and switching functions of attention that are most likely to be influenced by anxiety (Eysenck, Derakshan, Santos & Calvo, 2007).

4.1.2 The Foreign Language Learning Anxiety of Students With SpLDs

With regard to the emotions and attitudes of students with SpLDs in the academic domain in general, Riddick (1996) found that these children felt "disappointed, frustrated, fed up, ashamed, sad, depressed, angry and embarrassed by their difficulties" (p. 129). Similarly, in the field of language learning, important anxiety effects have been identified. In an early study, Sparks and Ganschow (1991) found that students who experienced high levels of foreign language anxiety were more likely to score lower on tests assessing foreign language aptitude and L1 ability. This provided some initial evidence that students at risk of L2 learning difficulties might be prone to significant anxiety effects due to the challenges they face in L2 learning. Sparks and Ganschow (1991) concluded that anxiety effects can be seen as "symptoms—behavioural manifestations—of a deeper problem" (p. 6).

In one of the few later studies investigating the interrelationship of anxiety and SpLDs, Piechurska-Kuciel (2008) administered a questionnaire to investigate the anxiety levels that occur in the three stages of language processing, input, processing and output, for Polish secondary school students with what she called developmental dyslexia symptoms. Developmental dyslexia symptoms were assessed with the help of a questionnaire: The Revised Adult Dyslexia Checklist (Vinegrad, 1994). The results of the study revealed that students with developmental dyslexia symptoms exhibited higher levels of anxiety in most stages of language processing in comparison to students who reported no dyslexic symptoms. In the first year of their secondary school studies, it was only processing anxiety that differed between the two groups, but the next year all three types of anxiety showed significant differences between them. In the 3rd year of study, the students with developmental dyslexia symptoms showed higher levels of anxiety than their peers in terms of input and output processing. The anxiety experienced by the group with no dyslexic symptoms in the input and processing stages decreased significantly after the 1st year of secondary school, then remained stable throughout the subsequent 2 years of secondary education. Nevertheless, anxiety at the output stage in students with dyslexia symptoms was found to remain permanently high throughout their whole secondary school career (see Figure 4.1 for an illustration).

The results of Piechurska-Kuciel's study (2008) yield several important insights into the kinds of anxiety experienced by students with SpLDs in foreign language classroom contexts. First of all, they reveal that the anxiety experienced while processing L2 knowledge, that is, building new knowledge representations and automatizing L2 skills, remains consistently high for secondary students with signs of SpLDs at almost all stages of foreign language learning. This creates a vicious circle for these students, as they might already face challenges due to their potentially lower working memory and phonological short-term memory capacity that can hinder the processing of new L2 knowledge (see Section 3.2 for more details). As argued in Eysenck and Calvo's (1992) Processing Efficiency Theory, the additional processing anxiety that learners with SpLDs are affected by might further interfere with working memory resources, thus closing the circle and contributing to additional L2 learning difficulties (see Figure 4.2).

Piechurska-Kuciel's (2008) study also indicates that producing output, that is using the L2 actively in communication in classroom contexts, can also be anxiety

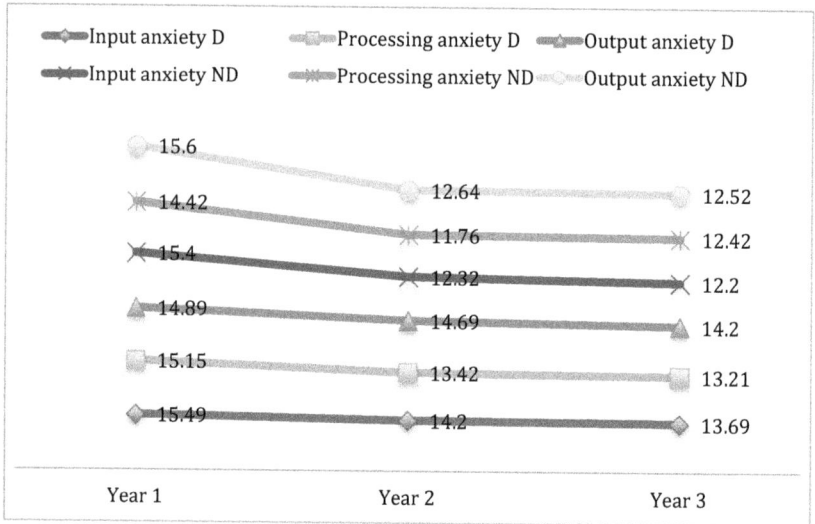

FIGURE 4.1 The Levels of Anxiety Experienced Across Years in Piechurska-Kuciel's (2008) Study

Note: D = students with dyslexic symptoms; ND = students with no dyslexic symptoms

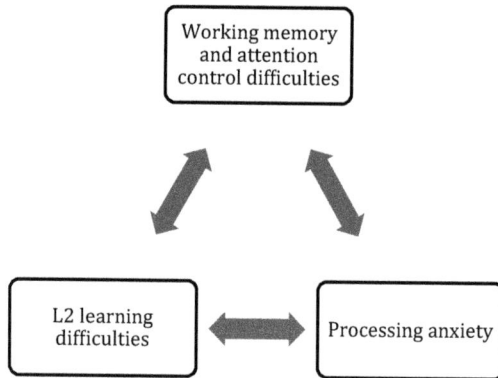

FIGURE 4.2 The Interrelationship of Processing Anxiety and Cognitive Functioning in Dyslexic L2 Learners

provoking for learners with SpLDs. Piechurska-Kuciel (2008) explains that anxiety at the output stage might stem from these individuals' low self-esteem and negative self-concept as language learners (for more details see Section 4.2.3) on the one hand, and from the potentially lower level of L2 competence they acquire in comparison with their peers on the other. She also highlights that output anxiety might arise from a fear of negative evaluation and the demands that oral communication make on coordinating different linguistic processes under time pressure. Finally, Piechurska-Kuciel (2008) draws attention to the possibility that the initially situation-specific anxiety experienced by learners with SpLDs can turn into a more stable trait-level anxiety that can have pervasive effects on their self-concept and behaviour (see e.g. Carroll and Illes, 2006, for a study of the anxiety of dyslexic university students).

In an interview study, Kormos, Csizér and Sarkadi (2009) investigated the foreign language learning experiences of learners with a formal diagnosis of dyslexia in a Hungarian context. The participants gave accounts of several classroom, teacher and group-level factors that they felt contributed to their anxiety in foreign language learning. Assessment, especially the high emphasis on accuracy and spelling in written work, was one of the most important causes of anxiety among the 15 interviewees. Other significant causes of anxiety included teachers' negative attitude to SpLDs and an unwillingness to accommodate learners with SpLDs in the classroom. For example, one of the interviewees explained that "they did not try to help me, but they emphasized that I am having problems, but not like wanting to help me but as a kind of humiliation" (Kormos et al., 2009, p. 123). With regard to their peers, the interviewees mentioned a lack of acceptance and understanding of the nature of difficulties that SpLDs can cause, and low levels of patience with their slower pace of learning. These social dimensions of anxiety seemed to be strongly prevalent in Kormos et al.'s (2009) data, which is a finding also emerging from other studies on emotions in SLA (e.g. Bown & White, 2010; Garrett & Young, 2009). Therefore, it seems that the anxiety-provoking factors described above, rooted in the educational context, do not seem to be unique to students with SpLDs.

In this section on the interrelationship of language learning anxiety and SpLDs, it was shown how cognitive factors can interact with the affective correlates of SpLDs. I also briefly explained how the instructional environment can contribute to feelings of anxiety. The effects of context and students' agency within a particular situation will be elaborated further in Section 4.2. Nevertheless, it is important to highlight that anxiety does not only arise as a result of the language learning difficulties of students with SpLDs. The effects of anxiety can be both mitigated and enhanced by the students' environment. In inclusive contexts where language learners with SpLDs are carefully accommodated (for more details see, Sections 6.1 and 6.2), anxiety might not be a correlate of SpLDs. A quote from Csizér, Kormos and Sarkadi's interview study (2010) illustrates that, in some cases, even small-scale accommodations in instructional practices can significantly change learners' affective state.

> My Hebrew teacher did not get any training in teaching dyslexics, but he does not consider spelling and that's it. This was all I needed and now I can speak one more language . . . So if your spelling is not assessed, it

will be easier for you, and you don't have butterflies in your stomach anymore that, my God, I have to get this right. Once you are relieved of this stress, you will do better. It will be much better.

(Kormos et al., 2009, p. 125)

4.2 Motivation and Language Learners With SpLDs

Barriers in the educational context and persistent difficulties experienced in learning an additional language may not only result in language learning anxiety, but can also undermine the motivation of students with SpLDs (see Csizér et al., 2010). This lack of motivation, in turn, may contribute to further challenges and difficulties. The vicious circle these learners might get into can pose a threat to the development of the students' L2 abilities. From interviews conducted with language learners with SpLDs and their teachers, it is also apparent that strong motivational forces are needed for these learners to overcome their difficulties in language learning and achieve success (Csizér et al., 2010; Kormos & Kontra, 2008). Therefore, it is important to examine what motivates individuals with SpLDs in language learning and how various internal and external factors interact and influence their motivational processes.

Motivation explains why people select a particular activity, how long they are willing to persist, and what effort they invest in it (Dörnyei, 2001). These three components of motivation correspond to goals and the initiation and maintenance of learning effort, which are the aspects of motivation that this section will focus on with regard to the language learning processes of individuals with SpLDs. This section will follow the structure of the interactive hierarchical motivational model proposed by Kormos, Kiddle and Csizér (2011). In this model, at the top of the interactive system of motivation we can find motivated behaviour, which acts as a volitional system controlling the effort and persistence invested in language learning and which is linked to actual language learning behaviour. At the next level, learners' self-guides and language learning attitudes can be located. Self-guides include the learners' own internalized views of the value and importance of L2 learning, L2 self-concept and self-efficacy beliefs, as well as external views of their environment. The third layer of the interactive model includes distal goals of language learning. These goals foster the establishment of self-guides and attitudes, but self-related beliefs and language learning experience can also modify language learning goals.

4.2.1 The Language Learning Goals of Students With SpLDs

With regard to the question of why people learn additional languages, in the field of SLA, a number of different language learning goals have been proposed. Gardner (Gardner, 1985, 2006; Gardner & Lambert, 1959; Masgoret & Gardner, 2003) differentiated instrumental goals, which are associated with the utilitarian values of speaking another language, from integrative goals, which express individuals' wish to learn the language in order to become integrated into the target language culture. Although the differentiation of integrative and instrumental motivation might be important with regard to the learning of modern foreign languages such as Italian, Spanish or French in a number of contexts, the case with English language learning motivation is more complex. By the end of the 20th century, English had become an international language serving as a lingua franca in a globalized world (e.g. Jenkins, 2007; Seidlhofer, 2005; Widdowson, 1993). Therefore, English has become separated from its native speakers and their cultures (Skutnabb-Kangas, 2000). Consequently, a new language learning goal has emerged: international posture, which includes "interest in foreign or international affairs, willingness to go overseas to study or work, readiness to interact with intercultural partners . . . and a nonethnocentric attitude toward different cultures" (Skutnabb-Kangas, 2000, p. 57; Yashima, 2002). As a result, international orientation often replaces integrative orientation in a large number of foreign language learning contexts (see e.g. Kormos et al.'s (2011) study in Chile and Kormos & Csizér (2008) study in Hungary). Further language learning goals may also include friendship, travel and knowledge orientations (Clément & Kruidenier, 1983).

Goals, however, are only effective motivators if they become internalized to some extent (Deci, Koestner & Ryan, 1999), an assumption which is expressed in Deci and Ryan's (1985) important distinction between intrinsic and extrinsic motivation. Intrinsically motivated individuals engage in the learning process because they find it interesting and enjoyable, whereas extrinsically motivated learners carry out the learning activity in order to gain a reward or avoid punishment. In the field of language learning motivation, Noels, Clément and Pelletier (2001) also identified intrinsic language learning goals, which are related to the feelings of enjoyment and enhancement experienced during the process of language learning.

The language learning goals of students with SpLDs were examined in a qualitative interview study conducted by Csizér et al. (2010). The participants of the study were 15 Hungarian language learners with a formal diagnosis of dyslexia who varied with regard to their age and educational background and also the foreign languages they studied in addition to English. In this study, three goals emerged as important reasons for language learning: *international posture*, *instrumental orientation* and *cultural orientation*. Csizér et al. highlighted that these orientations were not specific to learners with dyslexia, as in previous studies of Hungarian language learners, the participants gave very similar reasons as to why they studied a particular foreign language (Csizér & Kormos, 2008; Dörnyei, Csizér & Németh, 2006). However, their research showed that, generally, language learners with a formal diagnosis of dyslexia had a primarily extrinsic interest in language learning, whereas motivation research in the Hungarian context with groups of a similar age indicated that nondyslexic students tended to have internalized goals and an intrinsic interest in language learning (Csizér & Kormos, 2008).

International orientation was mentioned by 14 out of the 15 interviewees in Csizér et al.'s study (2010), and this was due to the importance of English as an international language. It was for this reason that most of the respondents thought that no one with dyslexia should be exempted from language learning. Interestingly, the international status of English was perceived to be demotivating for two of the interviewees, who stated that they disliked English because it is a world language, and because they felt that studying this language was prescribed for them: "I feel that English is really forced on me, I do not really like it, I know that it's an important language in the world, but I am unable to feel positive towards it" (Participant H in Csizér et al., 2010, p. 479). A questionnaire study investigating the differences between the motivational characteristics of dyslexic and nondyslexic primary school learners of English in Hungary, by Kormos and Csizér (2010), also showed that dyslexic learners with a formal diagnosis reported significantly lower intensities of international orientation than did their nondyslexic peers.

As for the instrumental orientation of learners with dyslexia, most of the participants in Csizér et al.'s (2010) study wanted to improve their knowledge of the L2 in order to be able to pass a language exam. The participants were also conscious of the work-related advantages one could gain with proficiency in an L2. Travelling or living abroad, or both, were also included in the instrumental category for the purposes of this study. Cultural orientation was found to be another important aspect of the motivation to study a foreign language among the formally identified dyslexic language learners in Csizér et al.'s study (2010). English served as a useful tool for these participants and helped them to gain access to a range of L2 cultural products and artefacts, such as films, videos, books, magazines and music.

Sparks, Patton, Ganschow and Humbach's (2009) study only indirectly investigated language learning goals and attitudes, as the composite score of a motivational questionnaire tapping into several motivational constructs was used. They found that low-achieving L2 learners who were at risk of learning difficulties displayed less favourable motivational profiles than high achievers. Interestingly, their research also indicated that negative motivational dispositions were already present before the students started learning an additional language. These results suggest that learners with SpLDs might approach the task of L2 learning with a low expectation of success, a negative attitude and no clear goals.

Based on the findings of studies conducted in the Hungarian context, it can be hypothesized that the general motives for learning additional languages for individuals with SpLDs might not be different from those of their peers. Language learning goals are strongly embedded in the social and educational context (see e.g. the model of motivation for dyslexic students proposed by Csizér et al. (2010) in Figure 4.3), and are thus less likely to vary based on the cognitive

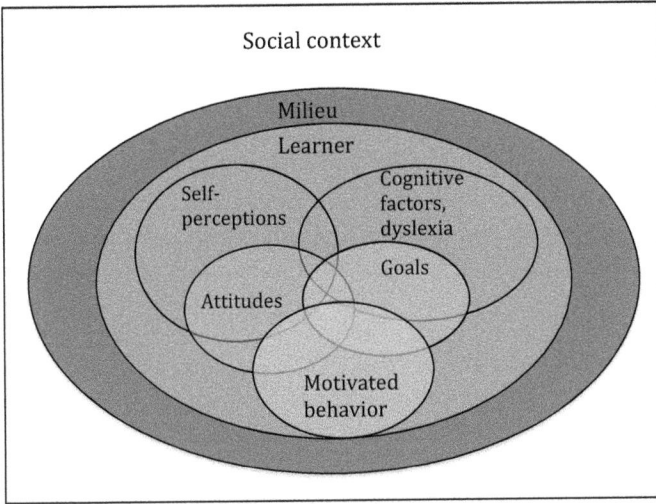

FIGURE 4.3 A Representation of the Motivational System in Csizér, Kormos and Sarkadi's (2010) Study

Source: Reproduced from the *Modern Language Journal* with permission of Blackwell Publishing Inc.

characteristics and SpLD status of learners. SpLDs, however, might exert an influence on how strongly the learners endorse these goals and to what extent they internalize them, as shown in the research findings of Csizér et al. (2010) and Kormos and Csizér (2010). Their results reveal that the difficulties individuals with SpLDs experience in language learning, which are often aggravated by a lack of sufficient educational support, contribute greatly to a loss of interest and the formation of negative attitudes to language learning. It also needs to be remembered that L2 learners with a history of literacy-related difficulties might also transpose their experiences of acquiring literacy skills in L1 to L2 learning and might lack specific goals at the onset of the L2 learning process (see Sparks et al., 2009).

Although this chapter is primarily concerned with the affective character-istics of language learners with SpLDs, it is important to remember that indi-vidual learner goals are socially constructed and shaped by how individuals view the cultural capital (Bourdieu, 1991) they can attain by learning an additional language (for a recent review see Norton and Toohey, 2011). Increased access to knowledge and cultural products, both of which contribute to learn-ers' cultural capital, was often mentioned by the formally diagnosed dyslexic participants in Csizér et al.'s (2010) study. Nevertheless, as will be shown in Section 4.2.4, due to barriers in the educational system and local classroom practices, learners with SpLDs might not be willing to make sufficient invest-ment in L2 learning.

4.2.2 The Language Learning Attitudes of Students With SpLDs

Language learning goals exert their motivational influence through emotional arousal (Ford, 1992). In educational psychology, emotional arousal is often conceptualized as either the intrinsic enjoyment derived from learning (see e.g. Ryan & Deci, 2000) or an attitude to the object of learning (Ajzen, 2005). MacIntyre (2002) highlighted the important role of emotions in L2 learning when he argued that "emotion has the capacity to explain cases where students endorse orientations but might not be energized to take action, and also cases where action is prevented by emotional arousal" (p. 63). In the field of L2 motivation, attitudes have been identified as one of the most significant emotional precursors of the initiation of learning behaviour.

Existing research on the attitudinal dispositions of students with SpLDs is scarce and has mostly been conducted with formally diagnosed dyslexic Hungarian language learners. In the interview study by Csizér et al. (2010) described previously, the analysis of the language learning attitudes showed that the most important learner-internal cause for the interviewees' negative attitudes, such as lack of enjoyment of language learning, was related to their dyslexia. Students voicing negative attitudes expressed the view that English was a difficult language due to its nontransparent orthography. This difficulty caused them much frustration and resulted in a lack of enjoyment in language learning. This finding shows how the cognitive appraisal of difficulties can result in negative emotional reactions and the establishment of stable negative affective states towards the process of language learning and particular learning tasks. The quantitative survey comparing the motivational characteristics of formally identified dyslexic and nondyslexic learners of English and German by Kormos and Csizér (2010) also revealed that dyslexic learners had significantly less favourable attitudes toward language learning than their nondyslexic peers. Interestingly, in their questionnaire study, Kormos and Csizér (2010) found that even though German has more transparent orthography than English, dyslexic language learners displayed less favourable attitudes to both German and English as foreign languages than their nondyslexic peers.

Csizér et al.'s study (2010) also documented how the attitudes of dyslexic language learners underwent changes in the course of their learning history. For example, two of their participants reported that, at the beginning of their language learning careers, they liked learning English, but as they encountered more and more difficulties, they gradually developed a negative attitude. As one participant described, "At the beginning I enjoyed learning English, but then I started doing poorly in class and then I didn't like English so much anymore" (Csizér et al., 2010, p. 478). The language learning histories of the participants revealed that initially positive attitudes either decreased gradually as they experienced difficulties in language learning due to their dyslexia, or the change was dramatic and caused by a sudden sense of failure.

An interesting finding in Csizér et al.'s (2010 study) is that while many learners reported strong negative emotions with regard to the first foreign language they were studying, usually English, the participants often displayed a positive attitude towards the second additional language which they could choose after they had already started learning an L2. For example, two participants expressed a positive attitude towards Russian. They reported that despite its different script, it was easier for them than English, because its spelling was predictable. Another participant took up Spanish in order to counterbalance the difficulties with English, while another dyslexic learner chose Italian. The more transparent orthography of these languages provided the participants with a greater sense of success than did English, and these positive experiences enhanced their attitudes and evoked positive emotions. As one of their participants explained,

> I really like Italian because it is such a beautiful language and it has a melody. I also like that whatever is written down can be read out easily. The rules are very simple, so this is a language that one can really get to like. . . . So you can really love a language that you learn because you chose it for yourself.
>
> *(Csizér et al., 2010, p. 480)*

The participants in Csizér et al.'s research (2010) also mentioned anxiety and negative attitudes in the same context. A regression analysis of questionnaire data in Kormos and Csizér's (2010) study revealed that the language learning experience variable was the strongest predictor of language learning attitudes, for both formally diagnosed dyslexic and nondyslexic learners, and the factor that correlated most strongly with language learning experience was the participants' evaluation of their teachers' instructional practices and behaviours. These results provide support for the qualitative findings of Csizér et al.'s (2010) study with regard to the environmental causes of negative emotions, including anxiety and enjoyment of language learning. They highlight how pedagogical practices can be the cause of negative emotional reactions and contribute to the formation of unfavourable attitudes towards language learning for learners with SpLDs. In another study, Csizér (2010) found evidence of how teachers' attitudes to SpLDs, available accommodations and students' language learning attitudes form a dynamically changing system.

In a small-scale study, McMullen (2013) found that primary schoolchildren with ASD studying English and Putonghoa as additional languages in Hong Kong displayed positive attitudes to English, which they could use outside the classroom context, as opposed to Putonghoa, which served only as a tool for written literacy. As already mentioned in Chapter 3, most of these learners with high-functioning autism did not experience considerable difficulties in learning additional languages and performed above the average level of their class in English. They liked the fact that they could use English for nonsocial entertainment purposes, mostly playing computer games but also watching films and reading. Although this study had a very small sample size and thus limited generalizability, the findings tentatively suggest that, in certain contexts, L2 learners with high-functioning autism might even have more favourable motivational profiles than their peers.

4.2.3 The Self-Concept of Students With SpLDs

Key elements of motivation which regulate goal-setting and influence the translation of goals into action are personal agency beliefs, which in educational psychology are embodied in two constructs: self-efficacy beliefs (Bandura, 1986) and self-concept (Shavelson, Hubner & Stanton, 1976). Self-efficacy beliefs express one's view as to whether one is capable of performing a given learning task and is consequently future oriented, whereas self-concept beliefs are based on past experiences and "control the processing of self-relevant information" (Campbell & Lavallee, 1993, p. 4). Within the construct of self, self-esteem embodies the evaluations of one's general self-worth or esteem (Bong & Skaalvik, 2003), and the Ideal Self describes the "ideal standards of behavior or particular skills which are valued by the individual" (Lawrence, 1996). These self-concepts have been somewhat neglected in SLA research until now (but see Mercer, 2011), with the exception of the Ideal L2 Self which forms part of the Motivational Self System Theory proposed by Dörnyei (2005), who argues that the main driving force in language learning is the learners' future self-image. His model of motivation contains two self-related components: Ideal L2 Self and Ought-to L2 Self. In this model, Ideal L2 Self is one's ideal self-image expressing the wish to become a competent L2 speaker. The Ought-to L2 Self contains "attributes that one believes one ought to possess (i.e. various duties, obligations, or responsibilities) in order to avoid possible negative outcomes" (Dörnyei, 2005, p. 106) associated with not being able to speak the L2 in question.

Academic achievement was shown to play an important role in the development of children's self-concept, regardless of the status of having learning difficulties or not, because one's views and evaluations of oneself are to a large extent based on school performance (Pajares & Schunk, 2005). Self-concept is also shaped by the environment and social comparisons (Bandura, 1997), and hence the relationship between achievement and self-concept is interactive. With regard to students with SpLDs, a number of studies have shown that students with dyslexia, as well as those more generally labelled as having 'special educational needs', have lower self-esteem than their peers (e.g. Humphrey, 2002; Riddick, 1996). Possible reasons for the lower self-esteem lie in the fact that children with learning difficulties might often be less accepted by their peers (Eaude, 1999), and from the age of 8, students' self-evaluation becomes dependent on comparisons with others (Gurney, 1988). There are two potential additional factors that have been found to influence the self-esteem of children with SpLDs, namely whether they study in mainstream classrooms or in segregated SpLDs units, and whether they have received an official identification and are labelled as having SpLDs in general or dyslexia in particular.

The findings with regard to mainstream students with SpLDs and those in segregated learning contexts have been mixed. In some studies, students who studied in segregated units showed higher self-esteem due to the availability of more resources, better trained teachers and comparisons with peers with similar types of learning difficulties (Gurney, 1988). In a more recent study, Humphrey (2002) found that although the self-esteem of students in specialized SpLD units, as measured by a standardized questionnaire of self-esteem, was generally higher in a number of academic domains than that of students who studied in mainstream classes, when another instrument assessing the discrepancy between the students' actual and ideal selves was used, the self-esteem of both groups with SpLDs was lower than that of their peers. One of the most important conclusions from this line of studies, despite their somewhat contradictory findings, is that, in addition to peer comparisons, the nature of the instructional environment, especially with regard to how the students' academic, emotional and social needs are addressed, plays a key role in the formation of self-concept.

The role of labelling in the formation of students' self-esteem has also been found to be complex. Riddick's (1996) interview study suggested that the identification of students' SpLD and subsequent labelling in the private domain was felt to be helpful by the children as it provided an explanation for their difficulties and granted them access to certain resources. It also allowed students to see that there are other people with similar difficulties and offered an opportunity for identification with a particular group. An additional benefit of labelling might be that, if it is based on timely identification of learning differences, children might develop successful coping strategies that prevent the formation of negative self-related beliefs (McNulty, 2003). In contrast, labelling was often felt to be detrimental to self-esteem when, in the public domain, it was used for highlighting students' difference from their peers and resulted in segregation. In an interesting recent study, Taylor, Hume and Welsch (2011) found that students aged 8–15 in the United Kingdom who were formally identified as dyslexic did not show significantly lower self-esteem than students with no dyslexia. In contrast, the group which was labelled as having general 'special educational needs' differed from both nondyslexic and dyslexic students significantly in terms of their self-esteem. Taylor et al. (2011) explain their findings with reference to heightened public awareness of dyslexia in the United Kingdom and the effective inclusion of these students in the school system in recent years. They also highlight that the identification of the exact nature of the students' learning difficulty in the case of dyslexia, as opposed to the more general special educational needs, is more beneficial for the students' self-esteem as it allows them access to targeted educational programmes and provides a clear explanation of the challenges they face.

The self-concept of language learners with SpLDs was investigated in Csizér et al.'s (2010) study in a Hungarian context. From among their 15 participants who all held an official diagnosis of dyslexia, only four students evaluated themselves positively; the remaining 11 all gave accounts of negative views of themselves as language learners. Two of the students with high self-esteem told the interviewers that they believed that they had a high level of language learning aptitude and good cognitive skills in general, suggesting that students transferred their general academic self-concept to the domain of language learning. The other two students with a positive self-concept in the L2 learning domain attributed their success to very hard work and a solid knowledge of the basics of the language, that helped them throughout their language learning careers. A reanalysis of the original interview data of Csizér et al. (2010) revealed that all four students were proactive learners who exercised strong agency over their learning processes. Among the learners who had negative self-perceptions, four interviewees held the view that they had failed as language learners and explained their lack of success with reference to a lack of effort and a low level of language aptitude. As will be shown below, the interview data concerning effort and investment confirmed the students' self-evaluation. While all these students attributed their lack of progress to internal factors rather than the environment, it was interesting to observe that only one of the students explicitly mentioned dyslexia as a source of his negative self-concept and difficulties in learning foreign languages. Nevertheless, this participant considered his dyslexia to be only one of his difficulties:

> It is very strange that it is quite difficult for me to learn foreign languages. Three things contribute to my difficulties. First, I am lazy, and that's entirely my fault. Second, I am dyslexic. Third, my foreign language learning aptitude is very low, just like my mother's. She is not dyslexic. She has very good writing and reading skills but no foreign language aptitude. She has been learning English for six years, but could not get anywhere with it.
>
> *(Csizér et al., 2010, p. 480)*

There were three other participants in Csizér et al.'s (2010) study who held similar views and used the word *lazy* to describe themselves. This view was probably internalized as the result of an environmental reaction to the students' difficulties in language learning. As one of the participants in the study explained, "It was difficult because I was always told that I am not good at English because I am lazy. But that was not true. I was studying for hours" (p. 480). The findings of Csizér et al.'s (2010) study are important as they show that evaluations stemming from the students' environment can be detrimental to self-esteem and lead to the internalization of the views of peers and teachers into the L2 self-concept.

With regard to the Ideal L2 self, Kormos and Csizér's (2010) questionnaire study showed that formally identified dyslexic language learners had significantly weaker visions of themselves as successful language learners than their nondyslexic peers. Similar to the findings concerning language learning attitudes, no interaction between the language studied and dyslexia was found, suggesting that whether the dyslexic students studied German or English made no difference in terms of their Ideal L2 self. It is noteworthy, however, that when regression analyses were conducted to explain variations in motivated behaviour, the Ideal L2 self played a less important role in the case of dyslexic learners of German than for dyslexic students who studied English. This seems to indicate that the future vision of what one can potentially achieve had a more important energizing function for dyslexic learners of English in this Hungarian context than for those studying German.

4.2.4 Motivated Behaviour, Investment and Agency of Students With SpLDs

No model of motivation is complete without considering the final outcome of the motivational processes, which is called *volition* in educational psychology and *motivated learning behaviour* in the field of SLA. Volition is defined by Corno (1993) as a "dynamic system of psychological control processes that protect concentration and directed effort in the face of personal and/or environmental distractions, and so aid learning and performance" (Corno, 1993, p. 16). In the field of language learning motivation, the parallel construct for volition is motivated behaviour, which is usually seen to consist of effort and persistence (e.g. Csizér & Dörnyei, 2005; Dörnyei, 2001, 2005; Gardner, 1985, 2006).

As Norton Peirce (1995) argued, motivated behaviour also needs to be viewed through the lens of the individual as a member of society. She showed how the social context and instructional practices in teaching the L2 might result in a lack of investment, despite highly positive motivational characteristics at the individual learner level. She defined investment with reference to the learners' situated and dynamically changing social identity and the cultural capital learners can gain by means of investing in language learning. Although the primary focus here is on the affective characteristics of individual learners with SpLDs, as is evident in this chapter, the emotional consequences of SpLDs cannot be separated from the social and educational context. Hence I will also briefly consider the social aspect of motivation: the investment and the agency that one exercises over their learning and in their environment.

In an interview study, Csizér et al. (2010) investigated the motivated behaviour of Hungarian language learners with a formal diagnosis of dyslexia. A considerable number of their interviewees reported high levels of motivated behaviour and these learners often compared their efforts, seeing them as being considerably greater than those of their nondyslexic peers. Out of the 15 participants, five reported that they spent a lot of time studying and practicing the L2 outside the language classroom. These participants were also aware that the success they achieved in L2 learning was mainly due to the energy they had invested in language learning. As one of the interviewees said, "This [my success] is the prize for the lot of hard work and studying" (p. 480).

A reanalysis of the interview data also revealed that these learners exercised active agency over their learning processes and made considerable efforts to change their learning environment. If they found that the classroom environment did not afford enough opportunities to them for development, they either asked for help from family members or opted for private tuition. Two of the students also repeatedly approached both the school management and their language teachers to request the use of accommodations in their assessment. These strongly motivated learners also had clear future goals with the language they were studying and were making a conscious investment in it. On the one hand, their investment was high because of the social, economic and cultural resources they could potentially gain by speaking an additional language. On the other, the interview data also suggest that these learners either studied in an environment, or created such an environment for themselves, in which they felt it was worth investing in language learning.

Language learners with SpLDs, however, can often become demotivated and may not make an investment in language learning, as found in Csizér et al.'s (2010) study. The lack of effort on the part of the learners in this study was explained by persistent difficulties in language learning and a lack of support in the given educational context. Csizér et al.'s interview data (2010) yield an insight into how demotivation might be linked to a lack of opportunities for dyslexic language learners to take control of their learning and exercise agency. They recount the experience of a Hungarian dyslexic language learner whose teacher in secondary school repeatedly ignored the parents' request for accommodations in assessment. As a result, the student lost interest in language learning and invested no effort in it; in her words, "I write my homework, study the words a little bit, but I feel that this is hopeless. To be honest, I have already given it up." The situation of dyslexic language learners in these contexts clearly underscores Pavlenko and Lantolf's (2000) argument that "agency is crucial at the point where the individuals must not just start memorizing a dozen new words and expressions but have to decide on whether to initiate a long, painful, inexhaustive and, for some, never-ending process of self-translation" (p. 170).

The interviews in Csizér et al.'s (2010) study also revealed that, as did their attitudes, the participants' language learning efforts fluctuated throughout their language learning careers. This fluctuation in motivated behaviour was often in parallel with changes in attitudes to language learning. These findings highlight that the motivated behaviour, investment and agency of language learners with SpLDs are not stable and given a priori characteristics, but rather change dynamically in response to the social and educational context.

4.3 Conclusion and Implications

This chapter has discussed the role that affective factors play in the second language learning processes of students with SpLDs. In the first part of the chapter, I reviewed the existing research on the anxiety experienced by students with SpLDs and pointed to an important link between cognitive characteristics, especially working memory capacity, and feelings of anxiety. It was argued that the difficulties students face in L2 learning often provoke anxiety, and these feelings of worry in turn further reduce their attentional capacity. I also highlighted that the source of anxiety for students with SpLDs is not only related to cognitive factors, but also associated with the educational context and the barriers present in the language classroom.

Most previous studies concerning the emotional correlates of learning differences have focused on students with a formal diagnosis of dyslexia, but the findings discussed in this chapter may be relevant for a wider range of learning difficulties. This is especially true for the findings concerning the sociocontextual and educational aspects of the motivation of students with SpLDs. A recurring theme throughout this chapter has been the important role played by peers' and teachers' classroom behaviour and attitudes to SpLDs and accommodations. Although these need to be considered within a wider context of educational policy and practices, when it comes to individual learners with SpLDs, the most immediate barriers they face are present in the classroom and at school level. These barriers significantly impact on the learners as individuals in terms of their emotional reactions, self-concept and motivation. They also have important consequences for them at the social level, including the investment they make in language learning and the agency they can exercise over their learning.

5

ASSESSING THE SECOND LANGUAGE SKILLS OF STUDENTS WITH SPECIFIC LEARNING DIFFICULTIES[1]

In many countries, a certificate of proficiency in a foreign language is a prerequisite for obtaining a university degree, and sometimes even for being admitted to university in the first place. Yet, in many high-stakes testing contexts special arrangements are rarely made for students with specific learning difficulties (SpLDs) taking language exams; and if they are made, those accommodations are far from sufficient to ensure equal opportunities for most of these learners. It is therefore of crucial importance that language proficiency tests do not unfairly disadvantage test-takers with SpLDs. In this chapter, I discuss the construct of test fairness and validity from the perspective of SpLDs and review recent research efforts in large-stakes and classroom contexts in this regard. I then consider the effect of various types of accommodation and modification on the performance of students with SpLDs. Next, I describe the kinds of accommodation in terms of test tasks and administration procedures that are necessary to give learners with SpLDs a fair chance to display their knowledge of a foreign language. The chapter concludes with a discussion of how stakeholders, including test-takers and representatives of major international language-test providers, view accommodations and practices related to the provision of special arrangements.

5.1 Validity and Fairness

The most fundamental issue in assessment is the accuracy of measurement, in other words, the validity of the test. Henning (1987) defines validity as follows:

> Validity refers to the appropriateness of a given test or any of its component parts as a measure of what it is purported to measure. A test is said to be valid to the extent it measures what it is supposed to measure. It follows,

that the term *valid* when used to describe a test should usually be accompanied by the preposition *for*. Any test then may be valid for some purposes but not for others.

(p. 89)

Messick' (1989) defines validity as "an integrated evaluative judgement of the degree to which empirical evidence and theoretical rationales support the *adequacy* and *appropriateness of inferences* and *actions* based on test scores or other modes of assessment" (p. 13, his emphasis). This definition also highlights that validity is not an inherent characteristic of a test itself, but depends on the context in which the test is used and on how the scores are interpreted. Messick argues that there are two major threats to validity: construct underrepresentation, when a test fails to measure what it intends to measure by ignoring relevant aspects of the construct (e.g. a dictation test used to measure writing skills), and construct-irrelevant variance, when a test also measures factors which are not central to the construct (e.g. a writing test which also involves criteria assessing the neatness of handwriting). The latter threat to validity might result in bias towards particular groups of test-takers and might result in unfair disadvantages to other groups (see the discussion of fairness below). Messick also highlights that validity includes the relevance and utility of a test in a given context, as well as its social consequences.

In the language-testing field, there has been a recent debate over the relationship between validity and fairness (see Davies, 2010; Kane, 2004, 2010; Kunnan, 2010; Xi, 2010). Some standards for assessment regard fairness as being entirely independent of validity (e.g. The Code of Fair Testing Practices in Education (Joint Committee on Testing Practices, 1998, 2004) and the Standards for Fairness and Quality by Educational Testing Service (ETS, 2002)). In contrast, Davies (2010) sees fairness as an irrelevant construct, "first because it is unattainable and second because it is unnecessary" (p. 171). Kunnan (2004) views fairness as an overarching concept that encompasses validity and claims that a test is only valid if it is fair. Finally, the Standards for Educational and Psychological Testing (AERA/APA/NCME, 1999) conceptualize fairness as distinct from but at the same time strongly interrelated to validity (see Figure 5.1 for an illustration of the possible relationships between fairness and validity). Kane (2010) outlines a similar conceptualization when he argues that:

> An assessment that is unfair, in the sense that it systematically misrepresents the standing of some individuals or some groups of individuals on the construct being measured or that tends to make inappropriate decisions for individuals or groups is, to that extent, not valid for that interpretation or use. Similarly, an assessment that is not valid in the sense that it tends to generate misleading conclusions or inappropriate decisions for some individuals or groups will also be unfair.

(p. 181)

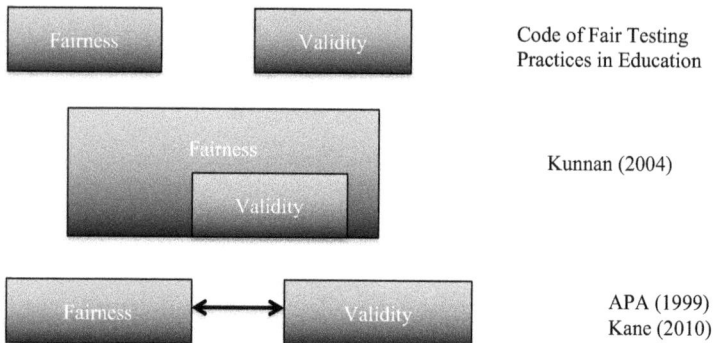

FIGURE 5.1 Different Conceptualizations of the Relationship of Fairness and Validity

Fairness as defined by the American Educational Research Association (AERA/APA/NCME, 1999) has four principal characteristics: lack of bias, equitable treatment in the testing process, equality in the outcomes of testing, and fairness as an opportunity to learn. Lack of bias means that a test does not have "construct irrelevant components that result in systematically lower or higher scores for identifiable groups of examinees" (AERA/APA/NCME, 1999, p. 76). Bias can be generated by the content of a test, such as including culture-specific background knowledge in a reading test, which creates negative bias for those who are not familiar with the particular culture in question. Bias can also result from the response format. In this case, the task requires the application of knowledge or skills which are irrelevant to the aspect of language competence to be measured, and it impedes the successful completion of the task. For example, asking students to draw a picture based on a listening test might disadvantage those who have difficulty with drawing, such as test-takers with dyspraxia. It is very important to consider bias resulting from the response format when testing students with SpLDs, and hence tasks used in assessment should be carefully examined in terms of construct-irrelevant features which might pose difficulties for these learners. If such bias is found, alternative tasks and response formats need to be employed in assessment.

Fairness as equitable treatment in the assessment process involves careful consideration of the context and purpose of the assessment. With regard to SpLDs, the most important aspect of fairness concerns appropriate testing conditions. Tests need to be administered under circumstances which allow students to demonstrate what they know and which do not prevent them from performing to the best of their knowledge. Therefore, test administration procedures often need to be modified to ensure appropriate testing conditions for students with SpLDs. For example, students with attention deficit hyperactivity disorder (ADHD) might need to be tested in a separate room from other candidates so that their attention will not be distracted from the test tasks.

Fairness as equality in outcomes of testing requires that different subgroups of test-takers, such as those from different first language or social backgrounds, who have similar levels of ability, should show comparable distributions of scores. In other words, this means that the fact that someone belongs to a particular group of test-takers should not affect their likelihood of passing a test. Finally, fairness as an opportunity to learn means that test-takers should have equal opportunities in preparing for a test.

It is important to acknowledge that, in certain cases, ensuring fairness might be beyond the test designers' or administrators' control. Social and educational factors might contribute to the fact that certain groups of students cannot fully demonstrate their ability in tests and might not have equal opportunities for learning the content or skills that are assessed in a test. In this case, the test is neither fair nor valid for the particular group of test-takers (Davies, 2010). Even though, in certain cases, fairness might be beyond the control of the test designer, it must still be an important consideration in the practice of language-test developers. The two most important international language-test associations, the International Language Testing Association (ILTA) and the Association of Language Testers in Europe (ALTE), also include fairness in their ethical guidelines and principles of practice. The ALTE's Principles of Good Practice (1994) explicitly state that "fairness is an overriding concern in all aspects of assessment". They add, however, that accommodations for "handicapped candidates" [sic] should be made "when feasible". In the ILTA's Guidelines for Practice (2000), it is the responsibility of the institution administering the test to "provide facilities for the administration of the test that do not disadvantage any test taker". Disabled test-takers "have the right to enquire and receive information about testing accommodations". As we will see below, the vaguely worded and broad statements in ethical guidelines concerning the fair treatment of candidates with disabilities result in a wide variety of practices when it comes to offering and granting accommodations to test-takers with SpLDs.

5.2 Accommodations and Modifications

Although fairness and validity are closely interrelated, and in most cases a valid test is fair and a fair test is valid, in the case of special arrangements, it is important to consider how being fair to a particular group of test-takers might adversely affect the validity of the exam. In the case of SpLDs, the most serious concern is to what extent the accommodations and modifications granted in terms of test content and test-taking procedures affect the construct validity of the test. "Accommodations provide unique and differential access (to performance) so certain students or groups of students may complete the test and tasks without other confounding influences of test format, administration, or responding" (Hollenbeck, Tindal & Almond, 1998, p. 175). In other words, accommodations should not affect the validity of the test, including the interpretation of scores, but at the same time they should ensure that the test is accessible to test-takers with various disabilities. In contrast, "modifications result in a change in the test (how it is given, how it is completed, or what construct is being assessed) and work across the board for all students with equal effect" (Hollenbeck et al., 1998, p. 176).

Distinguishing between what is an accommodation and what is a modification is not always easy. In the case of SpLDs, the most serious concern is to what extent the accommodations and modifications granted in test content and test-taking procedures affect the construct validity of the test. Hansen, Mislevy, Steinberg, Lee & Forer (2005) created a preliminary framework for investigating accommodations in relation to tasks types and the constructs they are supposed to measure in the field of language testing. To demonstrate the model, they use the case of a dyslexic student receiving a read-aloud accommodation on a reading comprehension task. Since the two main underlying features of a reading comprehension task are decoding (whether one is able to decode the written text) and comprehension (whether one is able to understand what is decoded), the read-aloud gives an unfair advantage to the dyslexic student since the examinee does not have to decode the written text. Thus, they claim that this is not an accommodation, but a modification that affects the construct validity of the test. On the other hand, allowing the student to answer reading comprehension questions orally and not in writing does not affect the construct of reading which is being tested, and consequently this adjustment does not affect the validity of the exam. Hansen et al.'s (2005) model is a useful one and it can be applied in both high-stakes proficiency testing and classroom-based assessment as it allows for a distinction between accommodations and modifications in language testing.

The issue of how accommodations affect validity is, however, more complex than is presented in Hansen et al.'s (2005) model, and it is often difficult to decide whether a particular accommodation has an impact on validity. Phillips (1994) lists a number of questions that would need to be answered in order to decide whether an accommodation should be granted to examinees. Three of her questions are of particular relevance:

- Does the accommodation change the construct being measured?
- Does the accommodation change the meaning of the scores?
- Would examinees without an SpLD also benefit from the accommodation?

In order to be able to answer these questions, it is important to carry out studies which compare the performance of students with and without SpLDs under testing conditions with and without accommodations. In one view, which is called *the interaction hypothesis*, accommodations that do not impinge on validity would result in overall score gains for students with SpLDs but in no gains for those without them (Shepard, Taylor, & Betebenner, 1998; Zuriff, 2000). If students with no apparent SpLDs would also benefit significantly from accommodations it means that they too are not performing to the best of their knowledge under standard administration procedures, and consequently the validity of the test is questionable (see the flowchart in Figure 5.2).

Research evidence in the field of general educational testing suggests that certain accommodations, especially allowing extended time in tests that have a time limit, might also advantage students with no SpLDs (for a review see Sireci, Scarpati & Li, 2005). One implication of these findings is that certain test administration procedures, such as making a test timed, disadvantage students with SpLDs, but allowing them extended time does not necessarily give them an advantage (Camara, Copeland & Rothchild, 1998). This does not mean, however, that students with SpLDs should not be granted extra time to complete the test, but rather that the relevance of the timed nature of the test to the construct it is supposed to measure should be reconsidered. Some experts in educational measurement argue for a *universal test design*, "which mandates that

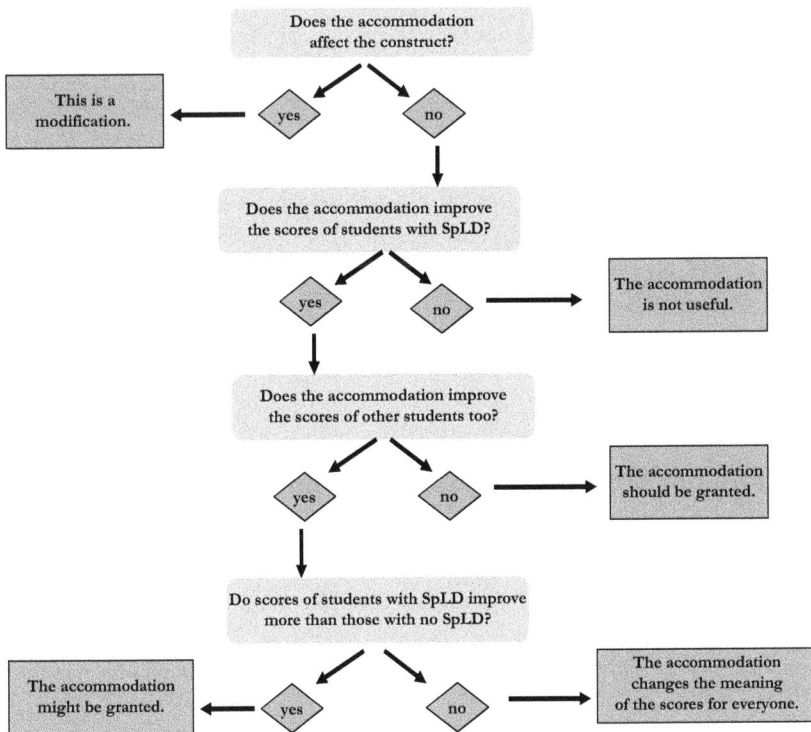

FIGURE 5.2 A Flowchart of How Accommodations Might Affect the Construct and Test Scores

Source: Reproduced from Kormos and Smith (2012), *Teaching Languages to Students with Specific Learning differences*, p. 151, with permission of Multilingual Matters.

tests be constructed and administered more flexibly so that accommodations become unnecessary" (Sireci et al., 2005; Thompson, Blount & Thurlow, 2002). Although, in theory, the fundamentals of universal test design point in a promising new direction, in fact they restate the basic conditions of test fairness, namely that tests should be designed and administered in such a way that they do not create bias for any group of test-takers. It is certainly true that certain advantages in technology, such as the wide availability of computer-based tests, might solve a number of accessibility issues with regard to testing. Nevertheless, practicalities in test administration will always constrain the creation of tests which are entirely flexible. For example, even computer-based tests are usually group-administered, which might be distracting for a student with ADHD, who might consequently require the accommodation of being tested in a separate room.

An additional question that needs to be asked in relation to time extensions is whether students with SpLDs benefit more from being given extra time than those with no SpLDs. According to the *differential boost hypothesis* (Fuchs & Fuchs, 1999; Pitoniak & Royer, 2001), making accommodations might be meaningful and might not pose a threat to the validity of the test, if it affects students with SpLDs (or other types of disability) differentially (see Figure 5.1). For example, a recent meta-analysis by Gregg and Nelson (2012) found that both adult and adolescent students with SpLDs scored significantly higher in tests of numeracy and literacy skills by being given extended time than did their peers with no SpLDs. Therefore, one should consider not only to what extent an accommodation benefits the test-takers, but also whether granting certain accommodations has a differential effect on students with SpLDs. Nevertheless, future research needs to take into account that it is possible that students with no SpLDs might not gain from accommodations because of ceiling effects (Koenig & Bachman, 2004). Therefore, when examining differential boost, the possibility that a test accommodation does not allow students with no SpLDs to further increase their scores should be excluded.

5.3 Types of Accommodations in Assessment

The Standards for Educational and Psychological Testing (AERA, 1999) list six types of test modifications, four of which can be considered accommodations rather than modifications and might not affect the construct being tested: modifying the presentation format, the response format, timing and the test setting (see also Gregg, 2009). The remaining two modifications: using only portions of a test and using substitute tests or alternate assessments have an effect on the construct being tested, but they might frequently be implemented by teachers in classroom settings. Accommodations to the presentation format might involve an alteration to the way in which test instructions or test items are presented to students. For example, a larger font size or spacing might be employed when testing students with SpLDs. Additional accommodations in the form of adjustment to the presentation format might include the use of a screen reader or an assistant reader and the use of simplified language in task instructions. Coloured overlays are another accommodation offered but currently no empirical evidence supports that they might enhance reading fluency (Gregg, 2009). Accommodation in the response format allows test-takers to respond to test items in another modality, such as answering comprehension questions orally rather than in writing, which is a frequent accommodation for students with dyspraxic-type difficulties. Using scribes to whom students dictate their responses might also be offered as an accommodation in this case. Another frequently applied accommodation is allowing students more time to complete the test. Finally, accommodations in the test setting might involve the allocation of a separate room for test-takers, making the location accessible for wheel-chair users or altering the lighting conditions. For a list of different types of accommodations available for students with SpLDs see Table 5.1.

Educational research on the effect of accommodations in high-stakes standardized tests, which has mainly been carried out in the United States, indicates that approximately two-thirds of students with SpLDs have been granted accommodations in these exams (Bolt & Thurlow, 2004). The most frequent accommodations have been extended time and alternative setting. In mathematics, assessment of task input and instructions have also been frequently read aloud to students with SpLDs (Bolt & Thurlow, 2004). Hansen et al.'s (2005) analysis of the read-aloud accommodation and their conclusion concerning the threats this accommodation poses to the validity of a test was discussed in Section 5.2. Researchers' views about whether read-aloud constitutes an accommodation or

TABLE 5.1 Accommodations Available for Students With SpLDs

Accommodations in Presentation Format	Accommodations in Response Format	Accommodations in Timing	Accommodations in Setting
Oral reading	Using a computer	Extended time	Administering the test individually
Large print	Using a scribe	Multiple or frequent breaks	Testing in a separate room
Magnification devices	Responding directly in the test booklet rather than on an answer sheet	Change in testing schedule	Testing in a small group
Screen reader	Using organizational devices such as spelling assistive devices, visual organizers	Testing over multiple days	Adjusting the lighting Providing noise buffers

Source: Reproduced from Kormos and Smith (2012), *Teaching Languages to Students with Specific Learning Differences*, p. 152, with permission of Multilingual Matters.

a modification in reading comprehension tests in students' first language are divided. Laitusis (2008) reports conflicting practices in different American states with regard to the classification of read-aloud as accommodation or modification. Research findings with regard to whether the read-aloud accommodation provides a differential boost to students with SpLDs in an L1 reading comprehension test have also been mixed. In some studies, no significant difference in the increases in scores between students with and without SpLDs was found (e.g. Kosciolek & Ysseldyke, 2000; McKevitt & Elliott, 2003; Meloy, Deville & Frisbie, 2002). In some studies (e.g. Crawford & Tindal, 2004; Fletcher et al., 2006; Laitusis, 2010), however, students with SpLDs, especially those with word-level decoding difficulties, benefited more from the read-aloud accommodation than those with no SpLDs. Laitusis (2010) also shows that a differential boost is detectable even when ceiling effects are controlled for, although older schoolchildren tend to benefit less overall from this change to the presentation format. Despite the beneficial effects of read-aloud on test scores, its influence on the validity of a test is still problematic. If the accuracy of word-level decoding is part of the construct to be assessed in a reading test, a read-aloud administration of the test makes it impossible to make a valid judgement of students' ability in this component of reading.

Accommodations in the response format in high-stakes testing have been less frequently investigated in educational research. The only area where research findings are currently available is the role of word-processors in writing assessment. Early studies found no differences between scores awarded for word-processed and handwritten versions of timed essays (Hollenbeck et al., 1998; MacArthur & Graham, 1987). More recently, however, Gregg, Coleman, Davis and Chalk (2007) have reported that raters were influenced by the quality of handwriting in assigning a score to the essays produced by students with SpLDs. Word-processing tools can enhance the fluency of writing and can be helpful in the editing, revision and monitoring process. Due to these beneficial effects, the use of word-processing tools might be useful for all test-takers, not just for those with SpLDs. With the more widespread application of computer-based assessment, word-processing tools will hopefully cease to serve as an accommodation and become a standard element of universal test design.

The role of extended time in tests of L1 reading comprehension has been the subject of extensive research. Sireci et al.'s (2005) conclusions with regard to the beneficial effect of extended time for students with and without SpLDs have already been mentioned in Section 5.2. The slower speed of text decoding often characteristic of students with SpLDs is one of the most important reasons why this accommodation might prove helpful in reading tests. Students with SpLDs do not only need time to process the input text but also for reading the test items that they need to answer in order to demonstrate their understanding of the text. Schulte, Elliott and Kratochwill's (2001) study shows that an accommodation granting extended time is particularly useful for students with SpLDs in multiple-choice tests of reading comprehension. In tests that require constructed answers, test-takers with and without SpLDs were found to benefit to a similar degree from extended time. Research evidence also indicates that if students do not understand the content of the text, they are not advantaged by having more time to read it (for a summary, see Gregg, 2011). Therefore providing extra time in reading comprehension tests does not seem to threaten construct validity.

Extended time is also helpful in writing assessment because it gives students an opportunity to plan, edit and monitor their writing more carefully. Nevertheless, empirical research on the differential effect of extended time on the performance of students with and without SpLDs is currently lacking. Indirect evidence for the potential benefits of extra time in writing is provided by Gregg, Coleman, Stennett and Davis (2002), whose study shows that the length of essays strongly correlates with text quality scores. Students with SpLDs were found to produce shorter essays, which received lower ratings. One can hypothesize that, given extended time, students with SpLDs might have produced longer texts of higher quality.

Although accommodations in scheduling (i.e. giving more frequent breaks, or test sessions on separate days) and setting are frequently recommended, little research is available on their effectiveness. Gregg (2011) explains that some students with word-decoding difficulties prefer to read a text aloud to themselves because this helps them to pay attention to what they are reading. Some other students with SpLDs or with ADHD use earplugs to eliminate external noise that would distract their attention (Shaywitz, 2003). These preferences of some students with SpLDs make it important to consider accommodations in the test setting.

Overall, one needs to pay close attention to the individual and often differing needs of students with SpLDs when granting accommodations. Research findings indicate that some accommodations might lower students' scores instead of raising them (Elliott, Kratochwill & McKevitt, 2001). This may happen when the accommodations granted are not matched to the students' needs and when the students have not had an opportunity to practice using the accommodation before taking the test (e.g. practicing how to work with a scribe or a reader, or using assistive devices such as screen-readers). There is also research evidence which shows that teachers are not always able to predict which students will need accommodations in tests and what accommodations would be beneficial for them (Helwig & Tindal, 2003). Therefore, students' views on what strategies and devices they generally use to overcome their problems in learning, what accommodations they have tried before, how these accommodations have helped them and how they think the use of accommodations might be improved need to be taken into account. Teachers and testing agencies also need to consider whether a student needs accommodations, how the accommodations will make the test both fair and valid, and how accommodations can be provided in terms of the practical realities of the assessment context. Further issues for consideration include how accommodations can be improved and how students can be helped to make the best possible use of accommodations granted.

5.4 Accommodations in High-Stakes Second Language Proficiency Tests

Providing accommodations in high-stakes assessment tests is regulated by law, but it also relies on the professional judgement of experts from the testing organization (Gregg, 2009). Expert judgement is involved in making decisions about eligibility criteria, in the provision of information on accommodations and the procedures involved in applying for applications. These aspects of the provision of accommodations are crucial because they can act as gatekeepers to access to fair assessment procedures.

The first step which learners usually take in deciding whether to apply for accommodations and in selecting appropriate access arrangements is searching for information on the websites of exam boards. Information on accommodations is used not only by the candidates but also their teachers, who help them prepare for exams. Learners with SpLDs might experience difficulties in orienting themselves on web pages and finding relevant information; therefore, it is of great importance that guidelines on how to apply for accommodations and data on the different types of accommodations are displayed in a prominent place on the website. The information provided to test-takers should also be clearly worded and sufficiently detailed so that they will not have to engage in email correspondence with the examination centre to find the information they require. Kormos, Sarkadi and Kálmos (2010) interviewed nine students with an official certificate of dyslexia who had recently taken a high-stakes language proficiency exam in Hungary. All the participants highlighted the importance of having clear and concise information about accommodations.

Kormos and Smith (2012) surveyed the variety of accommodations in high-stakes international language proficiency tests that were available to learners with SpLDs. They found that the system of granting accommodations, the types of accommodations offered and the information provided to the public on the accommodations showed great variation across exam boards, which made it difficult for learners with SpLDs to exercise advocacy concerning accommodations. Kormos, Sarkadi, et al. (2010) came to similar conclusions with regard to accredited language proficiency exams in Hungary. These reviews were conducted in 2010, but a recent analysis of the websites of major language-testing organizations indicates very little change since then.

In 2015, I surveyed the websites of five major international language-test providers: IELTS, ETS (Educational Testing Service), Pearson Academic Tests of English, Cambridge English Language Assessment and Trinity College London. This more recent review revealed that only two of these exam boards display readily accessible information on their websites. These two, ETS (www.ets.org/

disabilities/test_takers) and Cambridge English Language Assessment (www. cambridgeenglish.org/help/special-requirements), were already found to offer relevant and clearly presented guidelines and information on their websites in the review conducted by Kormos and Smith (2012) and they continue to be good models in this regard. Trinity College London only outlines how to submit requests for special arrangements (www.trinitycollege.com/site/?id=2933). It provides no information on what accommodations are available and instead directs applicants to a policy document. This document is intended for use by the exam board and does not target test-takers, neither in terms of relevant content nor the complexity of the language in which information is conveyed. The website of Pearson Academic Tests offers even less information and asks candidates to make a telephone call to their local office to discuss access arrangements (http://pearsonpte.com/faqs). The new IELTS exam website lists a small number of possible accommodations to test-takers with different types of disability (www.ielts.org/test_takers_information/what_is_ielts/special_needs.aspx), it also directs test-takers to contact their local test centre. The number of officially approved local test centres was reduced in 2015, which means that candidates often have to make international telephone calls.

Cambridge English Language Assessment is one of the few language-testing exam boards that have made its figures for the application of special arrangements for particular tests and different parts of tests publicly available (see e.g. Geranpayeh & Taylor, 2013; Khalifa & Weir, 2009; Shaw & Weir, 2007). Although published data only cover certain time periods, Taylor and Geranpayeh (2013) rightly note that "the fact that the number of requests for accommodated tests seems not to reflect the likely distribution of EFL learners with disabilities in the wider population constitutes some reason for concern" (p. 325). For example, in 2006, only 639 candidates with an official certificate of dyslexia requested additional time or supervised breaks in the reading component of the most popular English language exams offered by Cambridge ESOL (Khalifa & Weir, 2009). Similarly low numbers, 66 dyslexic students out of 24,000, submitted applications for special arrangements for the Test of German as a Foreign Language (TestDaF) in 2012 (Arras, Müller-Karabil & Zimmermann, 2013). Field (2013) hypothesizes that the small numbers of students applying for special arrangements might be due to low levels of awareness about the accommodations available to various groups of stakeholders, including candidates, their teachers and the test centres themselves. Another important reason listed by Taylor and Geranpayeh (2013), and confirmed by a review of the documentation available about special arrangements on Cambridge ESOL's website, is that the procedures for applying accommodations might be perceived to be complex by students and their parents. The application involves reading and processing technical information in English as well as completing complicated forms. Moreover, obtaining an official certificate with a diagnosis of SpLDs is in many contexts expensive and might not be affordable by students in addition to the cost of the exam.

The procedure for applying for accommodations usually involves the submission of documentation concerning the nature of the candidate's SpLD and a statement about the requested accommodation. Among the five international language-testing boards surveyed, only ETS specifies in detail what documentation they require from candidates to qualify for accommodations. ETS requests official documentation, prepared by a specialist, which describes the nature of the learning difference and lists all the testing instruments used in the diagnosis, as well as the student's achievement on these diagnostic instruments. They also ask candidates to submit a description of the types of accommodations they are applying for and to provide support for the need for the requested accommodations. The examination centres, however, differ with regard to how recent the official documentation of an SpLD should be. In the review conducted by Kormos and Smith (2012), some UK-based exam boards, such as Cambridge English Language Assessment, asked candidates to submit documents which were less than 2 years old, whereas ETS accepted documents no older than 5 years for learning difficulties or 3 years for ADHD. In 2015, information about the necessary documentation and dates were no longer available on the Cambridge English Language Assessment website.

One of the few testing agencies that systematically reports its accommodation practices for students with SpLDs and reviews these practices regularly is Cambridge English Language Assessment. This testing boards offers so-called Special Arrangements which:

> are intended to remove as far as possible the effects of the disability on the candidate's ability to demonstrate his or her true level of attainment in relation to the assessment objectives; to ensure that candidates with disabilities are not given an unfair advantage over other candidates; and to avoid misleading the user of the certificate about the candidate's attainment.
>
> *(Khalifa, 2005, p. 8)*

Cambridge English Language Assessment offers various accommodations to candidates with SpLDs in the assessment of listening, reading and writing skills. Elliott (2013) reports that, in listening tests, candidates with SpLDs are entitled to a modified version of the test, and this differs from the original test paper only in its presentation format. The candidates take this test in a separate room, they listen to the recording once and, on a second listening, the supervisor of the test pauses the recording at predetermined points. This allows the candidate enough time to read the test items, answer them and review their answers. The supervisor receives clear guidelines where to stop the recording but can decide, depending on the candidate's needs, how long the pauses should be. The points for pausing the recording are predetermined so that they will neither be too frequent to break the flow nor draw the candidate's attention to key information points and thereby give an unfair advantage in comparison to other candidates.

Coloured paper and coloured overlays are also offered although, as discussed earlier, their usefulness is not proven for students with SpLDs (Elliott, 2013). Candidates with SpLDs are given an additional accommodation, in the response format, which allows them to use a scribe if their handwriting is not easily legible. The scribe can copy the students' answers in the relevant part of the answer sheet. The candidate is present when the scribe transcribes his or her answers as written and can provide clarification if necessary.

In the reading component of the exams offered by Cambridge English Language Assessment, candidates with SpLDs might be allowed extended time and supervised breaks. Students with dyslexia, however, are not entitled to have a reader to read out the text or task instructions. Candidates with dyspraxia might be allowed to use some form of assistive technology to type their answers or to dictate them. In the speaking test, candidates who require more time to read exam prompts can apply for time extensions. With regard to writing tasks, dyslexic candidates can request extra time, which can range from 25 to 50%. Supervised breaks can also be granted for candidates in addition to or instead of extra time. Test-takers can also use assistive technology or writing and might not need to transfer their answers to the answer sheet.

Until 2004, Cambridge English Language Assessment offered separate marking for dyslexic students, in the process of which spelling was not taken account in the scores awarded in writing tasks. When students requested this accommodation, an additional endorsement on the certificate was added, which stated that "The candidate was exempt from satisfying the full range of assessment objectives in the examination." Shaw and Weir (2007) report a case study in which the use of this accommodation was reviewed by the exam board. In the first phase of the study, the views of an expert on dyslexia were considered with regard to the writing difficulties of dyslexic students. The expert's report highlighted the fact that language learners with dyslexia do not only have difficulties with spelling, but also with other areas of producing written texts. The report suggested that additional time might be the most beneficial accommodation for dyslexic students. Following this, a small-scale analysis of exam scripts produced by dyslexic L2 learners was compared to texts produced by learners from the same first language background in the Cambridge Learner Corpus. The analysis of 24 texts showed that, overall, dyslexic students made more spelling errors and a considerable proportion of their errors could also be identified as 'dyslexia-related' spelling errors. In the case study, the exam board also asked the evaluators of the scripts written by dyslexic students who requested that their spelling be disregarded in the assessment process to indicate whether this special arrangement made a difference to their final mark for writing. The results showed that in 2001, in the case of 46% of candidates, and in 2002 in the case of 63%, this special arrangement made a difference to the grade. From these figures the exam board concluded that in approximately 50% of the cases, students received an unnecessary endorsement on their certificate that they did not fulfil the full range of requirements for the exam. Based on the findings from this case study, the use of this special arrangement was discontinued.

The overview of accommodations offered by different language-testing boards conducted by Kormos and Smith (2012) showed that the practices of major international language examinations differ with regard to what special arrangements they offer to test-takers. Likewise, great variation was observed in the review conducted by Kormos, Sarkadi, et al. (2010) of nationally accredited language exams in Hungary. On the one hand, the variation in accommodation practices across language exams is due to the fact that the ethical guidelines and principles of language-testing associations that many exam providers are members of are relatively vague when it comes to offering accommodations to disabled students (see Section 5.1). It is probably impossible to establish uniform principles for fair assessment and providing equal access to language exams due to large cultural and social differences in the contexts in which various exams are sat. Nevertheless, large international exams operate in a global international market, and therefore more uniformity would certainly be welcome. On the other hand, the test providers are certainly constrained because the practicalities of offering accommodations often limit the options available to candidates. Therefore, O'Sullivan and Green (2011) rightly suggest that fairness in international tests can only be guaranteed if stakeholders in specific contexts are involved in the decisions about accommodation practices.

5.5 Stakeholders' Views About Accommodations in High-Stakes Language Assessment

In previous sections of this chapter, studies examining the effect of accommodations on test-takers' performance, reviews of documents and case studies of a specific exam board were presented. It is useful to investigate assessment practices not only from an outsider's perspective, as was done earlier in this chapter, but also from the point of view of stakeholders in the assessment process. An important group of stakeholders is the test-takers themselves.

Unfortunately, very few studies have been conducted on test-takers' perceptions of accommodations in language proficiency exams. Kormos, Sarkadi, et al. (2010) interviewed nine Hungarian language learners with SpLDs who had recent experience of taking different nationally accredited language tests. Two of the nine interviewees did not apply for any accommodations because they were confident they would pass the test without any special arrangements. These participants felt it important to demonstrate that they could succeed in the exam despite the challenges they face as a result of their SpLDs. Nevertheless, except for one participant, they were all familiar with the kinds of accommodations they would be entitled to in the given exam. Some of the students encountered difficulties when they requested special arrangements because either the exam centre refused to accept their request or they could not provide accommodations due to difficulties with the logistics of arranging a separate room where candidates can work for an extended time period.

The participants in Kormos, Sarkadi, et al.'s (2010) study found extra time to be one of the most helpful accommodations. Many accredited exams in Hungary set a translation task for which the use of electronic dictionaries was an additional useful tool. Word-processing tools were also listed as beneficial, especially for students with dyspraxia. The students mentioned that many of the language exams were too long for them and they would have preferred more frequent and longer breaks, but very few exam boards were willing to offer this accommodation.

Taylor and Khalifa (2013) asked candidates who took one of the exams offered by Cambridge English Language Assessment and who were granted special arrangements to respond to a small number of questions about accommodations by email. Unfortunately, they provide no information on how many responses were received or how many of the respondents had SpLDs. No data are given on the response rate either, which is important, since it can be assumed that only a limited number of students with SpLDs would take the initiative to respond in writing in English. From excerpts from the students' responses it is apparent that, overall, the candidates were satisfied with the special arrangements they received and how these were arranged.

In their study, Taylor and Khalifa (2013) also surveyed the views of other stakeholders, including test developers, examiners and test administrators. This part of the research focused on special arrangements in general, not specifically for students with SpLDs. From the responses of 144 test centres globally, it was apparent that the majority of special arrangement requests concerned extended time and separate invigilation. Other frequent accommodations included the use of assistive technology and requests for special listening which, as described above, is also offered to candidates with SpLDs. The administrators of the test centres were, overall, satisfied with the level and details of information they received from Cambridge English Language Assessment concerning the provision of special arrangements. The qualitative comments of the test-centre administrators, however, echo some of the views of the test-takers in Kormos, Sarkadi, et al.'s (2010) study. They voiced the concern that "organizing a special arrangement is time consuming and expensive" (Taylor & Khalifa, 2013, p. 237). The test centres of Cambridge English Language Assessment might be well-resourced in comparison with other exam boards that organize high-stakes exams in other international and national contexts. Therefore, ensuring that the needs of candidates with special needs are met puts a considerable burden on exam centres. Given that the ethical guidelines of language-testing associations such as ALTE state that accommodations should be provided 'when feasible', exam providers might not take all the necessary steps to provide appropriate and adequate special arrangements for test-takers. This was also reflected in the experiences of test-takers in Kormos, Sarkadi, et al.'s (2010) study.

The test-material developers interviewed by Taylor and Khalifa (2013) called attention to a further issue, namely that because accommodations differ across contexts, test-takers might not be entitled to the same special arrangements as they are used to in their home country. The interviewees also admitted that lack of access to certain accommodations in international exams such as those offered by Cambridge English Language Assessment might disappoint candidates and cause them anxiety. Conversely, in certain contexts, students might not be eligible for special arrangements at all or only be able to make use of a smaller number of test accommodations. Moreover, there are countries where, due to the low level of public and institutional awareness of SpLDs, test-takers might not even be cognizant of accommodations.

5.6 Conclusions and Implications

Fairness is an essential consideration in testing the second language competence of learners with SpLDs. Both high-stakes language exams and classroom assessment should apply tasks that are free of bias and should be conducted in a setting that allows students with SpLDs to demonstrate the best of their knowledge. Ideally tests should be designed so that they are accessible for every test-taker. Due to logistic constraints and limitations on resources, however, this might not always be possible. In these cases, test-takers with SpLDs should be granted accommodations, and relevant adjustments to the test settings, tasks, task format and administration and response mode should be made. Extended time is one of the most frequent and highly beneficial accommodations offered to learners with SpLDs, which can potentially boost their performance in reading and writing tests. It is also important that test-takers are consulted in the choice of accommodations and that they are provided with opportunities to practice using them before exams.

The review of a number of international language exam providers has revealed a large variation of practices with regard to offering accommodations to candidates with SpLDs. The findings of Taylor and Khalifa's (2013) study also highlight the importance of international coordination for practices granting special arrangements in high-stakes language tests and specifying these arrangements in the guidelines of language-testing associations. Improvements in dissemination practices regarding the availability of special arrangements are also needed so that candidates can more strongly exercise their rights when taking language proficiency exams.

Note

1 Parts of this chapter are based on sections of Chapter 8 in Kormos, J., & Smith, A.-M. (2012). *Teaching languages to students with specific learning differences.* Bristol: Multilingual Matters. Reproduced with permission from Multilingual Matters.

6

TEACHING LANGUAGES TO STUDENTS WITH SPECIFIC LEARNING DIFFICULTIES

Earlier in the book, I introduced the concept of specific learning difficulties (SpLDs) and discussed how we can identify them in multilingual contexts. I also described the cognitive and affective correlates of SpLDs and their interactions with language learning processes. In the previous chapter, I considered how language learners with SpLDs can be assessed in a fair, yet valid and reliable manner. The time has now come to apply all this to language teaching pedagogy and classroom practice.

In this chapter, I will first outline conceptualizations of inclusion and the characteristics of inclusive teaching processes. Then, I will place the dyslexia-friendly school movement within the framework of inclusion and review what the available research findings reveal about inclusion and dyslexia-friendly teaching practices in second language teaching. This will be followed by a detailed discussion of specific intervention techniques that have been used to facilitate the language learning processes of students with SpLDs. I will start with a review of reading intervention programmes and their applications for teaching L2 learners, and then present a critical overview of multisensory teaching methods. Elements of the multisensory teaching programme will be evaluated in the light of recent research findings in the fields of second language acquisition and second language teaching. The book will conclude with suggestions for language teacher education and educational policies.

6.1 Inclusion and Dyslexia-Friendly Schools

The approaches to the education of students with SpLDs have undergone major changes in the past 50 years. It is helpful to recall the differences in the conceptualizations and definitions of SpLDs, because these are reflected in decisions at the level of educational policy and instructional practices. According to the medical view of disabilities, students with SpLDs have special educational needs resulting from their learning difficulties, and hence they require specially designed instruction to be able to acquire the skills and knowledge necessary for successful functioning in society. As a result of this view, which was reflected in the legislation of many countries including both the United States and the United Kingdom until the early 1970s (Baker & Zigmond, 1995; Frederickson & Cline, 2009), children with SpLDs, especially if their difficulties were severe, were taught in a segregated context.

By the 1970s, parallel to advances in human rights movements that stood up to segregation of any kind, it became evident that segregation not only results in stigmatization and isolation, but for many children with SpLDs, it does not ensure better educational outcomes than education in mainstream schools (Dunn, 1968). This led to a move to integrate children with SpLDs in mainstream schools, which was an important and welcome change. Nevertheless, the integration movement was underpinned by the assumption that in an integrated school, some adaptations are made to meet the diverse needs of students, but the ultimate responsibility for integrating into the life of the school lies with the students themselves (Ainscow, 1995). Integration policies were fraught with further problems, namely that there are situations where education in a mainstream classroom might not provide the most effective learning environment for certain children (Kauffman, 1989). Integration policies were also underlined by the theoretical assumption that there are certain universal principles of effective teaching that apply to all children, and hence there is no need for special education at all. Differences among children are naturally occurring, and 'good teachers' can adjust their teaching to adapt to these differences (for a review of these positions see Frederickson, 1993).

The social view of disabilities has brought an important change to integration policies and has seriously questioned their underlying assumptions. In the social view, disabilities arise because there are barriers in the environment that disable some students. Therefore, the main responsibility for making relevant changes in education lies with institutions. It is institutions, and not the students themselves, that need to take all possible steps within their means to remove barriers and ensure equal opportunities for diverse students. This view is embodied in the concept of *inclusion*, which "involves the school in the process of accommodation where the onus is on the school to change, adapting the curricula, methods, materials and procedures so that it becomes more responsive" (Frederickson & Cline, 2009, p. 65). It is important to note that inclusion is not an end-state or an outcome, but a process in which schools continuously "engage in a critical examination of what can be done to increase the learning and participation of the diversity of students within the school and its locality" (Booth, Ainscow, Black-Hawkins, Vaughan & Shaw, 2000, p. 12). Inclusion as a concept and its practical implementations have been further refined based on the interactionist view of disabilities. This view highlights that students with SpLDs experience difficulties in learning when compared to other students and these difficulties interact with the barriers within the educational system. For inclusion to be successful the difficulties should be identified, barriers arising from the interaction of these difficulties with the learning environment need to be removed, and if necessary additional support has to be provided.

The core of the issue concerning the inclusion of children with disabilities is striking a balance between access to mainstream education and the appropriate support needed for successful learning. It is essential that schools make all necessary accommodations to cater for the diverse needs of different types of learners, but it is unrealistic to assume that these arrangements will in themselves be sufficient. In other words, the creation of an inclusive school environment that is beneficial to all children does not necessarily mean that all the needs of students with disabilities will be met (Frederickson & Cline, 2009). It is important to stress this because the criteria for official diagnosis and entitlement to additional support often posit that students should be in need of specialized educational arrangements. If one assumes that schools can be fully inclusive and address the needs of all, then there remain no students with disabilities. To address this issue, Norwich (2007) proposed a set of *flexible interacting continua of educational provision*. Norwich argues that inclusion should be seen as a continuum along which educational systems make persistent efforts to enhance commonality. To illustrate, inclusion can have varying degrees in terms of academic, social and cultural *participation*, *location* (a separate school with links to an ordinary school vs. same learning group) and *curriculum and teaching* (different educational pathways vs. same goals but adjusted teaching approaches).

The question then is how best to cater for the needs of students with SpLDs within the framework of an inclusive educational system. To answer this, it is helpful to revisit the 5th edition of the *Diagnostic and Statistical Manual of Mental Disorders* of the American Psychiatric Association (DSM-5; APA, 2013) guidelines described in Section 2.1, that relate the severity of SpLDs to the level and intensity of support required. In DSM-5, individuals who "may be able to compensate and function well when provided with appropriate accommodations and support services" (p. 67) are classified as mild cases of SpLDs. These students can successfully learn in inclusive environments with a high level of commonality with other students and benefit from teaching approaches designed to meet the diversity of learners' needs. They might only require minor adjustments and a small amount of additional support. Students with moderate SpLDs need "some intervals of intensive and specialised teaching" (APA, 2013, p. 68), which then helps them to catch up with their peers and follow mainstream educational programmes. Learners with severe SpLDs require "ongoing intensive individualized and specialized teaching" (APA, 2013, p. 68). For these latter two groups of learners, schools need to have special programmes in place to assist them in developing their literacy skills. In these cases, there seems to be a legitimate need for advocating not only inclusive schooling, but also schools that are equipped to provide specialized support for learners with SpLDs (Norwich, 2009).

The Dyslexia-Friendly School (British Dyslexia Association, 1996) initiative in the United Kingdom aimed to raise awareness of the needs of students with SpLDs within an inclusive framework of education. The criteria they list for schools to become dyslexia friendly include features that also characterize principles of inclusive education, such as accurate identification of students' strengths, weaknesses and needs, regular assessment of students' progress and adjustment of targets and teaching methods based on this progress, opportunities for children to work in a variety of groupings, enhancing students' self-regulation skills, confidence and self-esteem, fair assessment of learning outcomes and cooperation with parents. The additional elements of the criteria emphasize teachers' awareness of SpLDs, their knowledge and skills in implementing appropriate literacy intervention programmes and providing classroom support as well as schools being committed to developing dyslexia-friendly practices. In dyslexia-friendly schools, specific assistance is offered to students with dyslexia with the right balance between in-class support and withdrawal. How this balance is achieved in the field of second language teaching is the focus of the next section.

6.2 Inclusion of Students With SpLDs in the Second Language Classroom

Although the importance of providing an inclusive language learning environment for students with SpLDs was pointed out in Canada as early as the middle of the 1980s (Cummins, 1981) and in the United States in the 1990s (see e.g. Sparks, Ganschow, Kenneweg & Miller, 1991), as two very recent articles reveal (Cobb, 2015; Wight, 2015) not much progress has been made in terms of enhancing the language learning opportunities for learners with SpLDs since then. Cobb's (2015) study demonstrates the lack of support for students with additional needs in a Canadian French immersion programme, while Wight (2015) reports the still prevalent practice in many US states of exempting students with SpLDs from learning additional languages. Arries (1999) has called for more research on inclusive language teaching practices, yet few have responded to his call.

In a case study of an American college student with an SpLD, Abrams (2008) investigated how curricular adjustments and exam accommodations succeeded in removing barriers from completing a German course. The student was assigned alternative assessment tasks that he could complete outside class without time pressure and was offered weekly tutorial sessions to help him review vocabulary and grammar. These curricular and assessment modifications were very positively received by the student and ensured that he completed the course successfully and could graduate with a college degree. Abrams, however, pointed out that the organization and coordination of the additional support and alternative assessment tasks required a lot of time and effort from the teaching team, even in the case of a single student. Thus she highlighted the need for close collaboration within the teaching team as well between course instructors and learning support services. She also added that institutional acknowledgement of the extra workload involved is crucial. Abrams' (2008) study is an example of how a devoted team of language teachers can take the first step towards creating an inclusive language teaching environment at college level, and thereby "change the entire learning experience and even college career of a student with disabilities" (p. 426).

Inclusive language teaching practices in the sphere of public education were investigated by Kontra and Kormos (2010) in a study with five groups of teachers in Hungary. In this research, we conducted focus group interviews in primary and secondary schools that participated in a grant scheme set up by the Hungarian Ministry of Education to enhance language learning opportunities for disadvantaged schoolchildren. The schools had different geographical locations, varying from big cities to small towns and represented different socioeconomic contexts. The focus groups consisted of a team of teachers of various foreign languages (English, German and Italian) and special needs teachers working in the given school. Prior to the interviews, the members of the teaching teams implemented a language teaching programme, which they designed for children with SpLDs in their school and for which they received financial support from the grant scheme. Most of the teachers participating in the interviews had many years of experience teaching or working with students with SpLDs, and for most, the language teaching programme they developed was a continuation of their earlier inclusive practices.

In the analysis of the data, a large number of common themes emerged across the five investigated teaching contexts. Just as in Abrams' (2008) case study, all the participants advocated the need for adjusting the curriculum and methods of assessment to the needs and abilities of the students with SpLDs. The language teachers argued that if they had autonomy over the choice of curricular objectives, they would mainly focus on oral communication and authentic language tasks that the students might need to perform outside school. They mentioned, however, that the national curriculum and school leaving exam requirements often do not make adjustments to the curriculum possible. The findings of the interviews were also in line with Abrams' (2008) recommendations with regard to the demand for additional out-of-class support for language learners with SpLDs. Most of the Hungarian language teachers interviewed believed that in addition to participation in mainstream language classes, language learners with SpLDs should be offered 1 or 2 hours of extra language classes per week that specifically address their needs. The programme sponsored by the grant provided financial assistance towards the provision of these classes, which usually consisted of four to eight learners with SpLDs, and in many schools, these were taught by two teachers. These classes were reported to be highly successful in giving children with SpLDs the opportunity to progress at their own pace and practice language areas that they found difficult, and in raising their self-confidence in L2 learning. Nevertheless, sadly, as the grant scheme came to end, none of the schools could continue to offer these additional classes, which finding highlights the crucial role of support at the level of educational policy in developing inclusive practices.

From among the features of inclusive teaching and dyslexia-friendly practices, the teachers interviewed in Kontra and Kormos' (2010) study also discussed the central role of supportive teacher attitudes and the use of motivational strategies to actively engage children with SpLDs in the process of language learning. The language teachers involved in this study found it an invaluable experience that they could cooperate with special needs teachers and psychologists in the framework of the grant scheme. In this collaboration they did not only learn more about the nature of SpLDs, and thereby could assess the strengths and weaknesses of their learners better, but they also acquired techniques used in literacy intervention programmes and special education support classes that they could adopt in their teaching practice.

In a follow-up to this interview study, Kormos, Orosz and Szatzker (2010) examined the inclusive language teaching practices in three Hungarian schools using a multiple case study approach. The schools selected, one primary and two secondary, were pioneers in teaching languages to students with SpLDs in different ways. In the primary school, which was located in a rural town, students with SpLDs learned either English or German as a foreign language in mainstream language classes given by teachers who were specifically trained in teaching languages to SpLDs. For over 5 years, these teachers had been applying multisensory teaching methods (see Section 6.3.4) and educational adjustments to meet the needs of students with SpLDs. In one of the secondary schools, students with SpLDs studied either English or German in mainstream classes as well as in self-contained classes. Their language teachers were also highly experienced and well trained in working with students with SpLDs. In the third school, all the secondary school students with SpLDs studied languages in a mainstream class. Their teachers had around 10 years of teaching experience, including several years of working with students with SpLDs, but they had no formal training in this field. In this case study research, we observed a number of English and German classes taught in these schools and interviewed the teachers as well as two children per observed class.

Despite the differences in the age groups, geographical location, socioeconomic status of the children and the expertise and training of the language teachers, we found a number of common features of inclusive practices and dyslexia-friendly teaching techniques. The classroom observations showed that in every context all the learners were actively involved in the learning process and none of the students seemed either to be excluded or disengaged. The interviews with the students also confirmed that they perceived the language classes to be enjoyable and relevant to their future needs. The teachers appeared to have an excellent rapport with the groups they taught and in-depth knowledge of their students. They employed personalized motivational techniques, and their feedback was always constructive and encouraging. Each observed class contained a warm-up or lead-in phase and the last minutes of the lesson were usually used for consolidation and review. The activities tended to be relatively short and varied in either response format or organizational pattern (e.g. frontal teaching was followed by group work). Without exception, all the lessons were carefully planned and logically structured, but the interviewed teachers told us that they adapted their lesson plans flexibly depending on the progress of the students or their fatigue and level of attention. Group and pair work was frequently employed and in the interviews the teachers told us that they often used games, drama techniques and computer-assisted technology. On a few occasions we saw that teachers either discussed specific vocabulary learning strategies or modelled listening strategies for the students. In the interviews the teachers reported devoting a substantial amount of class time to how students could assist their own learning processes at the beginning of the school year, and periodically later in the term too. These observations provide evidence of many of the elements of inclusive teaching practices in these contexts. Specific techniques that have been recommended for teaching languages to students with SpLDs, such as the use of multisensory teaching methods, were also applied by all the teachers, making the classes dyslexia friendly (for a detailed discussion of multisensory teaching methods see Sections 6.3.4–6.3.6). From among the list of four specific strategies for teaching languages to students with SpLDs recommended by Arries (1999), we saw examples of enhancing phonological awareness in a primary school context that facilitated vocabulary learning. The remaining three general instructional strategies for facilitating memory, reducing anxiety and distractions were prominent themes in the interviews and were characteristic of actual teaching practice in every observed class.

As the above overview shows, there exist excellent examples of inclusive language teaching practices in different parts of the world. Nevertheless, in order to present a balanced view, it is also important to consider the obstacles to the implementation of inclusive practices. In the studies, barriers to inclusive practice were mentioned either by the participating teachers (Kontra & Kormos, 2010; Kormos, Orosz et al., 2010) or by the researchers who conducted the study (Abrams, 2008). These include the demand for institutional support, the need for close collaboration within the teaching team and, most importantly, the time and effort required on the part of the teachers. In mainstream educational contexts, the slower pace of learning that might characterize learners with SpLDs, the need for frequent revision and alternative assessment methods can also pose considerable challenges to successful inclusion (Abrams, 2008; Kontra & Kormos, 2010). The constraints of inflexible curricula and lack of appropriate legislation that would ensure educational rights can also seriously affect teachers, learners and other stakeholders, such as parents (Cobb, 2015; Sarkadi, 2008; Wight, 2015).

6.3 Intervention Programmes

As I have argued above, although an inclusive learning environment is essential for the provision of efficient language education to students with SpLDs, without additional outside class support and specific intervention programmes, few learners of SpLDs make sufficient progress. In the following sections I will describe specific intervention programmes that have been used in teaching additional languages or literacy skills in L2 for students with SpLDs. Some of these intervention programmes can be easily incorporated into regular classroom teaching practices and have been found to be beneficial for all learners, not just those with SpLDs. Some others might work better or provide additional benefits if they are administered in small-group contexts as additional support classes. The discussion of these programmes, below, will start with those which target the smallest units of language and move on to those that offer a comprehensive framework for teaching general language competencies.

6.3.1 Phonological Awareness-Raising Programmes

One of the early intervention programmes in the area of first language literacy education is concerned with raising children's phonological awareness (PA). In these programmes, children are explicitly taught how to manipulate sounds and syllables, and they also practice phoneme and syllable segmentation, blending, deletion and addition using a variety of activities. As pointed out in Section 2.3, PA is an important predictor of first language reading attainment and plays a key role in the development of word-decoding skills, especially in the first 2 years of literacy instruction (Share, Jorm, Maclean, & Matthews 1984). The National Reading Panel report (2000) reviewed the available intervention studies that investigated the success of PA-raising programmes in enhancing PA and its concomitant effect on word-level reading skills. The results of the meta-analyses were reported for three groups of children: those at at-risk of developing reading difficulties who were first graders or younger with a low phonological awareness score, children who were classified as having 'reading disabilities' based on their reading assessment scores, and typically developing readers. The findings indicated that PA training was the most efficient type for typically developing readers, and it also had a large effect on at-risk readers. PA training had a significant impact on the PA of children with 'reading disabilities' but its effect was considerably smaller than for the other two groups of children. The authors of the report speculated that the lower level of effectiveness of PA training for 'disabled readers' might be due to the fact that they were older and therefore might have already scored at a ceiling level when they began the training. The effects of PA training were found to transfer to word-level decoding skills, with at-risk readers again benefiting the most from the training. Children with reading difficulties made only moderate gains in word-level reading as a result of the PA training and a review of the available research evidence indicated no impact on their spelling skills. The meta-analysis of the National Reading Panel revealed that the effect size for the impact of PA-raising interventions was considerably larger for children whose first language was English than for speakers of other languages. This might be due to the fact that phonological awareness, especially at the phonemic level, seems to play a more important role in the acquisition of word-level decoding and spelling skills in English than in languages that have a more transparent orthographic system (see Section 2.4). The findings also showed that small-group interventions were more effective than programmes conducted with a whole class of children or with individual learners, and that the ideal length of the intervention was from 5 to 18 hours. No recommendation was made, however, with regard to how this instruction time should be distributed over a period.

Based on the review of the National Reading Panel (2000) and further studies conducted after its publication (e.g. Al Otaiba & Torgesen, 2007), it can be concluded that PA-raising programmes in the early years of literacy development can prove to be beneficial in helping at-risk readers to catch up with their typically developing peers, and thus this might prevent the development of reading difficulties. Nevertheless, as indicated by the relatively low effect size values for reading disabled students in the meta-analysis of the National Reading Panel (2000), there are children for whom PA training does not seem to work. Vellutino, Scanlon, Small and Fanuele (2006) estimate the percentage of 'nonresponders' to be between 1.5% and 8%.

Compared to the large number of studies in the field of L1 literacy development, there are very few studies that have investigated the effectiveness of PA training among multilingual speakers. Gerber, Jimenez, Leafstedt, Villaruz and Richards (2004) organised an explicit PA training programme for Spanish-L1-speaking children aged 5 in the United States. In the framework of the programme, children identified to be at risk of developing reading difficulties worked on rime and onset detection and phoneme segmentation and blending during nine 20-minute sessions. The intervention was conducted in Spanish, the first language of the children, and pre- and post-PA tests were administered in both English and Spanish. Word-level decoding was assessed only in English. Despite the short duration of the programme, the at-risk children whose PA was significantly below their Spanish-speaking non-at-risk peers at the onset of the study attained a similar level of PA in almost all measures as their peers at the end of their 1st school year. Importantly, the at-risk and not-at-risk groups did not differ significantly in word-level decoding skills at the end of Grade 1. These results show that young multilingual children who might be at risk of developing reading difficulties benefit from PA programmes conducted in their first language and can transfer these gains in PA to word-level reading in another language.

Leafstedt, Richards and Gerber (2004) replicated Gerber et al.'s (2004) study with a training period of 5 hours distributed over 10 weeks. They also varied the training, depending on whether students scored low, high or in the medium range of PA pretests. This grouping helped the researchers to adjust the intervention programme to the strengths and weaknesses of the children. The study confirmed previous findings of Gerber et al. (2004) by showing that all the participating bilingual children successfully increased their PA and word-level decoding skills as a result of the training provided in their L1. They also performed significantly better than their peers who did not receive any PA training. Furthermore, the findings indicated that participants who initially scored in the high and middle range of the PA tests benefited most from the intervention. The children with initially low PA skills gained in *early emerging PA skills* of onset and rime identification but, disappointingly, made no significant improvement in *late emerging PA skills* of phoneme segmentation and word-decoding skills. Leafstedt et al. explain the lack of effect on these skills by pointing out that in the training delivered to students with initially low PA, the emphasis was on early PA skills to provide sufficient foundation for more complex PA skills. They hypothesize that continued training in late emerging PA skills would probably have beneficial results. Therefore, prolonged training in PA for multilingual speakers who are at risk of developing reading difficulties might be needed.

While Gerber et al.'s (2004) and Leafstedt et al.'s (2004) studies were conducted in multilingual settings where children are exposed to the language of schooling outside the school context, Yeung, Siegel and Chan's (2013) recent study investigated how PA interventions can help children in an environment where the children rarely use the second language outside the classroom. In their research, they administered an intensive PA programme in English to Cantonese-speaking children aged approximately 5 years in kindergartens in Hong Kong. The programme consisted of twenty-four 30-minute sessions spread over 12 weeks, which aimed to raise children's PA skills at the syllable and sound level. The comparison group received English language instruction primarily focusing on enhancing children's vocabulary knowledge. The programme was found to have a significant impact on the development of the children's PA skills in English and it also enhanced their English word-reading and spelling skills and productive vocabulary knowledge in English. Yeung et al.'s (2013) study did not specifically focus on children who were at risk of reading difficulties or identified as having an SpLD. Nevertheless, the results of the study concerning the relatively large effect of an early PA programme in a language that is primarily used in a classroom context are important because they show that PA can be developed through the medium of a language that is different from the students' first language in both second and foreign language learning environments.

6.3.2 Phonics Instruction

Another programme of intervention, which was originally used to enhance the skills of students with reading difficulties, is phonics instruction. Phonics programmes have now been widely adopted in early primary school years, and they provide direct and explicit instruction in sound–letter correspondences to help children develop accurate and fluent word-level decoding and spelling skills. The various programmes differ in how they integrate phonics instruction into literacy teaching and what aspects of sound–letter correspondences they focus on. Nevertheless, they are all similar in that "they delineate a planned, sequential set of phonic elements and they teach these elements explicitly and systematically" (National Reading Panel, 2000, p. 89). They contrast with whole-language or sight-word programmes in which children engage in meaning-focused literacy activities or are taught a basic repertoire of sight words. In these programmes, children are either expected to work out sound–letter correspondences themselves or are taught these correspondences incidentally as the need arises for them.

A meta-analysis of studies on the effectiveness of phonics instruction conducted by the National Reading Panel (2000) revealed that the systematic and explicit teaching of phonics significantly increases children's word-decoding skills, irrespective of the type of phonics programme. The increase observed was substantially higher than those found in whole-language or sight-word programmes. The positive impact of phonics programmes on spelling was smaller, especially after Grade 1, and the results for effects on reading comprehension were mixed. Phonics instruction was shown to be beneficial, regardless of whether it was delivered individually, in a small group or to a whole class, but it had a greater impact in early school years than for older students. Parallel to what we saw with regard to the value of PA programmes, phonics instruction was also more facilitative of the reading development of at-risk children than of those identified as having reading disabilities. The effect size of phonics programmes on word-decoding skills for children with reading disabilities was small in kindergarten and in Grade 1, and became nonsignificant from Grade 2 onwards. Phonics programmes, however, had a large effect on the development of reading comprehension skills of reading disabled children.

Very few studies have investigated how language learners with SpLDs improve their L2 reading skills as a result of a phonics-based instructional programme. One of these exceptions is Lovett et al.'s (2008) project conducted in Canada with multilingual children who were identified as having word-level decoding difficulties, that is dyslexia. Their study also included a group of dyslexic children whose first language was English. The children whose ages ranged from 6 to 13 years received 105 hours of training (1 hour per occasion, four to five occasions per week) in phonological awareness and word-decoding skills using a phonics-based approach in small groups, which were established taking the age and reading abilities of the children into account. A control group participated in regular instruction based on the school curriculum. All children in the treatment group, regardless of their first language status, showed significant growth in measures of phonological awareness, word decoding and reading comprehension, and their development was significantly different from that of the control group. This finding shows that children whose first language was not English and who spent more than 2 years in a target language environment benefited similarly from the programme as those whose first language was English. Interestingly, L2 speaking children demonstrated a steeper learning curve for phonological processing skills and one of the tests of word-level decoding. This shows that phonics-based reading programmes are especially useful for multilingual children with dyslexic-type reading difficulties. Another noteworthy finding of the study was that oral language skills, including measures of productive vocabulary knowledge and listening comprehension, also interacted with the rate of development. Children with initially lower oral language skills scores gained more from the intervention than children with higher oral language abilities, and this difference was observable for both L2 and L1 speaking participants. This suggests that phonics-based intervention programmes might also be effective for children who have a low level of oral proficiency, and who arrived later in the target language country than the L2 speaking children who were included in Lovett et al.'s (2008) study.

A recent study by Partanen and Siegel (2014) investigated the long-term outcomes of early intervention programmes among L1 and L2 speaking children in a Canadian context. All the children in this longitudinal study received explicit phonological awareness training and teaching on sound–letter relationships in kindergarten. Following this phonics-based approach in the 1st year of their literacy instruction, in Grades 1–7 the children were instructed in literacy skills with the help of a programme that focused more on effective strategies for reading comprehension than on phonological skills. The researchers administered a standardized test of word reading to the participants in this early intervention programme each year until Grade 7. The findings revealed that whereas, at the end of kindergarten, 21.5% of the children were at risk of developing reading difficulties, this percentage significantly decreased to 6% by Grade 7. The reduction in the number of participants experiencing persistent word-level decoding difficulties was similar for L1 and L2 speaking children, thus showing the beneficial effects of the programme regardless of language background.

Overall, only a small number of studies have been conducted on the impact of phonologically based intervention programmes on L2 speaking children's reading development, and there have been even fewer projects focusing on children with SpLDs. Nevertheless, the available findings to date suggest that early phonological awareness-raising interventions and phonics-based approaches to teaching reading skills are beneficial for L2 speaking children with SpLDs and that these benefits can potentially be long-lasting (see Partanen & Siegel, 2014). These phonological intervention programmes, however, need to be provided in the very early years of literacy teaching and be intensive, especially for L2 speaking children with SpLDs. The results of studies in this area also show that phonological awareness programmes can be effective even if they are delivered in a language the children are not yet fully proficient in (see Yeung et al., 2013). Furthermore, the gains made in a programme provided in the children's L1 can transfer to reading skills in the L2 (Gerber et al., 2004; Leafstedt et al., 2004).

6.3.3 Reading Comprehension Training

Many students with SpLDs demonstrate difficulties in reading comprehension (see Section 1.4). Students with reading comprehension difficulties might find it challenging to process the syntactic structure of sentences as well as the overall structure of written text, understand the functioning of cohesive ties, make appropriate inferences and monitor their comprehension (Cain et al., 2004; Nation, 2005). The difficulties of these students might be intensified by low levels of vocabulary knowledge and inadequate representation of the orthographic and phonological form of words in their mental lexicon (Perfetti, 2007). For L2 learners who are at risk of comprehension difficulties these challenges are even more serious because they might have smaller vocabulary size, less well-developed grammar skills and less background knowledge than their L1 peers. Therefore, reading comprehension training programmes can be particularly helpful in assisting students to overcome their difficulties.

One of the key elements of reading comprehension instruction programmes is the development of students' vocabulary knowledge (for a review see the National Reading Panel, 2000). This is usually done in the form explicit vocabulary teaching, such as preteaching of keywords before reading a text, providing glossaries within the reading text, giving practice activities on using the taught vocabulary and instruction in techniques that help memorization of new words. There exist programmes that encourage the incidental learning of words through extensive reading and multimedia and computer-assisted tools are also available (e.g. Kim et al., 2006). The National Reading Panel's review of studies on research that was conducted with English L1 speakers concluded that for measurable gains in knowledge, vocabulary needs to be taught both directly and indirectly and learners need to encounter words repeatedly in rich contexts. This recommendation is in line with pedagogical advice we can draw from existing research in the field of second language vocabulary learning (for a recent review see Dóczi & Kormos, 2016). Nevertheless, the evidence for the long-term effectiveness of vocabulary teaching and transfer to reading comprehension is limited with regard to L1-speaking children (National Reading Panel, 2000). Currently, we are not aware of any studies that have been conducted to examine the contribution of vocabulary instruction to the development of reading comprehension skills of L2-speaking learners with SpLDs.

Most reading enhancement programmes include the explicit teaching of reading comprehension strategies. Reading is a strategic process and many children, but not all, develop effective strategies to extract meaning from a written text with little guidance received from teachers. Students with reading comprehension difficulties, however, benefit considerably from instructional programmes that enhance their awareness of the cognitive processes involved in reading, teach them reading comprehension strategies explicitly and provide opportunities to practice and apply these strategies until they can use them autonomously (e.g. Oakhill et al., 2014; Palinscar & Brown, 1984; Pressley et al., 1994). This type of instruction is called *cognitive-behavioural* (Talbott, Lloyd & Tankersley, 1994) or *questioning/strategy instruction* (Berkeley, Scruggs & Mastropieri, 2010) and can include a variety of approaches and their combinations such as teaching students to pose questions that aid comprehension and monitor understanding, and explanations of how to analyse text structure and informational content. Strategy instruction can be teacher led and/or peer mediated. In the *reciprocal teaching* approach the teacher models the use of various reading strategies, explains these strategies and sets up opportunities for learners to practice the application of these strategies. Teacher-support is then gradually withdrawn and peers assist each other. Another type of reading intervention programme which is called *cognitive* (Talbott et al., 1994) or *text enhancement* training (Berkeley et al., 2010) uses additional text-embedded support such as highlighting main information, keywords and cohesive ties, illustrations and while-reading questions. In these programmes, text enhancement strategies are complemented with reading skills training, vocabulary instruction and repeated reading.

The above-described reading intervention programmes were found to be equally effective, particularly if strategies were taught in combination (Berkeley et al., 2010; National Reading Panel, 2000). Berkeley et al.'s (2010) meta-analysis shows that students with SpLDs can also make significant improvement in reading skills from reading comprehension instruction and their gains are comparable to students with no SpLDs. In a very recent review of the past 30 years of research on reading comprehension instruction, however, Scammacca, Roberts, Vaughn and Stuebing (2015) note a decreasing effect size of the treatment conditions. Some of the reasons for this reduction in effect size can be related to changes in research methodology over time. Furthermore, the narrowing gap between experimental and nonexperimental groups might signal that reading instruction in regular classroom settings has started to incorporate elements of reading enhancement programmes and students with SpLDs benefit from these.

Unfortunately, very little research has been conducted that has investigated the benefits of reading intervention programmes for L2 learners and even fewer studies involved L2 learners with SpLDs. With regard to students who are speakers of additional languages and receive an English language medium instruction in the target language environment, August and Shanahan (2010) conclude that the components and methods of effective reading instruction programmes are essentially the same for both L1- and L2-speaking children. In one of the few available studies Klingner and Vaughn (1996) implemented a reciprocal teaching programme to a group of Hispanic L2-English-speaking seventh and eighth graders in the United States. The programme consisted of 40-minute sessions and lasted for 27 days. The language of instruction was English, but students were encouraged to use their L1 for clarification when comprehension broke down. Almost all students made significant gains in reading comprehension measures as a result of the intervention, but initial reading abilities and oral language proficiency in English moderated the rate of improvement. The results of a more recent study by Denton, Wexler, Vaughn and Bryan (2008) were less encouraging. The participants came from the same background and were of the same age as the students in Klinger and Vaughn's study, but they had severe reading difficulties and limited vocabulary knowledge in both English and Spanish. The intervention consisted of 13 sessions of phonics, explicit vocabulary and reading strategy instruction. Neither the experimental nor the control group showed significant improvement after the training. The conclusions we can draw from this limited pool of studies is that effective intervention programmes need to be intensive and long-term and supplemented with focused instruction that also enhances the students' L2 proficiency.

6.3.4 Multisensory Structured Learning Programmes in Foreign Language Teaching

One of the most frequently recommended teaching methods for foreign language learners with SpLDs is the Multisensory Structured Learning (MSL) approach, which was developed by Sparks et al. (1991) based on the dyslexia remedial programme of the Orton-Gillingham (OG) approach (Gillingham & Stillman, 1960). The MSL approach developed by Sparks et al. (1991), and also endorsed in numerous adaptations (e.g. Nijakowska, 2008, 2010; Schneider & Crombie, 2003; Schneider & Evers, 2009), gives children explicit and direct teaching in sound–letter correspondences and activates different sensory channels simultaneously. The MSL approach is highly structured, proceeds in small and cumulative steps and provides L2 learners with SpLDs with sufficient practice and revision opportunities. Its aim is to develop children's phonological, morphological and syntactic awareness, and thereby help them to acquire L2 skills successfully.

Variations exist with regard to the exact procedures recommended in different adaptations of the MSL approach. In the original version of the approach, Sparks et al. (1991) suggest four basic principles. First of all, the language of instruction in the classroom should be the target language, and the first language of the students should only be used for explanations of grammatical constructions. Second, each lesson should be clearly structured with "well-defined daily activities" (p. 107). Third, frequent revision is needed and, finally, teachers should "emphasize simultaneous writing and pronunciation so that students can 'see', 'hear' and 'do' the language" (p. 107). Sparks et al. (1991) also provide a lesson outline, which starts with blackboard drills for sounds and grammar, followed by oral drills, which review the sounds of the target language and include an introduction to and review of grammar concepts, vocabulary teaching and reading and communicative activities. The detailed description of their suggested lesson plan, with its heavy emphasis on drills and the use of presentation–practice–produce sequences, strongly resembles the Audiolingual Method (Fries, 1945). The features that distinguish it from audiolingualism include the additional communicative activities, the use of multiple sensory channels for the provision of language input and the production of learners' output, and the lack of any explicit focus on preventing errors that would arise from first language interference.

Schneider and Ganschow (2000) in a later article modify the teaching procedure suggested by Sparks et al. (1991). They complement the MSL approach with principles of dynamic assessment (see also Section 2.2), which is a form of continuous classroom assessment that teachers apply to adjust the learning materials and the pace of learning to the progress of the students. Dynamic assessment is not only a method of testing what students have learned, but it also provides a means to help students develop learner autonomy. Just like Sparks et al.'s (1991) MSL approach, the teaching procedures suggested by Schneider and Ganschow (2000) contrast with communicative language teaching (e.g. Krashen, 1981) and the 'focus on meaning' approaches in language teaching, in which learners are exposed to meaningful input and are expected to acquire linguistic regularities incidentally. Schneider and Ganschow (2000) emphasize the importance of explicit language knowledge for students with SpLDs and consequently argue for the need to develop metalinguistic awareness of language learners with SpLDs. In their conceptualization, metalinguistic awareness does not only include explicit knowledge about regularities of the language system, but also the skills to apply this metalinguistic knowledge in relevant contexts.

Schneider and Ganschow's (2000) teaching approach retains some elements of the original MSL procedures outlined by Sparks et al. (1991) but introduces a number of innovations, which makes it align better with current conceptualizations of language teaching pedagogies. They see the role of the teacher as that of a facilitator of learning and strongly encourage guided-discovery procedures. They also place strong emphasis on learner autonomy and the development of learners' self-monitoring skills. They list five specific stages of the teaching process which are based on dynamic assessment (see Figure 6.1). In the first two stages, the teacher elicits information from the students and instead of giving direct feedback, whether an answer is correct or not, guides the students through the process of discovering the solution to the

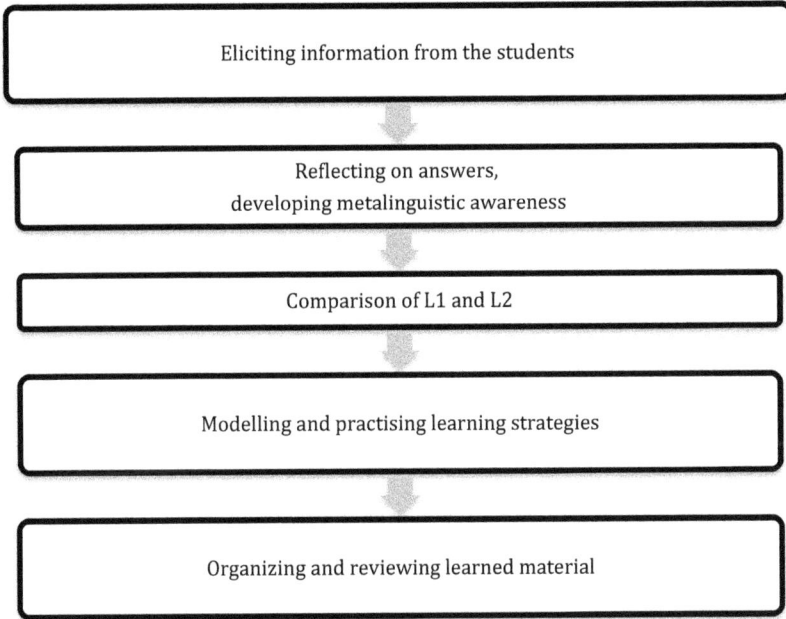

FIGURE 6.1 Stages of the Teaching Process Using Dynamic Assessment

task. The next stage involves the explicit comparison of the linguistic structure to be learned in the target language with the learners' L1. They argue for the beneficial effects of contrastive analysis on the acquisition of language structures based on the facilitative role of transfer (Koda, 2007) and Cummins' (1981) Linguistic Interdependence Hypothesis, which highlights the role of L1 as a resource and a supportive tool for L2 learning. Although this might not always be easy in multilingual classrooms and in situations where the teacher does not speak the students' L1, contrasting L1 and L2 linguistic patterns is assumed to promote learners' understanding of the phonological, syntactic and morphological structure of the L2 (Koda, 2007; Sparks & Ganschow, 1993). In the final two stages, learning strategies are taught and practised, and learners are given explicit guidance in how to organize and review the material they have covered. Schneider and Evers (2009) recommend further features of the MSL approach used in L1 literacy programmes (for a review see Kelly & Phillips, 2011) for the teaching of additional languages to students with SpLDs. They suggest that linguistic structures should be taught "in logical, sequential steps from simple to more complex tasks" (p. 58). They also stress that teaching should be cumulative and build on previously taught material (see also Nijakowska, 2008, 2010 for similar guidelines).

6.3.5 Theoretical and Empirical Underpinnings of MSL Instruction

The MSL approach consists of numerous elements that facilitate learning for every student, not just those with SpLDs. The parallel use of several sensory channels enhances the efficiency of encoding in memory for a number of reasons. First, based on Paivio's (1991) Dual Coding Theory, visual clues presented along with verbal information aid the memorization of new information and its integration into the knowledge system. The use of imagery along with the verbal code establishes associative links, called referential connections, between the verbal and nonverbal memory systems, and thereby stronger and more deeply engrained memory representations can be created. Second, the application of multiple modalities in learning results in more elaborate processing which, according to Craik and Lockhart's (1972) depth of processing theory, leads to more efficient learning. Extended practice activities in MSL instruction also serve a similar purpose. Finally, there are limitations on verbal and visual attentional resource pools and working memory (Baddeley, 2012), which can be overcome if information is presented in both visual and verbal modalities. This is especially helpful for students with SpLDs who often have lower phonological short-term memory and working memory capacity and, as a result, have difficulties processing complex verbal information (see Chapter 2). If, however, they have the opportunity to learn through additional sensory channels, their weaknesses in phonological processing can be counterbalanced.

The MSL approach takes another important characteristic of students with SpLDs into consideration, namely their general difficulties in committing verbal information to long-term memory. Learning another language requires the memorization of different types of verbal information: sound sequences, letter combinations, words, phrases and larger linguistic constructions, which might be particularly challenging for learners with SpLDs, whose phonological short-term memory might be able to hold less information than that of their peers. According to the assumptions of the MSL approach, L2 learners with SpLDs can succeed in encoding these elements of language in their long-term memory if they are presented in small units and are practised extensively in different settings. In other words, the MSL approach stresses the importance of practicing different aspects of the L2 until they become automatic. From the perspective of second language acquisition theory, the MSL approach seems to be built on the strong interface position, which claims that, in the course of learning another language, one first acquires explicit knowledge of specific linguistic constructions which, with practice, turns into implicit knowledge. This implicit knowledge can then be applied automatically and without conscious attention for communication (DeKeyser, 1997). The strong interface position is in stark contrast with the no interface position underlying communicative language teaching and *Focus on Meaning* approaches to language teaching, which posit that there is a complete dissociation of explicit and implicit knowledge (Krashen, 1981). The intermediary position called the weak interface position (N. Ellis, 2005; R. Ellis, 1994) argues that explicit knowledge can potentially play a role in the development of implicit knowledge but language teaching should predominantly focus on supporting the acquisition of implicit knowledge.

Although it is still an unresolved question whether explicit knowledge can turn into implicit knowledge, and if yes how (for a recent review see Ellis & Shintani, 2014), there seems to be evidence for the beneficial effects of explicit instruction in second language learning. In both Norris and Ortega's (2000) and Spada and Tomita's (2010) meta-analyses of previous studies, explicit instruction was found to result in substantially higher improvement in various posttest scores than implicit instruction, in which no explicit explanation of the grammatical construction or instruction to pay attention to specific constructions in the input was provided. The advantage of explicit instruction continued to be upheld even when delayed posttests were analysed (Spada & Tomita, 2010). It is also interesting that in Norris and Ortega's (2000) meta-analysis, the kind of explicit teaching advocated in the MSL approach, which focuses on linguistic constructions in isolation, was found be as effective as the *Focus on Form* approach, in which grammar instruction is embedded in the context of communicative interaction. Furthermore, Spada and Tomita's (2010) analysis indicated that explicit instruction was helpful not only for simple syntactic constructions, but also for more complex ones. The effect of explicit instruction was found to be larger than that of implicit learning conditions, even in free production tasks that can be assumed to require students to rely on implicit knowledge.

Not only might the explicit teaching of grammatical constructions be helpful for promoting second language development, but it has also been shown that explicit teaching of vocabulary can result in more efficient learning than purely incidental exposure (File & Adams, 2010; Tian & Macaro, 2012). Research evidence seems to suggest that the teaching of words in isolation might be somewhat more beneficial than integrated vocabulary learning activities (File & Adams, 2010; Laufer, 2006). Dóczi and Kormos (2016) explain that incidental vocabulary learning through meaningful input is constrained by working memory capacity limitations, and this has particular relevance for language learners with SpLDs. Repeated exposure and extended practice are also essential for encoding words, and all the rich information associated with a word, in long-term memory. For students with no SpLDs, repetitions between five to 16 occasions might be necessary for fully acquiring a word (Nation, 1990). Webb's (2007) study showed that even 10 encounters were not sufficient for learners to develop all the different types of word knowledge about targeted items. If we consider the difficulties that students with SpLDs might experience in vocabulary acquisition because of their reduced phonological short-term memory capacity (see Chapter 3), the recommendations of the MSL approach concerning frequent repetition are certainly well founded.

In the field of second language acquisition research, as well as in language teacher training, the mainstream approach advocated for teaching a second language is the Focus on Form approach and its various incarnations (for a review see Ellis & Shintani, 2014). In this approach, linguistic constructions including syntax, morphology, phonology and vocabulary are taught unobtrusively in communicative contexts and through communicative tasks. As we saw above, the MSL approach tends to fall within the *Focus on FormS* approach, where grammatical constructions are preselected for teaching and are often taught in isolation from a communicative context. It is not difficult to notice the obvious contrast between mainstream language teaching pedagogies and the MSL approach. There are numerous arguments, however, for abandoning the one-size-fits-all principle in the field of language teaching. Kubota (1998) enumerates a variety of situations in which languages are taught to culturally, linguistically and cognitively diverse populations and calls for the need to hear the voices of language teachers in these contexts. In her review of the MSL approach, she highlights that this approach takes the needs of students with SpLDs into account, which means "to understand and manipulate the structural aspects of language" (p. 403). She rightly points out that it is essential that instead of mechanically implementing inflexible and authoritarian teaching methodologies, teachers should be responsive to the specific needs of students.

There are not only cultural, social and contextual reasons for the need to apply different pedagogical approaches to teaching languages to students with SpLDs, but also cognitive ones. In the field of educational psychology, Snow (1992) introduced the concept of aptitude-treatment interaction, which expresses that students with different cognitive profiles might benefit from different instructional approaches (see also Skehan, 1998). Based on a review of relevant empirical studies, he argued that unstructured learning situations are more favourable for "able, independent, mastery-oriented and flexible" (p. 28) individuals, whereas highly structured learning contexts are more suitable for "less able, less independent, less mastery-oriented learners" (Skehan, 1998). Kirschner, Sweller and Clark (2006) drew a similar conclusion, namely that minimally guided instruction might be more useful for students who have preexisting knowledge in the field they study. They cite a variety of research findings in educational psychology that suggest that novices learn more efficiently with direct instructional guidance.

In the field of second language acquisition research, empirical findings with regard to the relationship between working memory and learning outcomes under different instructional conditions are somewhat contradictory. Some studies have found that aptitude as well as working memory capacity are predictive of learning outcomes in both explicit and incidental learning conditions (e.g. De Graaf, 1997) and that working memory is associated with the gains made in explicit learning conditions but not in incidental conditions (Robinson, 2005b). In these studies, however, participants had to learn a language previously unknown to them. In contrast, Erlam's (2005) study, which involved teaching a novel grammatical construction to learners of French, indicated that explicit instruction on the grammatical construction followed by production practice opportunities seemed to be beneficial for all learners, regardless of their language aptitude and working memory capacity (Erlam, 2005). Therefore, there seems to exist compelling evidence from both educational psychology and second language acquisition that explicit and guided instruction might assist students with lower levels of language aptitude and working memory capacity, especially in the initial stages of language learning. These findings can be transferred to the group of language learners with SpLDs who are generally characterized by lower levels of aptitude and working memory capacity (see Section 3.5.1, for more details).

In discussions of the theoretical and empirical underpinnings of the MSL approach, the emphasis thus far has been on teaching the target language. The MSL approach, however, does not only propose the use of specific methods to assist learners with the acquisition of linguistic structures. It also includes both metacognitive instruction, which makes students aware of the cognitive processes involved in using and learning an additional language and reflecting on those cognitive processes, and explicit learning strategy training. Language learning strategies can be subsumed under the broader concept of self-regulation, which refers to "the degree that individuals are metacognitively, motivationally and behaviourally active participants in their learning process" (Zimmerman, 1989, p. 329). The need for learning strategy training and enhancing the self-regulation of students with SpLDs is supported by studies that have shown that the use of strategies that assist students with planning, executing and monitoring learning tasks and consciously attending to and acquiring new information is strongly related to the academic success of university students with SpLDs (Trainin & Swanson, 2005). High-achieving students with SpLDs seem to be able to skilfully apply a variety of these strategies to help them overcome the difficulties resulting from their SpLDs (Reis, McGuire, & Neu, 2000). Recent research has also demonstrated that students with SpLDs tend to use fewer metacognitive reading and learning strategies than those with no history of SpLDs (Chevalier, Parrila, Ritchie & Deacon, 2015). These empirical findings underscore the need for enhancing metacognitive awareness and the use of self-regulation strategies among students with SpLDs. Available research findings suggest that learning and reading strategy instruction for learners with SpLDs has positive effects on various academic domains, including reading comprehension, and that students with SpLDs seem to benefit most from combined direct instruction in literacy skills with learning strategy training (for a review see Swanson & Hoskyn, 1998). In the field of second language acquisition research, it has also been demonstrated that learning strategy training enhances students' strategy use and consequently can result in the development of second language skills (Chamot, 2005).

To summarize, the MSL approach to teaching languages to students with SpLDs seems to have a firm grounding in relevant theories in the field of second language acquisition and educational and cognitive psychology. Although it differs from mainstream language teaching pedagogies concerning the role of explicit teaching and the importance attributed to metalinguistic awareness of the structural regularities of the target language, this difference should not be an argument against its adaptation in teaching languages to students with SpLDs. It is, however, critical to the success of the MSL approach that explicit teaching does not involve the use of complex metalanguage when the features of the target language are presented to the learners. Learners should not be expected to memorize these regularities as rules, but to apply them in communicative contexts. Another feature of the MSL approach, namely the extensive use of practice tasks, repetitions and drills, should also be considered carefully by language teachers. When possible, these practice tasks should not be devoid of context and should be meaningful to learners, and a sufficient variety should be included to ensure that the learning experience does not become tedious and uninspiring. Most importantly, teachers should not regard the MSL approach as yet another dogma that they should adapt unquestioningly without considering the needs of their learners and the context in which learning takes place.

6.3.6 Empirical Evidence for the Effectiveness of MSL Programmes

There exists substantial research evidence that supports the effectiveness of MSL instruction in a variety of contexts. In a series of pioneering studies, Sparks and his colleagues (Sparks & Ganschow, 1993; Sparks et al., 1992) investigated the effects of classroom instruction using the MSL approach on language learning aptitude and native language skills. The experimental groups consisted of teenage learners of Spanish in private college preparatory schools in the United States who were all *at-risk language learners*. These learners had either an official diagnosis of SpLD or a history of learning difficulties. In each group, there were also students who had not been identified as having an SpLD but experienced difficulties with learning additional languages in the past. In a study conducted by Sparks et al. (1992), two experimental groups followed the MSL training programme proposed by Sparks et al. (1991) (see Section 6.3.4). In one of the groups, the instructor spoke Spanish exclusively, whereas in the other group, the teacher used both English and Spanish. The control group was taught using the "natural communication approach emphasizing global skills used for oral and written communication" (p. 112). The results showed that the control group made no gains in any of the language aptitude measures or native language skills. The participants in whose classroom their first language, English, was not used at all in the MSL programme improved significantly in their aptitude test scores, but not in native language measures. The MSL group where both English and Spanish were used for instruction made significant improvements in all the aptitude measures as well as in tests of native language that assessed phonological

perception skills, word decoding and vocabulary size. These findings were replicated by a follow-up study conducted by Sparks and Ganschow (1993). The
beneficial effects of MSL instruction on language learning aptitude, phonological
perception and word decoding were also confirmed in Sparks and Ganschow's
(1993) study in which students with SpLDs were taught Latin.

The findings of the series of studies conducted by Sparks and his colleagues
are remarkable because, on the one hand, they show that explicit instruction in
the phonological and syntactic system of an additional language can enhance the
cognitive skills underlying second language acquisition. On the other hand, the
results also indicate that foreign language instruction using the MSL approach is
beneficial for students' phoneme awareness and word-level decoding skills in their
first language. These studies underscore the importance and value of teaching
additional languages to students with SpLDs. The findings also highlight the
facilitative role the students' first language can play in the instruction process (see
Figure 6.2 for an illustration of the effects of MSL instruction).

Sparks and his colleagues continued investigating the effects of MSL instruction in studies that also involved students with no SpLDs as a comparison group
(Ganschow & Sparks, 1995; Sparks et al., 1995, 1998). The comparison group
was taught using the aforementioned *natural communication approach*, whereas with
the group of SpLD learners the MSL approach was used. The students with no
SpLDs also showed improvement in language aptitude measures, but during 1
year of instruction did not achieve any development in phonological awareness.
Only Sparks et al.'s (1995) study that analysed changes over a period of 2 years
of Spanish instruction showed gains in phonological awareness for the group
with no SpLDs. Although the MSL instruction was clearly found to be beneficial

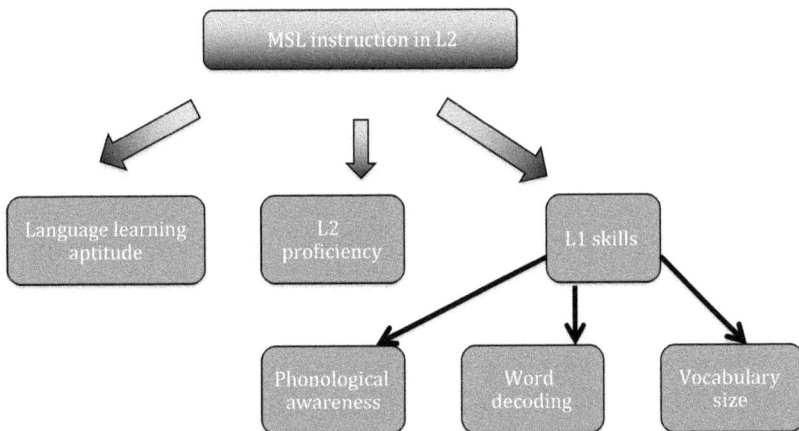

FIGURE 6.2 The Effects of MSL Instruction in Sparks, Ganschow, Pohlman, Skinner
and Artzer (1992) and Sparks et al.'s (1998) Studies

in these studies, the findings also revealed that the students with SpLDs still lagged behind their peers who had no history of learning difficulties in terms of their language aptitude and native language skills.

The question is, however, whether MSL instruction facilitates the development of second language competence, and not just the skills underlying successful second language acquisition. In order to answer this, Sparks et al. (1998) conducted another study with American teenage learners of Spanish in a college preparatory school. The study followed the development of the language skills of students who were classified as being 'at risk of language learning problems' and those who did not exhibit difficulties in their first language literacy skills. The not-at-risk students received regular classroom instruction in Spanish for a year. A group of at-risk students were taught via the MSL approach in self-contained classes, and another group of at-risk students studied in a self-contained class where the same instructional method as the not-at-risk group was applied. The fourth group of at-risk students studied in a mixed-ability class together with not-at-risk students but were granted educational accommodations, such as extended time on tests, audio presentation of readings and tests and extra support with spelling and homework. All four groups were administered a proficiency test consisting of reading comprehension, writing and listening/speaking components at the end of the academic year. A remarkable finding of the study was that the MSL at-risk-group showed a comparable level of attainment in all the components of the proficiency test and an additional measure of foreign word recognition as the not-at-risk group which was taught via the natural communication approach. Furthermore, the at-risk group taught via the MSL approach performed significantly better on all these assessments than the other two at-risk groups. Although Sparks et al. did not use a pretest to establish an initial level of language competence and hence they could only compare final achievement and not the rate of improvement, these results seem to provide evidence for the effectiveness of the MSL approach in the development of second language skills (see Figure 6.2).

The beneficial effects of the MSL programme were further investigated for other languages, such as English, the orthographic system of which is considerably less transparent than that of Latin or Spanish. Nijakowska (2008) conducted an experiment in which five dyslexic secondary school students in Poland received explicit MSL instruction on phoneme–grapheme correspondences and certain systematic features of the English spelling system. The intervention programme lasted for 6 months and involved 90-minute sessions in a self-contained class, which were offered in addition to regular classroom instruction in English as a foreign language. The control groups included 10 students with an official certificate of dyslexia and 10 students with no formal identification of SpLDs who attended mainstream English classes where no explicit teaching of orthographic awareness and spelling was provided. Nijakowska (2008) conducted both pre- and posttests and assessed the development in English word reading and spelling skills. The experimental group made large and statistically significant gains in both spelling and word reading during the intervention, while the dyslexic control group showed no improvement. The nondyslexic control group only made a significant increase in English word-spelling scores, but not on a word-reading test. A remarkable finding of Nijakowska's (2008) study was that the experimental group significantly outperformed even the nondyslexic control group in a word-reading and spelling posttest. Although these results need to be treated with caution due to the small sample size, they seem to provide additional support for the beneficial effects of direct, explicit and multisensory teaching of additional languages to students with SpLDs.

In a recent study, Pfenninger (2015) investigated the impact of the MSL approach using a computer-based instructional programme with participants who were younger than the students previously involved in the research of Sparks and his colleagues (1991, 1992, 1995) and Nijakowska (2008). Another interesting feature of Pfenninger's study was that her research was conducted in a Swiss context where the standard variety of German is the children's second language and English is the third language they acquire. The project aimed to assess not only how the MSL approach assists in the development of third language skills, that is in English, but also whether it has an impact on German-L2 word naming, word-level decoding and phonological awareness. Ten students aged between 9 and 11 who were identified as dyslexic and 10 nondyslexic students in the same age range received an experimental treatment for 3 months, 5 times a week for 20 minutes. The treatment, which was offered in addition to regular classroom instruction in English, involved the use of a computer programme that provided explicit teaching on how to read and spell words in English following the principles of the MSL approach. Specific and immediate feedback on students' performance was given by the programme and the children could also practice the newly presented material with the help of different tasks. The control groups, which comprised ten officially identified dyslexic and ten nondyslexic students, received regular classroom instruction and did not use the computer programme.

Pfenninger's (2015) research produced several noteworthy results. On the one hand, her study was the first one to show that MSL instruction is also beneficial for nondyslexic students as her participants using the computer programme improved significantly in a number of areas of L2 German and L3 English skills. The treatment had a significant effect on phonological awareness in L2 and L3, word decoding in L3, L3 vocabulary knowledge and rapid automated naming in L2 and L3 (except for a rapid digit-naming test in German). Little improvement was found for L2 word decoding and sentence reading fluency, which might be due to ceiling effects caused by the relatively transparent nature of German orthography. On the other hand, the statistical analyses also revealed that the dyslexic participants benefited significantly more from the MSL instruction than did their nondyslexic peers in terms of rapid automated picture naming

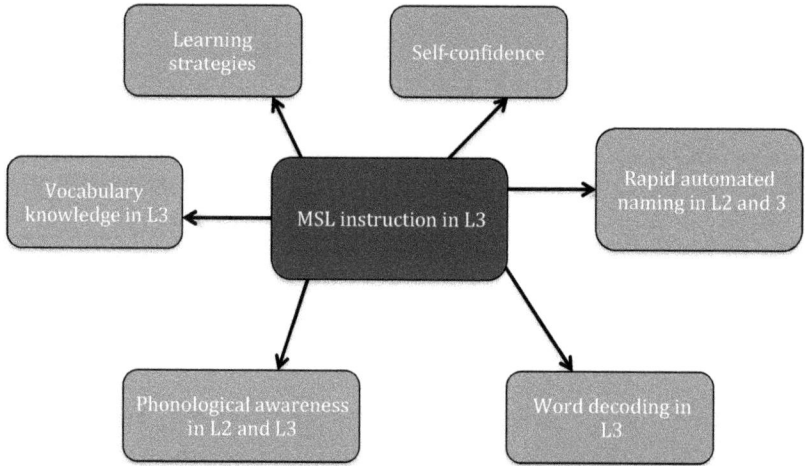

FIGURE 6.3 The Effects of MSL Instruction in L3 in Pfenninger's (2015, in press) Study

in L2 and L3, in phonological awareness in L2 and L3, in L2 spelling and in receptive and productive L3 vocabulary knowledge (see Figure 6.3 for an illustration). Pfenninger's study extends the available evidence on the usefulness of MSL programmes to younger children and to multilingual contexts where children acquire two additional languages in parallel in a predominantly classroom instructed language learning situation.

In a follow-up project, Pfenninger (in press) also investigated the effect of MSL instruction on motivation, self-confidence and the use of learning strategies. Overall, she found that the MSL instruction had a positive impact on these affective factors and was particularly beneficial for dyslexic students who gained substantially in self-confidence and reported using more learning strategies at the end of the treatment. Her results also indicated that there was a significant association between the gains the participants made in tests of L3 skills and motivational variables. Although these findings do not allow us to establish direct links of causality, Pfenninger's study seems to suggest that MSL instruction does not only have cognitive benefits and a positive impact on the development of L2/L3 skills, but it can potentially also enhance students' motivation, self-confidence and self-regulatory strategy use (see Figure 6.3).

6.4 Conclusion

While sporadic examples of successful inclusive and dyslexia-friendly programmes can be found, unfortunately, in most contexts, the needs of language learners with SpLDs are still neglected. On the one hand, this might stem from the lack of appropriate teacher knowledge of SpLDs. Results of studies examining the role of teacher knowledge in teaching literacy skills to SpLDs have demonstrated that insufficient familiarity with the nature of SpLDs, and their effect on learning processes can result in negative attitudes to inclusion, high anxiety in working with students with SpLDs, and ultimately low effectiveness for teaching and underachievement by students (Joshi et al., 2009; Washburn, Joshi & Cantrell, 2011). A recent European survey of language teacher's previous training and existing knowledge of SpLDs paints a bleak picture and shows that language teachers themselves describe their expertise in this area as poor and deficient (Nijakowska, 2014). Therefore, there is a clear and obvious need to incorporate courses, modules or units of study on SpLDs and inclusion in both in- and preservice teacher education programmes. One such course is Dyslexia for Teachers of English as a Foreign Language (Dystefl course—www.dystefl.eu), which offers materials for self-study and inclusion in a variety of teacher training contexts (for a review see also Nijakowska & Kormos, 2015).

On the other hand, the implementation of inclusive and dyslexia-friendly practices is an arduous undertaking because it is time-consuming and dependent on the successful collaboration of the teaching, management and administrative teams of the school (Abrams, 2008; Arries, 1999). It is also resource-intensive in terms of both teachers' time and other material resources, such as appropriate supportive technology. Therefore, it is not only crucial that schools as communities are strongly committed to inclusion, but that there is support available in terms of management, financing and legislation. Knowledge of another language is an influential resource in the 21st century, and speaking an additional language can be as empowering as literacy or numeracy skills. For this reason, both in legislation and at the level of educational policy, it should be ensured that no one is left out of learning additional languages. Exemption from learning languages should only be an option if, despite all the affordances of an inclusive environment, students experience failure. Just as additional support is offered to all students with SpLDs who are in need of it while developing their literacy skills, similar opportunities should be available for learning additional languages. Although schools and enthusiastic and committed communities of teachers can establish a dyslexia-friendly and inclusive environment, only sustained support at the level of educational policy and financial resources can contribute to making inclusion in language learning a norm rather than an exception. Endeavours for inclusion can also strengthen the voice and advocacy of learners with SpLDs.

In this book, I have given readers guidance on how signs of learning difficulties can be identified and described the tools with which teachers can systematically observe their learners and gain a better understanding of the challenges they face. I have also argued that an essential component of the identification process is not only the description of the learners' strengths and weaknesses, but also the thorough investigation of the barriers present in the educational context.

The creation of an inclusive learning environment and the removal of these obstacles are essential for successful second language development.

In addition to inclusive practices, most learners with SpLDs benefit from specialized instructional interventions. The L2 reading skills of young children with SpLDs can improve significantly if they participate in early phonological awareness-raising and phonics-based teaching programmes. L2 learners with SpLDs of all ages profit from the explicit teaching of vocabulary that focuses not only on form-meaning associations, but other aspects of word knowledge such as spelling, pronunciation, grammatical information and collocations. Reading strategy instruction, developing metacognitive awareness as well as more general training in the efficient use of self-regulation strategies enhances the L1 and L2 reading skills of learners of SpLDs and serves them well in performing academic learning tasks.

The multisensory learning programme provides an explicit, direct and carefully structured teaching of all levels of the L2 linguistic system and activates learners' different sensory channels simultaneously. This teaching framework benefits L2 learners with SpLDs at multiple levels. It helps them overcome their phonological short-term and working memory limitations and assists them to successfully memorize rules and regularities of the L2 as well as language items such as words. Frequent revision and recycling, as well multiple meaningful and varied practice opportunities aid the automatization of new L2 constructions. Through the application of guided-discovery procedures and explicit explanations, students are supported in the learning process and do not have to rely on implicit and incidental learning exclusively. In addition to developing the L2 competence of students with SpLDs, the multisensory learning programme has been found to increase L1 phoneme awareness and word-level decoding skills and enhance motivation, self-confidence and self-regulation skills.

I hope that this book has helped readers to understand and assist language learners with SpLDs so that they will no longer have to say: "I don't 'suffer' from dyslexia. I live with it and I work with it. I suffer from the ignorance of people who think they know what I can and cannot do" (Erica Cook).

REFERENCES

Aaron, P., Joshi, R., Gooden, R., & Bentum, K. (2008). Diagnosis and treatment of reading disabilities based on the component model of reading: An alternative to the discrepancy model of LD. *Journal of Learning Disabilities*, *41*, 67–84.

Abrams, Z. S. (2008). Alternative second language curricula for learners with disabilities: Two case studies. *The Modern Language Journal*, *92*, 414–430.

Abu Rabia, S., Share, D., & Mansour, S. M. (2003). Word recognition and basic cognitive processes among reading-disabled and normal readers of Arabic. *Reading and Writing: An Interdisciplinary Journal*, *16*, 423–442.

Abu Rabia, S., & Siegel, L. S. (2002). Reading, syntactic, orthographic and working memory skills of bilingual Arabic-English speaking children. *Journal of Psycholinguistic Research*, *31*, 661–678.

Ackerman, P. L. (2007). New developments in understanding skilled performance. *Current Directions in Psychological Research*, *16*, 235–239.

Adams, A.M., & Guillot, K. (2008). Working memory and writing in bilingual students. *International Journal of Applied Linguistics*, *156*, 13–28.

AERA/APA/NCME. (1999). *Standards for educational and psychological testing*. Washington, DC: Author.

Ainscow, M. (1995). Education for all: Making it happen. *Support for Learning*, *10*, 147–155.

Ajzen, I. (2005). *Attitudes, personality and behaviour*. New York: Open University Press.

Alderson, J. C., Brunfaut, T., & Harding, L. (2014). Towards a theory of diagnosis in second and foreign language assessment: Insights from professional practice across diverse fields. *Applied Linguistics*, *36*, 236–260.

Alderson, J. C., Haapakangas, E.-L., Huhta, A., Nieminen, L., & Ullakonoja, R. (2014). *Diagnosing reading in a second or foreign language*. London: Routledge.

Alloway, T. P., Gathercole, S. E., & Elliott, J. (2010). Examining the link between working memory behavior and academic attainment in children with ADHD. *Developmental Medicine & Child Neurology*, *52*, 632–636.

Al Otaiba, S., & Torgesen, J. (2007). Effects from intensive standardized kindergarten and first-grade interventions for the prevention of reading difficulties. In S. R. Jimerson, M. K. Burns & A. M. Van Der Heyden (Eds.), *Handbook of response to intervention* (pp. 212–222). New York: Springer.

American Psychiatric Association. (1994). *Diagnostic and statistical manual of mental disorders* (4th ed.). Washington, DC: Author.

American Psychiatric Association. (2013). *Diagnostic and statistical manual of mental disorders* (5th ed.). Washington, DC: Author.

Anderson, J. R. (1995). *Learning and memory: An integrated approach.* New York: Wiley.

Arras, U., Müller-Karabil, A., & Zimmermann, S. (2013). On equal footing? Accommodations for disabled candidates in the TestDaF. In D. Tsagari & G. Spanoudis (Eds.), *Assessing L2 students with learning and other disabilities* (pp. 271–286). Newcastle upon Tyne, UK: Cambridge Scholars.

Arries, J. F. (1999). Learning disabilities and foreign languages: A curriculum approach to the design of inclusive courses. *The Modern Language Journal, 83,* 98–110.

Association of Language Testers in Europe. (1994). *The Association of Language Testers of Europe code of practice.* Retrieved from http://www.alte.org.

August, D., & Shanahan, T. (2010). Response to a review and update on developing literacy in second-language learners: Report of the national literacy panel on language minority children and youth. *Journal of Literacy Research, 42,* 341–348.

Baddeley, A. D. (1986). *Working memory.* Oxford: Oxford University Press.

Baddeley, A. D. (2000) The episodic buffer: a new component of working memory? *Trends in Cognitive Science, 4,* 417–423.

Baddeley, A. D. (2003). Working memory: Looking back and looking forward. *Nature Reviews Neuroscience, 4,* 829–839.

Baddeley, A. D. (2012). Working memory: Theories, models, and controversies. *Annual Review of Psychology, 63,* 1–29.

Baddeley, A. D., & Hitch, G. J. (1974). Working memory. In G. A. Bower (Ed.), *Recent advances in learning and motivation* (Vol. 8, pp. 47–90). New York: Academic Press.

Baddeley, A. D., & Logie, R. H. (1999). Working memory: The multiple component model. In A. Miyake & P. Shah (Eds.), *Models of working memory: Mechanisms of active maintenance and executive control* (pp. 28–61). Cambridge: Cambridge University Press.

Baird, G., Simonoff, E., Pickles, A., Chandler, S., Loucas, T., Meldrum, D., & Charman, T. (2006). Prevalence of disorders of the autism spectrum in a population cohort of children in South Thames: The special needs and autism project (SNAP). *Lancet, 368(9531),* 210–215.

Baker, J. M., & Zigmond, N. (1995). The meaning and practice of inclusion for students with learning disabilities: Themes and implications from the five cases. *Journal of Special Education, 29,* 163–180.

Bandura, A. (1986). *Social foundations of thought and action: A social cognitive theory.* Englewood Cliffs, NJ: Prentice-Hall.

Bandura, A. (1997). *Self-efficacy: The exercise of control.* New York: W. H. Freeman.

Barkley, R. A. (1997). Inhibition, sustained attention, and executive functions: Constructing a unifying theory of ADHD. *Psychological Bulletin, 121,* 65–94.

Barkley, R. A. (2006). *Attention-deficit hyperactivity disorder.* New York, NY: Guilford Press.

Barnes, C. (1996). Theories of disabilities and the origin of oppression of disabled people in Western society. In L. Barton (Ed.), *Disability and society: Emerging issues and insights* (pp. 43–60). London: Longman.

Baron-Cohen, S. (2008). *Autism and Asperger syndrome.* Oxford: Oxford University Press.

Berkeley, S., Scruggs, T. E., & Mastropieri, M. A. (2010). Reading comprehension instruction for students with learning disabilities, 1995–2006: A meta-analysis. *Remedial and Special Education, 31*, 423–436.

Berninger, V. (2000). Development of language by hand and its connections to language by ear, mouth, and eye. *Topics in Language Disorders, 20*, 65–84.

Berninger, V. W., Abbott, R. D., Abbott, S. P., Graham, S., & Richards, T. (2002). Writing and reading: Connections between language by hand and language by eye. *Journal of Learning Disabilities, 35*, 39–56.

Besner, D., & Smith, M. (1992). Basic processes in reading: Is the orthographic depth hypothesis sinking? In R. Frost & L. Katz (Eds.), *Orthography, phonology, morphology and meaning* (pp. 45–66). Amsterdam: North Holland.

Bialystok, E., & Majumder, S. (1998). The relationship between bilingualism and the development of cognitive processes in problem solving. *Applied Pyscholinguistics, 19*, 69–85.

Bishop, D. V. M., & Snowling, M. J. (2004). Developmental dyslexia and specific language impairment: Same or different? *Psychological Bulletin, 130*, 858–886.

Bolt, S. E., & Thurlow, M. L. (2004). Five of the most frequently allowed testing accommodations in state policy. *Remedial and Special Education, 25*, 141–152.

Bong, M., & Skaalvik, E. M. (2003). Academic self-concept and self-efficacy: How different are they really? *Educational Psychology Review, 15*, 1–40.

Booth, T., Ainscow, M., Black-Hawkins, K., Vaughan, M., & Shaw, L. (2000). *Index for inclusion: Developing learning and participation in schools.* Bristol: Centre for Studies on Inclusive Education.

Borodkin, K., & Faust, M. (2014). Native language phonological skills in low proficiency second language learners. *Languages Learning, 64*, 132–159.

Bourdieu, P. (1991). *Language and symbolic power* (J. B. Thompson, ed.; G. Raymond & M. Adamson, trans.). Cambridge, UK: Polity Press (original work published in 1982).

Bowers, P. G., & Swanson, L. B. (1991). Naming speed deficit in reading disability: Multiple measures of a singular process. *Journal of Experimental Child Psychology, 51*, 195–219.

Bown, J., & White, C. (2010). A social cognitive approach to affect in SLA. *International Review of Applied Linguistics, 48*, 331–353.

British Dyslexia Association. (1996). *Dyslexia friendly schools good practice guide: Abridged version.* Bracknell, UK: British Dyslexia Association.

Burgoine, E., & Wing, L. (1983). Identical triplets with Asperger's syndrome. *British Journal of Psychiatry, 143*, 261–265.

Cain, K. (2006). Individual differences in children's memory and reading comprehension: An investigation of semantic and inhibitory deficits. *Memory, 14*, 553–569.

Cain, K., & Bignell, S. (2014). Reading and listening comprehension and their relation to inattention and hyperactivity. *British Journal of Educational Psychology, 84*, 108–124.

Cain, K., Oakhill, J., & Bryant, P. (2004). Children's reading comprehension ability: Concurrent prediction by working memory, verbal ability, and component skills. *Journal of Educational Psychology, 96*, 31–42.

Calvo, M. G., & Eysenck, M. W. (1996). Phonological working memory and reading test anxiety. *Memory, 4*, 289–305.

Camara, W., Copeland, T., & Rothchild, B. (1998). Effects of extended time on the SAT I: Reasoning Test: Score growth for students with learning disabilities. *College Board Research Report 98–7.* New York: The College Board.

Campbell, J. D., & Lavallee, L. F. (1993). Who am I? The role of self-concept confusion in understanding the behavior of people with low self-esteem. In R. F. Baumeister (Ed.), *Self-esteem, the puzzle of low self-regard* (pp. 3–36). New York: Plenum Press.

Caravolas, M. (2004). Spelling development in alphabetic writing systems: A cross-linguistic perspective. *European Psychologist, 9,* 3–14.

Caravolas, M., Hulme, C., & Snowling, M. J. (2001). The foundations of spelling ability: Evidence from a 3-year longitudinal study. *Journal of Memory & Language, 45,* 751–774.

Caravolas, M., Lervåg, A., Defior, S., Seidlová Málková, G., & Hulme, C. (2013). Different patterns, but equivalent predictors, of growth in reading in consistent and inconsistent orthographies. *Psychological Science, 24,* 1398–1407.

Caravolas, M., Lervåg, A., Mousikou, P., Efrim, C., Litavsky, M., Onochie-Quintanilla, E., . . . Seidlová-Málková. (2012). Common patterns of prediction of literacy development in different alphabetic orthographies. *Psychological Science, 23,* 678–686.

Carlisle, J. F. (2000). Awareness of the structure and meaning of morphologically complex words: Impact on reading. *Reading and Writing: An Interdisciplinary Journal, 12,* 169–190.

Carroll, J. B. (1981). Twenty-five years of research on foreign language aptitude. In K. C. Diller (Ed.), *Individual differences and universals in language learning aptitude* (pp. 119–154). Rowley, MA: Newbury House.

Carroll, J. B., & Sapon, S. M. (1959). *The modern language aptitude test.* San Antonio, TX: Psychological Corporation.

Carroll, J. M., & Illes, J. E. (2006). An assessment of anxiety levels in dyslexic students in higher education. *British Journal of Educational Psychology, 76,* 651–662.

Chamot, A. U. (2005). Language learning strategy instruction: Current issues and research. *Annual Review of Applied Linguistics, 25,* 112–130.

Chao, Y.-R. (1968). *A grammar of spoken Chinese.* Berkeley, CA: University of California Press.

Cheung, H. (1996). Nonword span as a unique predictor of second-language vocabulary learning. *Developmental Psychology, 32,* 867–873.

Chevalier, T. M., Parrila, R., Ritchie, K. C., & Deacon, S. H. (2015). The role of meta-cognitive reading strategies, metacognitive study and learning strategies, and behavioral study and learning strategies in predicting academic success in students with and without a history of reading difficulties. *Journal of Learning Disabilities.* DOI: 10.1177/0022219415.

Chiu, M. M., & Chow, B. W. Y. (2010). Culture, motivation, and reading achievement: High school students in 41 countries. *Learning and Individual Differences, 20,* 579–592.

Chiu, M. M., & McBride-Chang, C. (2006). Gender, context, and reading: A comparison of students in 43 countries. *Scientific Studies of Reading, 10,* 331–362.

Chiu, M. M., McBride-Chang, C., & Lin, D. (2012). Ecological, psychological, and cognitive components of reading difficulties: Testing the component model of reading in fourth graders across 38 countries. *Journal of Learning Disabilities, 45,* 391–405.

Chung, K. K. H., & Ho, C. S. H. (2009). Second language learning difficulties in Chinese children with dyslexia: What are the reading-related cognitive skills that contribute to English and Chinese word reading? *Journal of Learning Disabilities, 43,* 194–211.

Clément, R., & Kruidenier, B. G. (1983). Orientations in second language acquisition: I. The effects of ethnicity, milieu, and target language on their emergence. *Language Learning, 33*, 273–291.

Cobb, C. (2015). Is French immersion a special education loophole? . . . And does it intensify issues of accessibility and exclusion? *International Journal of Bilingual Education and Bilingualism, 18*, 170–187.

Coltheart, M. (1978). Lexical access in simple reading tasks. In G. Underwood (Ed.), *Strategies of information processing* (pp. 151–216). London: Academic Press.

Corno, L. (1993). The best-laid plans: Modern conceptions of volition and educational research. *Educational Researcher, 22*, 14–22.

Cowan, N. (1995). *Attention and memory*. Oxford, England: Oxford University Press.

Cowan, N. (1999). An embedded-process model of working memory. In A. Miyake & P. Shah (Eds.), *Models of working memory: Mechanisms of active maintenance and executive control* (pp. 62–101). Cambridge: Cambridge University Press.

Craik, F. I., & Lockhart, R. S. (1972). Levels of processing: A framework for memory research. *Journal of Verbal Learning and Verbal Behaviour, 11*, 671–684.

Crawford, L., & Tindal, G. (2004). Effects of a read-aloud modification on a standardized reading test. *Exceptionality, 12*, 89–106.

Crombie, M. (1997). The effects of specific learning difficulties (dyslexia) on the learning of a foreign language at school. *Dyslexia, 3*, 27–47.

Csizér, K. (2010). Diszlexia és nyelvtanuási motiváció [Dyslexia and language learning motivation]. In J. Kormos & K. Csizér (Eds.), *Idegennyelv-elsajátítás és részképességzavarok* [Foreign language acquisition and learning disabilities] (pp. 49–76). Budapest: Eötvös Kiadó.

Csizér, K., & Dörnyei, Z. (2005). The internal structure of language learning motivation and its relationship with language choice and learning effort. *Modern Language Journal, 89*, 19–36.

Csizér, K., & Kormos, J. (2008). The relationship of inter-cultural contact and language learning motivation among Hungarian students of English and German. *Journal of Multilingual and Multicultural Development, 29*, 30–48.

Csizér, K., Kormos, J., & Sarkadi, Á. (2010). The dynamics of language learning attitudes and motivation: Lessons from an interview study with dyslexic language learners. *Modern Language Journal, 97*, 470–487.

Cummins, J. (1981). Empirical and theoretical underpinnings of bilingual education. *Journal of Education, 163*, 16–29.

Cummins, J. (1991). Conversational and academic language proficiency in bilingual contexts. In J. Hulstifn & J. Matter (Eds.), *Reading in two languages* (pp. 75–89). Amsterdam, Netherlands: Free University Press.

Cummins, J. (2000). *Language, power, and pedagogy: Bilingual children in the crossfire*. Clevedon, UK: Multilingual Matters.

Cummins, J. (2012). The intersection of cognitive and sociocultural factors in the development of reading comprehension among immigrant students. *Reading & Writing, 25*, 1973–1990.

Daneman, M., & Carpenter, P. A. (1980). Individual differences in working memory and reading. *Journal of Verbal Learning and Verbal Behaviour, 19*, 450–466.

Davies, A. (2010). Test fairness: A response. *Language Testing, 27*, 171–176.

Deci, E. L., Koestner, R., & Ryan, R. M. (1999). A meta-analytic review of experiments examining the effects of extrinsic rewards on intrinsic motivation. *Child Development, 72*, 1135–1150.

Deci, E. L., & Ryan, R. M. (1985). *Intrinsic motivation and self-determination in human behavior.* New York: Plenum.

de Graaff, R. (1997). The eXperanto experiment: Effects of explicit instruction on second language acquisition. *Studies in Second Language Acquisition, 19,* 249–276.

de Jong, P. F., & van der Leij, A. (2003). Developmental changes in the manifestation of a phonological deficit in dyslexic children learning to read a regular orthography. *Journal of Educational Psychology, 95,* 22–40.

DeKeyser, R. M. (1997). Beyond explicit rule learning. *Studies in Second Language Acquisition, 19,* 195–221.

Denckla, M. B., & Rudel, R. G. (1976). Naming of objects by dyslexic and other learning-disabled children. *Brain and Language, 3,* 1–15.

Denton, C. A., Wexler, J., Vaughn, S., & Bryan, D. (2008). Intervention provided to linguistically diverse middle school students with severe reading difficulties. *Learning Disabilities Research & Practice, 23(2),* 79–89.

Department of Education and Science. (2005). *Guidance to support pupils with dyslexia and dyscalculia* (No. DfES 0512/2001). London: HMSO.

Dóczi, B., & Kormos, J. (2016). *Longitudinal developments in vocabulary knowledge and lexical organization.* Oxford: Oxford University Press.

Dörnyei, Z. (2001). *Teaching and researching motivation.* Harlow: Longman.

Dörnyei, Z. (2005). *The psychology of the language learner: Individual differences in second language acquisition.* Mahwah, NJ: Lawrence Erlbaum.

Dörnyei, Z. (2010). The relationship between language aptitude and language learning motivation. In E. Macaro (Ed.), *Continuum companion to second language acquisition* (pp. 247–267). London: Continuum.

Dörnyei, Z., Csizér, K., & Németh, N. (2006). *Motivational dynamics, language attitudes and language globalisation: A Hungarian perspective.* Clevedon, England: Multilingual Matters.

Dörnyei, Z., & Tseng, W.-T. (2009). Motivational processing in interactional tasks. In A. Mackey & C. Polio (Eds.), *Multiple perspectives on interaction: Second language research in honor of Susan M. Gass* (pp. 117–134). London: Routledge.

Downey, D., Snyder, L., & Hill, B. (2000). College students with dyslexia: Persistent linguistic deficits and foreign language learning. *Dyslexia, 6,* 101–111.

Dufva, M., & Voeten, M. (1999). Native language literacy and phonological memory as prerequisites for learning English as a foreign language. *Applied Psycholinguistics, 20,* 329–348.

Dunn, L. M. (1968). Special education for the mildly retarded—Is much of it justifiable? *Exceptional Children, 35,* 5–22.

Eaude, T. (1999). *Learning difficulties: Dyslexia, bullying and other issues.* London: Letts Educational.

Educational Testing Service. (2002). *ETS standards for quality and fairness.* Princeton, NJ: Author.

Ehlers, S., & Gillberg, C. (1993). The epidemiology of Asperger's syndrome: A total population study. *Journal of Child Psychology and Psychiatry, 34,* 1327–1350.

Ehri, L. C. (1997). Learning to read and learning to spell are one and the same, almost. In C. Perfetti, L. Rieben & M. Fayol (Eds.), *Learning to spell: Research, theory, and practice* (pp. 237–269). Mahwah, NJ: Lawrence Erlbaum.

Ehri, L. C. (2005). Learning to read words: Theory, findings, and issues. *Scientific Studies of Reading, 9,* 167–188.

Ehri, L. C., & Wilce, L. S. (1980). The influence of orthography on readers' conceptualization of the phonemic structure of words. *Applied Psycholinguistics, 1*, 371–385.

Elbeheri, G., Everatt, J., Mahfoudhi, A., Abu Al-Diyar, M., & Taibah, N. (2011). Orthographic processing and reading comprehension among Arabic speaking mainstream and LD children. *Dyslexia, 17*(2), 123–142.

Elbro, C., & Arnbak, E. (1996). The role of morpheme recognition and morphological awareness in dyslexia. *Annals of Dyslexia, 46*, 209–240.

Elbro, C., Daugaard, H. T., & Gellert, A. S. (2012). Dyslexia in a second language?—A dynamic test of reading acquisition may provide a fair answer. *Annals of Dyslexia, 62*, 172–185.

Elliott, M. (2013). Test taker characteristics. In A. Geranpayeh & L. Taylor (Eds.), *Examining listening: Research and practice in assessing second language listening* (pp. 36–76). Cambridge: Cambridge University Press.

Elliott, S. N., Kratochwill, T. R., & McKevitt, B. C. (2001). Experimental analysis of the effects of testing accommodations on the scores of students with and without disabilities. *Journal of School Psychology, 39*, 3–24.

Ellis, N. (2005). At the interface: Dynamic interactions of explicit and implicit language knowledge. *Studies in Second Language Acquisition, 27*, 305–352.

Ellis, N. C. (1994). Introduction: Implicit and explicit language learning—an overview. In N. Ellis (Ed.), *Implicit and explicit learning of languages* (pp. 1–31). London: Academic Press.

Ellis, N. C. (2002). Frequency effects in language acquisition: A review with implications for theories of implicit and explicit language acquisition. *Studies in Second Language Acquisition, 24*, 143–188.

Ellis, R. (1994). *The study of second language acquisition*. Oxford: Oxford University Press.

Ellis, R., & Shintani, N. (2014). *Exploring language pedagogy through second language acquisition research*. London: Routledge.

Engle, R. W., Laughlin, J. E., Tuholski, S. W., & Conway, A. (1999). Working memory, short-term memory, and general fluid intelligence: A latent-variable approach. *Journal of Experimental Psychology: General, 128*(3), 309–333.

Erlam, R. (2005). Language aptitude and its relationship to instructional effectiveness in second language acquisition. *Language Teaching Research, 9*, 147–171.

Everatt, J., Smythe, I., Adams, E., & Ocampo, D. (2000). Dyslexia screening measures and bilingualism. *Dyslexia, 6*, 42–56.

Eysenck, M. W. (1992). *Anxiety: The cognitive perspective*. Hove, UK: Erlbaum.

Eysenck, M. W., & Calvo, M. G. (1992). Anxiety and performance: The processing efficiency theory. *Cognition and Emotion, 6*, 409–434.

Eysenck, M. W., Derakshan, N., Santos, R., & Calvo, M. G. (2007). Anxiety and performance: Attentional control theory. *Emotion, 7*, 336–353.

Feldman, J., Kerr, B., & Streissguth, A. P. (1995). Correlational analyses of procedural and declarative learning performance. *Intelligence, 20*, 87–114.

Feuerstein, R. (1980). *Instrumental enrichment*. Baltimore, MD: University Park Press.

Field, J. (2013). Cognitive validity. In A. Geranpayeh & L. Taylor (Eds.), *Examining listening: Research and practice in assessing second language listening* (pp. 77–151). Cambridge: Cambridge University Press.

File, K. A., & Adams, R. (2010). Should vocabulary instruction be integrated or isolated? *TESOL Quarterly, 44*, 222–249.

Fletcher, J. M. (2012). Classification and identification of learning disabilities. In B. Wong & D. Butler (Eds.), *Learning about learning disabilities* (4th ed., pp. 1–26). New York, NY: Elsevier.

Fletcher, J. M., Francis, D. J., Boudousquie, A., Copeland, K., Young, V., Kalinowski, S., & Vaughn, S. (2006). Effects of accommodations on high stakes testing for students with reading disabilities. *Exceptional Children, 72*, 136–150.

Fletcher, J. M., Morris, R. D., & Lyon, G. R. (2004). Classification and definition of learning disabilities: An integrative perspective. In H. L. Swanson, K. R. Harris & S. Graham (Eds.), *Handbook of learning disabilities* (pp. 30–56). New York: Guilford.

Ford, M. (1992). *Motivating humans: Goals, emotions, and personal agency beliefs.* Newbury Park, CA: Sage.

Frederickson, N. (1993). Using soft systems methodology to rethink special educational needs. In A. Dyson & C. Gains (Eds.), *Rethinking special needs in mainstream schools: Towards the year 2000* (pp. 1–21). London: David Fulton.

Frederickson, N., & Cline, T. (2002). *Special educational needs, inclusion and diversity: A textbook.* Maidenhead, UK: Open University Press.

Frederickson, N., & Cline, T. (2009). *Special educational needs, inclusion and diversity: A textbook* (2nd ed.). Maidenhead, UK: Open University Press.

Frederickson, N., & Frith, U. (1998). Identifying dyslexia in bilingual children: A phonological approach with inner London Sylheti speakers. *Dyslexia, 4*, 119–131.

Frederickson, N., Frith, U., & Reason, R. (1997). *Phonological assessment battery.* Windsor, UK: NFER-Nelson.

Frick, P. J., Kamphaus, R. W., Lahey, B. B., Loeber, R., Christ, M., Hart, E., & Tannenbaum, L. E. (1991). Academic underachievement and the disruptive behavior disorder. *Journal of Consulting and Clinical Psychology, 59*, 289–294.

Fries, C. C. (1945). *Teaching and learning English as a foreign language.* Ann Arbor, MI: University of Michigan Press.

Frith, U. (1980). Unexpected spelling problems. In U. Frith (Ed.), *Cognitive processes in spelling* (pp. 495–515). London: Academic Press.

Frith, U. (1985). Beneath the surface of developmental dyslexia. In K. Patterson, M. Coltheart & J. Marshall (Eds.), *Surface dyslexia: Neuropsychological and cognitive studies of phonological reading* (pp. 301–330). Mahwah, NJ: Lawrence Erlbaum.

Frith, U. (1986). A developmental framework for developmental dyslexia. *Annals of Dyslexia, 36*, 69–81.

Frith, U. (1999). Paradoxes in the definition of dyslexia. *Dyslexia, 5*, 192–214.

Fuchs, L. S., & Fuchs, D. (1998). Treatment validity: A simplifying concept for reconceptualizing the identification of learning disabilities. *Learning Disabilities: Research and Practice, 4*, 204–219.

Fuchs, L. S., & Fuchs, D. (1999). Fair and unfair testing accommodations. *School Administrator, 56*, 24–29.

Ganschow, L., & Sparks, R. (1995). Effects of direct instruction in Spanish phonology on the native language skills and foreign language aptitude of at-risk foreign language learners. *Journal of Learning Disabilities, 28,* 107–120.

Ganschow, L., Sparks, R. L., Anderson, R., Javorshy, J., Skinner, S., & Patton, J. (1994). Differences in Language Performance among High-, Average-, and Low-Anxious College Foreign Language Learners. *The Modern Language Journal, 78*(1), 41–55.

Gardner, M. (2005). *Test of auditory processing skills.* Ann Arbor, MI: Academic Therapy Publications.

Gardner, R. C. (1985). *Social psychology and second language learning: The role of attitudes and motivation.* London: Edward Arnold.

Gardner, R. C. (2006). The socio-educational model of second language acquisition: A research paradigm. *EUROSLA Yearbook, 6*, 237–260.

Gardner, R. C., & Lambert, W. (1959). Motivational variables in second language acquisition. *Canadian Journal of Psychology, 13*, 266–272.

Gardner, R. C., & MacIntyre, P. D. (1993). On the measurement of affective variables in second language learning. *Language Learning, 43*, 157–194.

Garrett, P., & Young, R. F. (2009). Theorizing affect in foreign language learning: An analysis of one learner's responses to a communicative-based Portuguese course. *Modern Language Journal, 32*, 209–226.

Gass, S. (1997). *Input, interaction, and the second language learner.* Mahwah, NJ: Lawrence Erlbaum.

Gathercole, S. E. (1999). Cognitive approaches to the development of short-term memory. *Trends in Cognitive Sciences, 3*, 410–419.

Gathercole, S. E., Alloway, T. P., Kirkwood, H. J., Elliott, J. G., Holmes, J., & Hilton, K. A. (2008). Attentional and executive function behaviours in children with poor working memory. *Learning and Individual Differences, 18*, 214–223.

Gathercole, S. E., & Baddeley, A. D. (1990). Phonological memory deficits in language disordered children: Is there a causal connection? *Journal of Memory and Language, 29*, 336–360.

Genesee, F., Geva, E., Dressler, D., & Kamil, M. (2006). Synthesis: Cross-linguistic relationships. In D. August & T. Shanahan (Eds.), *Developing literacy in second-language learners: Report of the national literacy panel on language-minority children and youth* (pp. 153–174). Mahwah, NJ: Lawrence Erlbaum.

Georgiou, G. K., Parrila, R., & Kirby, J. R. (2009). RAN components and reading development from grade 3 to grade 5: What underlies their relationship? *Scientific Studies of Reading, 13*, 508–534.

Georgiou, G. K., Parrila, R., & Papadopoulos, T. C. (2008). Predictors of word decoding and reading fluency across languages varying in orthographic consistency. *Journal of Educational Psychology, 100*, 566–580.

Geranpayeh, A., & Taylor, L. (Eds.) (2013). *Examining listening: Research and practice in assessing second language listening.* Cambridge: Cambridge University Press.

Gerber, M., Jimenez, T., Leafstedt, J., Villaruz, J., & Richards, C. (2004). English reading effects of small-group intensive intervention in Spanish for K-1 English learners. *Learning Disabilities Research and Practice, 19*, 239–251.

Geva, E. (2006). Second-language oral proficiency and second-language literacy. In D. August & T. Shanahan (Eds.), *Developing literacy in second-language learners: Report of the national literacy panel on language-minority children and youth* (pp. 123–140). Mahwah, NJ: Lawrence Erlbaum.

Geva, E., & Lafrance, L. (2011). Linguistic and cognitive processes in the development of spelling in ELLs: L1 transfer, language proficiency, or cognitive processes. In A. Y. Durgunoglu & C. Goldenberg (Eds.), *Language and literacy development in bilingual settings* (pp. 245–279). London: Guilford Press.

Geva, E., & Massey-Garrison, A. (2013). A comparison of the language skills of ELLs and monolinguals who are poor decoders, poor comprehenders or normal readers. *Journal of Learning Disabilities, 46*, 387–401.

Geva, E., & Ryan, E. B. (1993). Linguistic and cognitive correlates of academic skills in first and second languages. *Language Learning, 43*, 5–42.

Geva, E., Wade-Woolley, L., & Shany, M. (1993). The concurrent development of spelling and decoding in two different orthographies. *Journal of Literacy Research, 25*, 383–406.

Geva, E., & Wiener, J. (2014). *Psychological assessment of culturally and linguistically diverse children and adolescents: A practitioner's guide.* New York: Springer Publishing Company.

Geva, E., & Yaghoub Zadeh, Z. (2006). Reading efficiency in native English-speaking and English-as-a-second-language children: The role of oral proficiency and underlying cognitive-linguistic processes. *Scientific Studies of Reading, 10,* 31–57.

Gillberg, C. (1989). Asperger's syndrome in 23 Swedish children. *Developmental Medicine and Child Neurology, 31,* 520–531.

Gillingham, A., & Stillman, B. (1960). *Remedial training for children with specific disabilities in reading, spelling, and penmanship.* Cambridge, MA: Educators Publishing Service.

Godfroid, A., Boers, F., & Housen, A. (2013). An eye for word: Gauging the role of attention in incidental L2 vocabulary acquisition by means of eye-tracking. *Studies in Second Language Acquisition, 35,* 483–517.

Goh, C. C. M. (2000). Cognitive perspective on language learners' listening comprehension problems. *System, 28,* 55–75.

Gold, B. T., Kim, C., Johnson, N. F., Kryscio, R. J., & Smith, C. D. (2013). Lifelong bilingualism maintains neural efficiency for cognitive control in aging. *Journal of Neuroscience, 33,* 387–396.

Gombert, J. E. (1992). *Metalinguistic development.* Chicago: University of Chicago Press.

Goswami, U., Thomson, J., Richardson, U., Stainthorp, R., Hughes, D., Rosen, S., & Scott, S. K. (2002). Amplitude envelope onsets and developmental dyslexia: A new hypothesis. *Proceedings of the National Academy of Sciences USA, 99,* 10911–10916.

Gough, P. B., & Tunmer, W. E. (1986). Decoding, reading and reading disability. *Remedial and Special Education, 7,* 6–10.

Granena, G., & Long, M. (Eds.) (2013). *Sensitive periods, language aptitude and ultimate L2 attainment.* Amsterdam: John Benjamins.

Gregg, N. (2009). *Assessment and accommodation of adolescents and adults with LD and AD/HD.* New York, NY: Guilford.

Gregg, N. (2011). Increasing access to learning for the adult basic education learner with learning disabilities: Evidence-based accommodation research. *Journal of Learning Disabilities, 45,* 47–63.

Gregg, N., Coleman, C., Davis, M., & Chalk, J. C. (2007). Timed essay writing: Implications for high-stakes tests. *Journal of Learning Disabilities, 40,* 306–318.

Gregg, N., Coleman, C., Stennett, B., & Davis, M. (2002). Discourse complexity of college writers with and without disabilities: A multidimensional analysis. *Journal of Learning Disabilities, 35,* 23–38.

Gregg, N., & Nelson, J. M. (2012). Meta-analysis on the effectiveness of extra time as a test accommodation for transitioning adolescents with learning disabilities more questions than answers. *Journal of Learning Disabilities, 45*(2), 128–138.

Grigorenko, E. L., Sternberg, R. J., & Ehrman, M. E. (2000). A theory based approach to the measurement of foreign language learning ability: The Canal-F theory and test. *Modern Language Journal, 84,* 390–405.

Gurney, P. (1988). *Self-esteem in children with special educational needs.* London: Routledge.

Hale, J., Alfonso, V., Berninger, V., Bracken, B., Christo, C., Clark, E., & Yalof, J. (2010). Critical issues in response-to-intervention, comprehensive evaluation, and specific learning disabilities identification and intervention: An expert white paper consensus. *Learning Disability Quarterly, 33,* 223–236.

Hambly, C., & Fombonne, E. (2012). The impact of bilingual environment on language development in children with autism spectrum disorders. *Journal of Autism and Developmental Disorders, 42,* 1342–1352.

Hansen, E. G., Mislevy, R. J., Steinberg, L. S., Lee, M. J., & Forer, D. C. (2005). Accessibility of tests for individuals with disabilities within a validity framework. *System*, *33*, 107–133.

Heath, S. B. (1983). *Ways with words: Language, life and work in communities and classrooms*. Cambridge: Cambridge University Press.

Helland, T., & Kaasa, R. (2005). Dyslexia in English as a second language. *Dyslexia*, *11*, 41–60.

Helwig, R., & Tindal, G. (2003). An experimental analysis of accommodation decisions on large-scale mathematics tests. *Exceptional Children*, *69*, 211–225.

Henning, G. (1987). *A guide to language testing: Development, evaluation, research*. Boston: Heinle and Heinle.

Hollenbeck, K., Tindal, G., & Almond, P. (1998). Teachers' knowledge of accommodations as a validity issue in high-stakes testing. *Journal of Special Education*, *32*, 175–183.

Hoover, W. A., & Gough, P. B. (1990). The simple view of reading. *Reading and Writing: An Interdisciplinary Journal*, *2*, 127–160.

Horwitz, E. K. (2000). It ain't over til it's over: On foreign language anxiety, first language deficits, and the confounding of variables. *The Modern Language Journal*, *84*, 256–259.

Horwitz, E. (2001). Language anxiety and achievement. *Annual Review of Applied Linguistics*, *21*, 112–126.

Horwitz, E. K., Horwitz, M. B., & Cope, J. A. (1986). Foreign language classroom anxiety. *Modern Language Journal*, *70*, 25–132.

Hu, M., & Nation, I. S. P. (2000). Vocabulary density and reading comprehension. *Reading in a Foreign Language*, *23*, 403–430.

Humphrey, N. (2002). Teacher and pupil ratings of self-esteem in developmental dyslexia. *British Journal of Special Education*, *29*, 29–36.

International Language Testing Association. (2000). *Code of ethics for ILTA*. Retrieved February 18, 2008 from http://www.iltaonline.com/code.pdf.

Jean, M., & Geva, E. (2012). Through the eyes and from the mouths of young heritage language learners: How children feel and think about their two languages and why. *TESL Canada Journal*, *29(6)*, 49–80.

Jeffries, S., & Everatt, J. (2004). Working memory: Its role in dyslexia and other specific learning difficulties. *Dyslexia*, *10*, 196–214.

Jegatheesan, B. (2011). Multilingual development in children with autism: Perspectives of South Asian Muslim immigrant parents on raising a child with a communicative disorder in multilingual contexts. *Bilingual Research Journal*, *34*, 185–200.

Jenkins, J. (2007). *English as a Lingua Franca: Attitude and identity*. Oxford: Oxford University Press.

Jiang, Y., & Chun, M. M. (2001). Selective attention modulates implicit learning. *The Quarterly Journal of Experimental Psychology*, *54A*, 1105–1124.

Jiménez, L., & Méndez, C. (1999). Which attention is needed for implicit sequence learning? *Journal of Experimental Psychology: Learning, Memory, and Cognition*, *25*, 236–259.

Johnson, E. S., Humphrey, M., Mellard, D. F., Woods, K., & Swanson, H. L. (2010). Cognitive processing deficits and students with specific learning disabilities: A selective meta-analysis of the literature. *Learning Disability Quarterly*, *33*, 3–18.

Joint Committee on Testing Practices. (1998, 2004). *Code of fair testing practices in education*. Washington, DC: Author.

Joshi, R. M., Binks, E., Hougen, M., Dahlgren, M. E., Ocker-Dean, E., & Smith, D. L. (2009). Why elementary teachers might be inadequately prepared to teach reading. *Journal of Learning Disabilities*, *42*, 392–402.

Juffs, A., & Harrington, M. W. (2011). Aspects of working memory in L2 learning. *Language Teaching: Reviews and Studies, 42,* 137–166.

Kane, M. T. (2004). Certification testing as an illustration of argument-based validation. *Measurement: Interdisciplinary Research and Perspectives, 2,* 135–170.

Kane, M. T. (2010). Validity and fairness. *Language Testing, 27,* 177–182.

Kanner, L. (1971). Follow up study of eleven children originally reported in 1943. *Journal of Autism and Schizophrenia, 1,* 119–145.

Kauffman, J. M. (1989). The regular education initiative as Reagan–Bush education policy: A trickle-down theory of education of the hard-to-teach. *Journal of Special Education, 23,* 256–278.

Kaufman, S. B., DeYoung, C. G., Gray, J. R., Jiménez, L., Brown, J., & Mackintosh, N. J. (2010). Implicit learning as an ability. *Cognition, 116,* 321–340.

Kelly, K., & Phillips, S. (2011). *Teaching literacy to learners with dyslexia: A multi-sensory approach.* New York: Sage.

Kendeou, P., Broek, P., Helder, A., & Karlsson, J. (2014). A cognitive view of reading comprehension: Implications for reading difficulties. *Learning Disabilities Research & Practice, 29,* 10–16.

Khalifa, H. (2005). Are test taker characteristics accounted for in Main Suite Reading papers? *Research Notes, 21,* 7–10.

Khalifa, H., & Weir, C. (2009). *Examining reading: Research and practice in assessing second language reading.* Cambridge: Cambridge University Press.

Kim, A., Vaughn, S., Klinger, J. K., Woodruff, A. L., Reutebuch, K. C., & Kouzekanani, K. (2006). Improving the reading comprehension of middle school students with disabilities through computer-assisted collaborative strategic reading. *Remedial and Special Education, 27,* 235–249.

Kintsch, W. (1998). *Comprehension: A paradigm for cognition.* Cambridge: Cambridge University Press.

Kirby, A., & Kaplan, B. J. (2003). *Specific learning difficulties.* Oxford: Health Press.

Kirby, J. R., Georgiou, G. K., Martinussen, R., & Parrila, R. (2010). Naming speed and reading: From prediction to instruction. *Reading Research Quarterly, 45,* 341–362.

Kirschner, P. A., Sweller, J., & Clark, R. E. (2006). Why minimal guidance during instruction does not work: An analysis of the failure of constructivist, discovery, problem-based, experiential, and inquiry-based teaching. *Educational Psychologist, 41,* 75–86.

Klingner, J. K., & Vaughn, S. (1996). Reciprocal teaching of reading comprehension strategies for students with learning disabilities who use English as a second language. *The Elementary School Journal, 96,* 275–293.

Koda, K. (2007). Reading and language learning: Crosslinguistic constraints on second language reading development. *Language Learning, 57(s1),* 1–44.

Koenig, J. A., & Bachman, L. F. (2004). *Keeping score for all: The effects of inclusion and accommodation policies on large-scale educational assess.* Washington, DC: National Academies Press.

Kontra, E., & Kormos, J. (2010). Tanítási módszerek és technikák a diszlexiások idegen-nyelv-oktatásában [Methods and techniques in teaching dyslexic language learners]. In J. Kormos & K. Csizér (Eds.), *Rész-képességzavarok és idegen nyelvtanulás* [Learning disabilities and foreign language acquisition] (pp. 163–184). Budapest: Eötvös Kiadó.

Kormos, J. (2013). New conceptualizations of language aptitude in second language attainment. In G. Granena & M. Long (Eds.), *Sensitive periods, language aptitude and ultimate L2 attainment* (pp. 131–152). Amsterdam: John Benjamins.

Kormos, J. (2015). Individual differences in speech production. In J. Schwieter (Ed.), *Cambridge handbook of bilingual language processing* (pp. 369–388). Cambridge: Cambridge University Press.

Kormos, J., & Csizér, K. (2008). Age-related differences in the motivation of learning English as a foreign language: Attitudes, selves and motivated learning behaviour. *Language Learning, 58,* 327–355.

Kormos, J., & Csizér, K. (2010). A comparison of the foreign language learning motivation of Hungarian dyslexic and non-dyslexic students. *International Journal of Applied Linguistics, 20,* 232–250.

Kormos, J., Csizér, K., & Sarkadi, Á. (2009). The language learning experiences of students with dyslexia: Lessons from an interview study. *Innovation in Language Learning and Teaching, 3,* 115–130.

Kormos, J., Kiddle, T., & Csizér, K. (2011). System of goals, attitudes and self-related beliefs in second language learning motivation. *Applied Linguistics, 32,* 495–516.

Kormos, J., & Kontra, H. E. (2008). Hungarian teachers' perceptions of dyslexic language learners. In J. Kormos & E. H. Kontra (Eds.), *Language learners with special needs: An international perspective* (pp. 189–213). Clevedon: Multilingual Matters.

Kormos, J., & Mikó, A. (2010). Diszlexia és az idegen-nyelvtanulás folyamata [Dyslexia and the process of second language acquisition]. In J. Kormos & K. Csizér (Eds.), *Idegennyelv-elsajátítás és részképességzavarok* [Foreign language acquisition and learning disabilities] (pp. 49–76). Budapest: Eötvös Kiadó.

Kormos, J., Orosz, V., & Szatzker, O. (2010). Megfigyelések a diszlexiás nyelvtanulók idegennyelv-tanulásáról: A terepmunka tanulságai [Observations on teaching foreign languages to dyslexic students: Lessons from a field-study]. In J. Kormos & K. Csizér (Eds.), *Rész-képességzavarok és idegen nyelvtanulás* [Learning disabilities and foreign language acquisition] (pp. 185–211). Budapest: Eötvös Kiadó.

Kormos, J., & Sáfár, A. (2008). Phonological short term-memory, working memory and foreign language performance in intensive language learning. *Bilingualism: Language and Cognition, 11,* 261–271.

Kormos, J., Sarkadi, Á., & Kálmos, B. (2010). Részképesség-zavarok és nyelvvizsgáztatás [Specific learning difficulties and language testing]. In J. Kormos & K. Csizér (Eds.), *Rész-képességzavarok és idegen nyelvtanulás* [Learning disabilities and foreign language acquisition] (pp. 77–96). Budapest: Eötvös Kiadó.

Kormos, J., & Smith, A.-M. (2012). *Teaching languages to students with specific learning differences.* Bristol: Multilingual Matters.

Kosciolek, S., & Ysseldyke, J. E. (2000). *Effects of a reading accommodation on the validity of a reading test* (Technical Rep. No. 28). Minneapolis: University of Minnesota, National Center on Educational Outcomes.

Kozey, M., & Siegel, S. L. (2008). Definitions of learning disabilities in Canadian provinces and territories. *Canadian Psychology, 49,* 162–171.

Krashen, S. D. (1981). *Second language acquisition and second language learning.* Oxford: Oxford University Press.

Kubota, R. (1998). Voices from the margin: Second and foreign language teaching approaches from minority perspectives. *Canadian Modern Language Review, 54,* 394–412.

Kunnan, A. J. (2004). Test fairness. In M. Milanovic & C. Weir (Eds.), *European language testing in a global context: Proceedings of the ALTE Barcelona conference* (pp. 27–48). Cambridge: Cambridge University Press.

Kunnan, A. J. (2010). Test fairness and Toulmin's argument structure. *Language Testing, 27,* 183–189.

Kyllonen, P. C., & Lajoie, S. P. (2003). Reassessing aptitude: Introduction to a special issue in honor of Richard E. Snow. *Educational Psychologist, 38,* 79–83.

Laitusis, C. C. (2008). State reading assessments and inclusion of students with dyslexia. *Perspectives on Language and Literacy, 34,* 31–33.

Laitusis, C. C. (2010). Examining the impact of audio presentation on tests of reading comprehension. *Applied Measurement in Education, 23,* 153–167.

Landerl, K., Ramus, F., Moll, K., Lyytinen, H., Leppänen, P. H., Lohvansuu, K., . . . Kunze, S. (2013). Predictors of developmental dyslexia in European orthographies with varying complexity. *Journal of Child Psychology and Psychiatry, 54,* 686–694.

Landerl, K., & Wimmer, H. (2008). Development of word reading fluency and spelling in a consistent orthography: An 8-year follow-up. *Journal of Educational Psychology, 100,* 150–161.

Landerl, K., Wimmer, H., & Frith, U. (1997). The impact of orthographic consistency on dyslexia: A German-English comparison. *Cognition, 63,* 315–334.

Lantolf, J. P., & Poehner, M. E. (2011). Dynamic assessment in the classroom: Vygotskian praxis for second language development. *Language Teaching Research, 15,* 11–33.

Laufer, B. (1989). What percentage of text-lexis is essential for comprehension? In C. Lauren & M. Nordman (Eds.), *Special language: From humans to thinking machines* (pp. 316–323). Clevedon, England: Multilingual Matters.

Laufer, B. (2006). Comparing focus on form and focus on form S in second language vocabulary learning. *Canadian Modern Language Review, 63,* 149–166.

Lawrence, D. (1996). *Enhancing self-esteem in the classroom.* London: Paul Chapman.

Leafstedt, J. M., Richards, C. R., & Gerber, M. M. (2004). Effectiveness of explicit phonological awareness instruction for at risk English learners. *Learning Disabilities Research & Practice, 19,* 252–261.

Lervåg, A., Bråten, I., & Hulme, C. (2009). The cognitive and linguistic foundations of early reading development: A Norwegian latent variable longitudinal study. *Developmental Psychology, 45,* 764–781.

Lesaux, N. K., & Siegel, L. S. (2003). The development of reading in children who speak English as a second language. *Developmental Psychology, 39,* 1005–1019.

Limbos, M. M., & Geva, E. (2001). Accuracy of teacher assessments of second-language students at risk for reading disability. *Journal of Learning Disabilities, 34,* 136–151.

Linck, J. A., Osthus, P., Koeth, J. T., & Bunting, M. F. (2014). Working memory and second language comprehension and production: A meta-analysis. *Psychonomic Bulletin and Review, 21,* 861–883.

Lindgrén. S.-A., & Laine, M. (2011). Cognitive linguistics performances of multilingual university students suspected of dyslexia. *Dyslexia, 17,* 184–200.

Lindsey, K. A., Manis, F. R., & Bailey, C. E. (2003). Prediction of first-grade reading in Spanish-speaking English-language learners. *Journal of Educational Psychology, 95,* 482–494.

Lovett, M. W. (1987). A developmental approach to reading disability: Accuracy and speed criteria of normal and deficient reading skill. *Child Development, 58,* 234–226.

Lovett, M. W., De Palma, M., Frijters, J., Steinbach, K., Temple, M., Benson, N., & Lacerenza, L. (2008). Interventions for reading difficulties a comparison of response to intervention by ELL and EFL struggling readers. *Journal of Learning Disabilities, 41,* 333–352.

Lovett, M. W., Steinbach, K. A., & Frijters, J. C. (2000). Remediating the core deficits of developmental reading disability: A double-deficit perspective. *Journal of Learning Disabilities, 33,* 334–358.

MacArthur, C., & Graham, S. (1987). Learning disabled students' composing under three methods of text production: Handwriting, word processing, and dictation. *Journal of Special Education, 21*, 22–42.

MacIntyre, P. (2002). Motivation, anxiety and emotion in second language acquisition. In P. Robinson (Ed.), *Individual differences and instructed language learning* (pp. 45–68). Amsterdam: John Benjamins.

MacIntyre, P. D. (1995). How does anxiety affect second language learning? A reply to Sparks and Ganschow: MLJ Response Article. *Modern Language Journal, 79*, 90–99.

MacIntyre, P. D., & Gardner, R. C. (1994). The subtle effects of language anxiety on cognitive processing in the second language. *Language Learning, 44*, 283–305.

Mackey, A., Philp, J., Egi, T., Fujii, A., & Tatsumi, T. (2002). Individual differences in working memory, noticing of interactional feedback, and L2 development. In P. Robinson (Ed.), *Individual differences and instructed language learning* (pp. 181–209). Amsterdam: John Benjamins.

Mackey, A., & Sachs, R. (2012). Older learners in SLA research: A first look at working memory, feedback, and L2 development. *Language Learning, 61*, 704–740.

Mahony, D., Singson, M., & Mann, V. (2000). Reading ability and sensitivity to morphological relations. *Reading and Writing: An Interdisciplinary Journal, 12*, 191–218.

Mann, V., & Wimmer, H. (2002). Phoneme awareness and pathways into literacy: A comparison of German and American children. *Reading and Writing, 15*, 653–682.

Martin, K. I., & Ellis, N. C. (2012). The roles of phonological STM and working memory in L2 grammar and vocabulary learning. *Studies in Second Language Acquisition, 34*, 379–413.

Martinussen, R., & Tannock, R. (2006). Working memory impairments in children with attention-deficit hyperactivity disorder with and without comorbid language learning disorders. *Journal of Clinical and Experimental Neuropsychology, 28*, 1073–1094.

Masgoret, A.-M., & Gardner, R. C. (2003). Attitudes, motivation and second language learning: A meta-analysis of studies conducted by Gardner and associates. *Language Learning, 53*, 123–163.

McKevitt, B. C., & Elliott, S. N. (2003). Effects and perceived consequences of using read-aloud and teacher-recommended testing accommodations on a reading achievement test. *School Psychology Review, 32*(4), 583–601.

McMullen, J. L. (2013). *Autism and additional language acquisition in Hong Kong.* Unpublished Masters Dissertation. Lancaster University, UK.

McNulty, M. (2003). Dyslexia and the life course. *Journal of Learning Disabilities, 36*, 363–381.

Melby-Lervåg, M., & Lervåg, A. (2014). Reading comprehension and its underlying components in second-language learners: A meta-analysis of studies comparing first- and second-language learners. *Psychological Bulletin, 140*, 409–430.

Meloy, L. L., Deville, C., & Frisbie, D. A. (2002). The effect of a read-aloud accommodation on test scores of students with and without a learning disability in reading. *Remedial and Special Education, 23*, 248–255.

Mercer, S. (2011). *Towards an understanding of language learner self-concept.* Dordrecht: Springer.

Messick, S. (1989). Validity. In R. Linn (Ed.), *Educational measurement* (3rd ed., pp. 13–103). Washington, DC: American Council on Education.

Miles, T. R. (1997). *Bangor dyslexia test* (2nd ed.). Cambridge: Learning Development Aids.

Miles, T. R., & Haslum, M. N. (1986). Dyslexia: Anomaly or normal variation. *Annals of Dyslexia, 36*, 103–117.

Miller, C. A., Kail, R., Leonard, L. B., & Tomblin, J. B. (2001). Speed of processing in children with specific language impairment. *Journal of Speech Language and Hearing Research, 44*, 416–433.

Miyake, A., Friedman, N. P., Emerson, M. J., Witzki, A. H., Howerter, A., & Wager, T. D. (2000). The unity and diversity of executive functions and their contributions to complex "frontal lobe" tasks: A latent variable analysis. *Cognitive Psychology, 41*, 49–100.

Moll, K., & Landerl, K. (2009). Double dissociation between reading and spelling deficits. *Scientific Studies of Reading, 13*, 359–382.

Monsell, S. (1996). Control of mental processes. In V. Bruce (Ed.), *Unsolved mysteries of the mind: Tutorial essays in cognition* (pp. 93–148). Mahwah, NJ: Lawrence Erlbaum.

Morris, N., & Jones, D. M. (1990). Memory updating in working memory: The role of the central executive. *British Journal of Psychology, 81*, 111–121.

Nation, I. S. P. (1990). *Teaching and learning vocabulary.* New York, NY: Newbury House.

Nation, K. (2005). Children's reading comprehension difficulties. In M. J. Snowing & C. Hulme (Eds.), *The science of reading: A handbook* (pp. 248–266). Oxford: Blackwell.

National Institute of Adult Continuing Education. (2009). *Making a difference for adult learners: NIACE policy impact report 2009.* Retrieved from http://www.niace.org.uk/sites/default/files/documents/policy/NIACE%20Policy%20Report%2028pg.pdf.

National Institute of Child Health and Human Development. (2000). *Report of the National Reading Panel: Teaching children to read: An evidence-based assessment of the scientific research literature on reading and its implications for reading instruction.* Retrieved August 8, 2015 from http://www.nichd.nih.gov/publications/nrp/smallbook.htm.

Ndlovu, K., & Geva, E. (2008). Writing abilities in first and second language learners with and without reading disabilities. In J. Kormos & E. H. Kontra (Eds.), *Language learners with special needs: An international perspective* (pp. 36–62). Clevedon: Multilingual Matters.

Nicolson, R. I., & Fawcett, A. J. (1990). Automaticity: A new framework for dyslexia research? *Cognition, 35*, 159–182.

Nicolson, R. I., & Fawcett, A. J. (2008). *Dyslexia, learning, and the brain.* Cambridge, MA: MIT Press.

Nijakowska, J. (2008). An experiment with direct multisensory instruction in teaching word reading and spelling to Polish dyslexic learners of English. In J. Kormos & E. H. Kontra (Eds.), *Language learners with special needs: An international perspective* (pp. 130–157). Bristol, UK: Multilingual Matters.

Nijakowska, J. (2010). *Dyslexia in the foreign language classroom.* Bristol: Multilingual Matters.

Nijakowska, J. (2014). Dyslexia in the European EFL teacher training context. In M. Pawlak & L. Aronin (Eds.), *Essential topics in applied linguistics and multilingualism* (pp. 129–154). New York: Springer International Publishing.

Nijakowska, J., & Kormos, J. (2015). Foreign language teacher training on dyslexia: DysTEFL resources. In L. Peer & G. Reid (Eds.), *Multilingualism, literacy and dyslexia* (pp. 104–114). London: Routledge.

Noels, K. A., Clément, R., & Pelletier, L. G. (2001). Intrinsic, extrinsic, and integrative orientations of French Canadian learners of English. *Canadian Modern Language Review, 57*, 424–442.

Norbury, C. F., & Sparks, A. (2013). Difference or disorder? Cultural issues in understanding neurodevelopmental disorders. *Developmental Psychology, 49*, 45–58.

Norris, J. M., & Ortega, L. (2000). Effectiveness of L2 instruction: A research synthesis and quantitative meta-analysis. *Language Learning, 50*, 417–528.

Norton, B., & Toohey, K. (2011). Identity, language learning and social change. *Language Teaching, 44*, 412–446.

Norwich, B. (2007). *Dilemmas of difference, inclusion and disability: International perspectives and future directions.* London: Routledge.

Norwich, B. (2009). How compatible is the recognition of dyslexia with inclusive education? In G. Reid (Ed.), *The Routledge companion to dyslexia* (pp. 177–193). London: Routledge.

Novick, J. M., Hussey, E., Teubner-Rhodes, S., Harbison, J. I., & Bunting, M. F. (2014). Clearing the garden-path: Improving sentence processing through cognitive control training. *Language and Cognitive Processes, 29*, 186–217.

Oakhill, J., Cain, K., & Bryant, P. E. (2003). The dissociation of word reading and text comprehension: Evidence from component skills. *Language and Cognitive Processes, 18*, 443–468.

Oakhill, J., Cain, K., & Elbro, C. (2014). *Understanding and teaching reading comprehension: A handbook.* London: Routledge.

Oakhill, J., Hartt, J., & Samols, D. (2005). Levels of comprehension monitoring and working memory in good and poor comprehenders. *Reading and Writing, 18*, 657–686.

O'Brien, I., Segalowitz, N., Collentine, J., & Freed, B. (2007). Phonological memory and lexical narrative, and grammatical skills in second language oral production by adult learners. *Applied Psycholinguistics, 27*, 377–402.

Ohashi, J. K., Mirenda, P., Marinova-Todd, S., Hambly, C., Fombonne, E., Szatmari, P., . . . Volden, J. (2012). Comparing early language development in monolingual- and bilingual-exposed young children with autism spectrum disorders. *Research in Autism Spectrum Disorders, 6*, 890–897.

Organization for Economic Cooperation and Development (OECD). (2009). *PISA 2009 results: What students know and can do: Student performance in reading, mathematics and science* (Vol. 1). Retrieved from http://www.oecd-ilibrary.org/education/pisa-2009-results-what-students-know-and-can-do9789264091450-en;jsessionid=7g7khrnsjphc2.x-oecd-live-01.

O'Sullivan, B., & Green, A. (2011). Test taker characteristics. In L. Taylor (Ed.), *Examining speaking: Research and practice in assessing second language speaking* (pp. 36–64). Cambridge: Cambridge University Press.

Paivio, A. (1991). Dual coding theory: Retrospect and current status. *Canadian Journal of Psychology, 45*, 255–287.

Pajares, F., & Schunk, D. H. (2005). Self-efficacy and self-concept beliefs. In H. W. Marsh, R. G. Craven & D. M. McInerney (Eds.), *International advances in self research* (Vol. 2, pp. 95–121). Greenwich, CT: Information Age Publishing.

Palinscar, A. S., & Brown, A. L. (1984). Reciprocal teaching of comprehension-fostering and comprehension-monitoring activities. *Cognition and Instruction, 1*, 117–175.

Papagno, C., & Vallar, G. (1995). Verbal short-term memory and vocabulary learning in polyglots. *Quarterly Journal of Experimental Psychology, 48A(1)*, 98–107.

Partanen, M., & Siegel, L. S. (2014). Long-term outcome of the early identification and intervention of reading disabilities. *Reading and Writing, 27*, 665–684.

Pavlenko, A., & Lantolf, J. P. (2000). Second language learning as participation and the (re)construction of selves. In J. P. Lantolf (Ed.), *Sociocultural theory and second language learning* (pp. 155–177). New York: Oxford University Press.

Pennington, B. F. (2006). From single to multiple deficit models of developmental disorders. *Cognition, 101*, 385–413.

Pennington, B. F., & Bishop, D. (2009). Relations among speech, language, and reading disorders. *Annual Review of Psychology, 60,* 283–306.

Pennington, B. F., Cardoso-Martins, C., Green, P. A., & Lefly, D. L. (2001). Comparing the phonological and double deficit hypotheses for dyslexia. *Reading and Writing, 14,* 707–755.

Pennington, B. F., & Olson, R. (2005). Genetics of dyslexia. In M. Snowling & C. Hulme (Eds.), *The science of reading: A handbook* (pp. 453–472). Oxford: Blackwell.

Perfetti, C. (2007). Reading ability: Lexical quality to comprehension. *Scientific Studies of Reading, 8,* 293–304.

Perfetti, C. A., Beck, I., Bell, L., & Hughes, C. (1987). Phonemic knowledge and learning to read are reciprocal: A longitudinal study of first grade children. *Merrill-Palmer Quarterly, 33,* 283–319.

Perfetti, C. A., & Harris, L. N. (2013). Universal reading processes are modulated by language and writing system. *Language Learning and Development, 9,* 296–316.

Perfetti, C. A., Liu, Y., & Tan, L. H. (2005). The lexical constituency model: Some implications of research on Chinese for general theories of reading. *Psychological Review, 12,* 43–59.

Perfetti, C. A., Zhang, S., & Berent, I. (1992). Reading in English and Chinese: Evidence for a "universal" phonological principle. In R. Frost & L. Katz (Eds.), *Orthography, phonology, morphology, and meaning* (pp. 227–248). Amsterdam: North-Holland.

Petersen, J., Marinova-Todd, S. H., & Mirenda, P. (2012). An exploratory study of lexical skills in bilingual children with autism spectrum disorder. *Journal of Autism and Developmental Disorders, 42,* 1499–1503.

Peterson, R. L., & Pennington, B. F. (2015). Developmental dyslexia. *Annual Review of Clinical Psychology, 11,* 283–307, Advance Access.

Pfenninger, S. (2015). MSL in the digital ages: Effects and effectiveness of computer-mediated intervention for FL learners with dyslexia. *Studies in Second Language Learning and Teaching, 1,* 109–133.

Pfenninger, S. E. (in press). Taking L3 learning by the horns: Benefits of computer-mediated intervention for dyslexic school children. *Innovation in Language Learning and Teaching (ahead-of-print),* 1–18. DOI: 10.1080/17501229.2014.959962.

Phillips, S., Kelly, K., & Symes, L. (2013). *Assessment of learners with dyslexic type difficulties.* London: Sage.

Phillips, S. E. (1994). High-stakes testing accommodations: Validity versus disabled rights. *Applied Measurement in Education, 7,* 93–120.

Piechurska-Kuciel, E. (2008). Input, processing and output anxiety in students with symptoms of developmental dyslexia. In J. Kormos & E. H. Kontra (Eds.), *Language learners with special needs: An international perspective* (pp. 86–109). Bristol: Multilingual Matters.

Pitoniak, M. J., & Royer, J. M. (2001). Testing accommodations for examinees with disabilities: A review of psychometric, legal, and social policy issues. *Review of Educational Research, 71,* 53–104.

Pižorn, K., & Erbeli, F. (2013). Assessment accommodations n EFL reading competence for Slovene EFL students with specific reading differences. In D. Tsagari & G. Spanoudis (Eds.), *Assessing L2 students with learning and other disabilities* (pp. 189–206). Newcastle upon Tyne, UK: Cambridge Scholars.

Podhajski, B., Mather, N., Nathan, J., & Sammons, J. (2009). Professional development in scientifically based reading instruction, teacher knowledge and reading outcomes. *Journal of Learning Disabilities, 42,* 403–417.

Prainsson, K. O. (2012). *Autism and second language acquisition.* Unpublished Bachelors Dissertation. University of Iceland, Reykjavik: Skemman.

Pressley, M., Almasi, J., Schuder, T., Bergman, J., Hite, S., El-Dinary, P. B., & Brown, R. (1994). Transactional instruction of comprehension strategies: The Montgomery County, Maryland, SAIL program. *Reading & Writing Quarterly: Overcoming Learning Difficulties, 10,* 5–19.

Puolakanaho, A., Ahonen, T., Aro, M., Eklund, K., Leppänen, P. H., Poikkeus, A. M., . . . Lyytinen, H. (2007). Very early phonological and language skills: Estimating individual risk of reading disability. *Journal of Child Psychology and Psychiatry, 48,* 923–931.

Ravid, D., & Malenky, D. (2001). Awareness of linear and nonlinear morphology in Hebrew: A developmental study. *First Language, 21,* 25–56.

Reber, A. S. (1993). *Implicit learning and tacit knowledge: An essay on the cognitive unconscious.* Oxford: Clarendon Press.

Reber, A. S., Walkenfeld, F. F., & Hernstadt, R. (1991). Implicit and explicit learning: Individual differences and IQ. *Journal of Experimental Psychology: Learning, Memory, and Cognition, 17,* 888–896.

Reis, S. M., McGuire, J. M., & Neu, T. W. (2000). Compensation strategies used by high-ability students with learning disabilities who succeed in college. *Gifted Child Quarterly, 44,* 123–134.

Riddick, B. (1996). *Living with dyslexia.* London: Routledge.

Riddick, B. (2001). Dyslexia and inclusion: Time for a social model of disability perspective? *International Studies in Sociology of Education, 11,* 223–236.

Robinson, P. (1997). Individual differences and the fundamental similarity of implicit and explicit adult second language learning. *Language Learning, 47,* 45–99.

Robinson, P. (2001). Individual differences: Cognitive abilities, aptitude complexes and learning conditions in second language acquisition. *Second Language Research, 17,* 368–392.

Robinson, P. (2002). Effects of individual differences in intelligence, aptitude and working memory on adult incidental SLA: A replication and extension of Reber, Walkenfeld and Hernstadt, 1991. In P. Robinson (Ed.), *Individual differences and instructed language learning* (pp. 211–266). Amsterdam: John Benjamins.

Robinson, P. (2005a). Aptitude and second language acquisition. *Annual Review of Applied Linguistics, 25,* 45–73.

Robinson, P. (2005b). Cognitive abilities, chunk-strength, and frequency effects in implicit artificial grammar and incidental L2 learning: Replications of Reber, Walkenfeld, and Hernstadt (1991) and Knowlton and Squire (1996) and their relevance for SLA. *Studies in Second Language Acquisition, 27,* 235–268.

Rooke, M. (2016). *Creative successful dyslexic: 23 high achievers share their stories.* London: Jessica Kingsley.

Ross, D. M., & Ross, S. A. (1976). *Hyperactivity: Research, theory, and action.* New York, NY: Wiley.

Ruthruff, E., Van Selst, M., Johnston, J. C., & Remington, R. (2006). How does practice reduce dual-task performance: Structural limitation or strategic postponement? *Psychological Research, 70,* 125–142.

Ryan, R. M., & Deci, E. L. (2000). Self-determination theory and the facilitation of intrinsic motivation, social development, and well-being. *American Psychologist, 55,* 68–78.

Saeigh-Haddad, E., & Geva, E. (2008). Morphological awareness, phonological awareness, and reading in English-Arabic bilingual children. *Reading and Writing: An Interdisciplinary Journal, 21,* 481–504.

Sáfár, A., & Kormos, J. (2008). Revisiting problems with foreign language aptitude. *International Review of Applied Linguistics in Language Teaching, 46*, 113–136.

Samson, J. F., & Lesaux, N. K. (2009). Language-minority learners in special education: Rates and predictors of identification for services. *Journal of Learning Disabilities, 42*, 248–162.

Sarkadi, Á. (2008). Vocabulary learning in dyslexia—The case of a Hungarian learner. In J. Kormos & E. H. Kontra (Eds.), *Language learners with special needs: An international perspective* (pp. 110–129). Clevedon: Multilingual Matters.

Sato, E., & Jacobs, B. (1992). From input to intake: Towards a brain-based perspective of selective attention. *Issues in Applied Linguistics, 3*, 267–293.

Sawyer, M., & Ranta, L. (2001). Aptitude, individual differences, and instructional design. In P. Robinson (Ed.), *Cognition and second language instruction* (pp. 319–353). Cambridge: Cambridge University Press.

Scammacca, N. K., Roberts, G., Vaughn, S., & Stuebing, K. K. (2015). A meta-analysis of interventions for struggling readers in grades 4–12: 1980–2011. *Journal of Learning Disabilities, 48*, 369–390.

Scarborough, H. (2001). Connecting early language and literacy to later reading (dis)abilities: Evidence, theory, and practice. In S. B. Neuman & D. K. Dickinson (Eds.), *Handbook of early literacy* (pp. 97–110). New York, NY: Guilford Press.

Scarborough, H. S., & Dobrich, W. (1990). Development of children with early delay. *Journal of Speech and Hearing Research, 33*, 70–83.

Schmidt, R. (1990). The role of consciousness in second language learning. *Applied Linguistics, 11*, 129–158.

Schneider, E., & Crombie, M. (2003). *Dyslexia and foreign language learning*. London: Routledge.

Schneider, E., & Evers, T. (2009). Linguistic intervention techniques for at-risk English language learners. *Foreign Language Annals, 42*, 55–76.

Schneider, E., & Ganschow, L. (2000). Dynamic assessment and instructional strategies for learners who struggle to learn a foreign language. *Dyslexia, 6*, 72–82.

Schoonen, R., Snellings, P., Stevenson, M., & van Gelderen, A. (2009). Towards a blueprint of the foreign language writer: The linguistic and cognitive demands of foreign language writing. In R. M. Manchon (Ed.), *Writing in foreign language contexts: Learning, teaching and research* (pp. 77–101). Bristol: Multilingual Matters.

Schulte, A. A., Elliott, S. N., & Kratochwill, T. R. (2001, March). Effects of testing accommodations on students' standardized mathematics test scores: An experimental analysis. *School Psychology Review, 30*, 527–547.

Schumann, J. (1998). *The neurobiology of affect in language*. Malden, MA: Blackwell.

Seidlhofer, B. (2005). English as a lingua franca. *ELT Journal, 59*, 339–341.

Service, E. (1992). Phonology, working memory and foreign language learning. *Quarterly Journal of Experimental Psychology, 45A*, 21–50.

Service, E., & Kohonen, V. (1995). Is the relation between phonological memory and foreign language learning accounted for by vocabulary acquisition? *Applied Psycholinguistics, 16*, 155–172.

Seymour, P. H. K., Aro, M., & Erskine, J. M. (2003). Foundation literacy acquisition in European orthographies. *British Journal of Psychology, 94*, 143–174.

Share, D., & Levin, I. (1999). Learning to read and write in Hebrew. In M. Harris & G. Hatano (Eds.), *A cross linguistic perspective on learning to read* (pp. 89–111). Cambridge: Cambridge University Press.

Share, D. L. (1995). Phonological recoding and self-teaching. *Cognition, 55*, 151–218.

Share, D. L., Jorm, A. F., Maclean, R., & Matthews, R. (1984). Sources of individual differences in reading acquisition. *Journal of Educational Psychology, 76*, 1309–1324.

Sharwood Smith, M. (1993). Input enhancement in instructed SLA. *Studies in Second Language Acquisition, 15*, 165–179.

Shavelson, R. J., Hubner, J. J., & Stanton, G. C. (1976). Self-concept: Validation of construct interpretations. *Review of Educational Research, 46*, 407–441.

Shaw, S. D., & Weir, C. J. (2007). *Examining writing: Research and practice in assessing second language writing*. Cambridge: Cambridge University Press.

Shaywitz, S. (2003). *Overcoming dyslexia: A new and complete science-based program for reading problems at any level*. New York: Alfred Knopf.

Shepard, L., Taylor, G., & Betebenner, D. (1998). Inclusion of limited-English proficient students in Rhode Island's Grade 4 Mathematics Performance Assessment (CSE Tech. Rep. No. 486). Los Angeles: University of California, National Center for Research on Evaluation, Standards, and Student Testing.

Siegel, L. S. (2008). Morphological awareness skills of English language learners and children with dyslexia. *Topics in Language Disorders, 28*, 15–27.

Sireci, S. G., Scarpati, S. E., & Li, S. (2005). Test accommodations for students with disabilities: An analysis of the interaction hypothesis. *Review of Educational Research, 75*, 457–490.

Skehan, P. (1986). Cluster analysis and the identification of learner types. In V. Cook (Ed.), *Experimental approaches to second language acquisition* (pp. 81–94). Oxford: Pergamon.

Skehan, P. (1998). *A cognitive approach to language learning*. Oxford: Oxford University Press.

Skutnabb-Kangas, T. (2000). *Linguistic genocide in education- or worldwide diversity and human rights?* Mahwah, NJ: Lawrence Erlbaum.

Smith, A.-M. (2013). Developing cognitive assessments for multilingual learners. In D. Tsagari & G. Spanoudis (Eds.), *Assessing L2 students with learning and other disabilities* (pp. 151–168). Newcastle upon Tyne, UK: Cambridge Scholars.

Snow, R. E. (1992). Aptitude theory: Yesterday, today, and tomorrow. *Educational Psychologist, 27*, 5–32.

Snowling, M., & Hulme, C. (2012). Annual research review: The nature and classification of reading disorders—A commentary on proposals for DSM-5. *Journal of Child Psychology and Psychiatry, 53*, 593–607.

Snowling, M. J. (2000). *Dyslexia* (2nd ed.). Oxford: Blackwell.

Snowling, M. J. (2008). Specific disorders and broader phenotypes: The case of dyslexia. *The Quarterly Journal of Experimental Psychology, 61*, 142–156.

Spada, N., & Tomita, Y. (2010). Interactions between type of instruction and type of language feature: A meta-analysis. *Language Learning, 60*, 263–308.

Sparks, R. L. (2001). Foreign language learning problems of students classified as learning disabled and non-learning disabled: Is there a difference? *Topics in Language Disorders, 21*, 38–54.

Sparks, R. L. (2012). Individual differences in L2 learning and long-term L1–L2 relationships. *Language Learning, 62*, 5–27.

Sparks, R. L., Artzer, M., Patton, J., Ganschow, L., Miller, K., Hordubay, D. J., & Walsh, G. (1998). Benefits of multisensory structured language instruction for at-risk foreign language learners: A comparison study of high school Spanish students. *Annals of Dyslexia, 48*, 239–270.

Sparks, R. L., & Ganschow, L. (1991). Foreign language learning differences: Affective or native language aptitude differences? *Modern Language Journal, 75,* 3–16.

Sparks, R. L., & Ganschow, L. (1993). The impact of native language learning problems on foreign language learning: Case study illustrations of the linguistic coding deficit hypothesis. *Modern Language Journal, 77,* 58–74.

Sparks, R., & Ganschow, L. (2001). Aptitude for learning a foreign language. *Annual Review of Applied Linguistics, 21,* 90–111.

Sparks, R. L., Ganschow, L., Fluharty, K., & Little, S. (1995). An exploratory study on the effects of Latin on the native language skills and foreign language aptitude of students with or without disabilities. *The Classical Journal, 91,* 165–184.

Sparks, R. L., Ganschow, L., Kenneweg, S., & Miller, K. (1991). Use of an orton-gillingham approach to teach a foreign language to dyslexic/learning-disabled students: Explicit teaching of phonology in a second language. *Annals of Dyslexia, 41,* 96–118.

Sparks, R. L., Ganschow, L., & Patton, J. (2008). L1 and L2 literacy, aptitude, and affective variables as discriminators among high and low-achieving L2 learners. In J. Kormos & E. Kontra (Eds.), *Language learners with special needs: An international perspective* (pp. 11–35). London: Multilingual Matters.

Sparks, R. L., Ganschow, L., Pohlman, J., Skinner, S., & Artzer, M. (1992). The effects of a multisensory, structured language approach on the native and foreign language aptitude skills of at-risk foreign language learners. *Annals of Dyslexia, 42,* 25–53.

Sparks, R. L., Humbach, N., & Javorsky, J. (2008). Comparing high and low achieving, LD, and ADHD foreign language learners: Individual and longitudinal differences. *Learning and Individual Differences, 18,* 29–43.

Sparks, R. L., & Javorsky, J. (1999). Students classified as learning disabled and the college foreign language requirement: Replication and comparison studies. *Journal of Learning Disabilities, 32,* 329–349.

Sparks, R. L., Patton, J., Ganschow, L., & Humbach, N. (2009). Long-term relationships among early language skills, L2 aptitude, L2 affect, and later L2 proficiency. *Applied Psycholinguistics, 30,* 725–755.

Sparks, R. L., Patton, J., Ganschow, L., Humbach, N., & Javorsky, J. (2006). Native language predictors of foreign language proficiency and foreign language aptitude. *Annals of Dyslexia, 56,* 129–160.Sparks, R. L., Patton, J., Ganschow, L., Humbach, N., & Javorsky, J. (2008). Early first-language reading and spelling skills predict later second-language reading and spelling skills. *Journal of Educational Psychology, 100,* 162–174.

Sparks, R., Philips, L., Ganschow, L., & Javorsky, J. (1999). Students classified as learning disabled and the college foreign language requirement: A quantitative analysis. *Journal of Learning Disabilities, 32,* 566–580.

Speciale, G., Ellis, N. C., & Bywater, T. (2004). Phonological sequence learning and short-term store capacity determine second language vocabulary acquisition. *Applied Psycholinguistics, 25,* 293–321.

Spielberger, C. D. (1983). *Manual for the state-trait anxiety inventory.* Palo Alto, CA: Consulting Psychologists Press.

Spolsky, B. (1989). *Conditions for second language learning.* Oxford: Oxford University Press.

Spolsky, B. (2004). *Language policy.* Cambridge: Cambridge University Press.

Stanovich, K. E. (1988). Explaining the differences between the dyslexic and the garden-variety poor reader: The phonological-core variable-difference model. *Journal of Learning Disabilities, 21,* 590–604.

Steffler, D., Varnhagen, C. K., Friesen, C. K., & Treiman, R. (1998). There's more to children's spelling than the errors they make: Strategic and automatic processes for one-syllable words. *Journal of Educational Psychology, 90*, 492–505.

Swain, M. (1995). Three functions of output in second language learning. In G. Cook & B. Seidlhofer (Eds.), *Principle and practice in applied linguistics: Studies in honour of H. G. Widdowson* (pp. 125–144). Oxford: Oxford University Press.

Swan, D., & Goswami, U. (1997). Phonological awareness deficits in developmental dyslexia and the phonological representations hypothesis. *Journal of Experimental Child Psychology, 66*, 18–41.

Swanson, H. L., & Hoskyn, M. (1998). Experimental intervention research on students with learning disabilities: A meta-analysis of treatment outcomes. *Review of Educational Research, 68*, 277–321.

Swanson, H. L., & Lussier, C. (2001). A selective synthesis of the experimental literature on dynamic assessment. *Review of Educational Research, 71*, 321–361.

Szatmari, P. (1992). The epidemiology of attention-deficit hyperactivity disorders. In G. Weiss (Ed.), *Child and adolescent psychiatric clinics of North America: Attention-deficit hyperactivity disorder* (pp. 361–372). Philadelphia: Saunders.

Talbott, E., Lloyd, J. W., & Tankersley, M. (1994). Effects of reading comprehension interventions for students with learning disabilities. *Learning Disability Quarterly, 17*, 223–232.

Tallal, P. (2004). Improving language and literacy is a matter of time. *Nature Reviews Neuroscience, 5*, 721–728.

Tallal, P., Curtiss, S., & Kaplan, R. (1988). The San Diego longitudinal study: Evaluating the outcomes of preschool impairments in language development. In S. G. Gerber Mencher (Ed.), *International perspectives on communication disorders* (pp. 86–126). Washington, DC: Gallaudet University Press.

Tallal, P., & Piercy, M. (1973). Developmental aphasia: Impaired rate of nonverbal processing as a function of sensory modality. *Neuropsychologia, 11*, 389–398.

Tannock, R. (2013). Rethinking ADHD and LD in DSM-5: Proposed changes in diagnostic criteria. *Journal of Learning Disabilities, 46*, 5–25.

Taylor, L., & Geranpayeh, A. (2013). Conclusions and recommendations. In A. Geranpayeh & L. Taylor (Eds.), *Examining listening: Research and practice in assessing second language listening* (pp. 322–334). Cambridge: Cambridge University Press.

Taylor, L., & Khalifa, H. (2013). Assessing students with disabilities: Voices from the stakeholder community. In D. Tsagari & G. Spanoudis (Eds.), *Assessing L2 students with learning and other disabilities* (pp. 229–252). Newcastle upon Tyne: Cambridge Scholars.

Taylor, L. M., Hume, I. R., & Welsh, N. (2011). Labelling and self-esteem: The impact of using specific vs. generic labels. *Educational Psychology: An International Journal of Experimental Educational Psychology, 30*, 191–202.

Teale, W. H., & Sulzby, E. (1986). *Emergent literacy: Writing and reading.* Norwood, NJ: Ablex.

Thomas, G., & Loxley, A. (2007). *Deconstructing special education.* Maidenhead, UK: Open University Press.

Thompson, S., Blount, A., & Thurlow, M. (2002). *A summary of research on the effects of test accommodations: 1999 through 2001* (Technical Rep. No. 34). Minneapolis: University of Minnesota, National Center on Educational Outcomes. Retrieved June 4, 2015 from http://education.umn.edu/NCEO/OnlinePubs/Technical34.htm.

Tian, L., & Macaro, E. (2012). Comparing the effect of teacher codeswitching with English-only explanations on the vocabulary acquisition of Chinese university students: A lexical focus-on-form study. *Language Teaching Research, 16*, 361–385.

Tobias, S. (1986). Anxiety and cognitive processing of instruction. In R. Schwarzer (Ed.), *Self related cognition in anxiety and motivation* (pp. 35–54). Hillsdale, NJ: Erlbaum.

Trainin, G., & Swanson, H. L. (2005). Cognition, metacognition, and achievement of college students with learning disabilities. *Learning Disability Quarterly, 28*, 261–272.

Treiman, R., & Kessler, B. (2005). Writing systems and spelling development. In M. J. Snowing & C. Hulme (Eds.), *The science of reading: A handbook* (pp. 120–134). Oxford: Blackwell.

Truscott, J., & Sharwood Smith, M. (2011). Input, intake and consciousness. *Studies in Second Language Acquisition, 33*, 497–528.

Tunmer, W. E., & Chapman, J. W. (2012). The simple view of reading redux. *Journal of Learning Disabilities, 45*, 453–466.

Tunmer, W. E., & Hoover, W. (1993). Components of variance models of language-related factors in reading disability: A conceptual overview. In M. Joshi & C. K. Leong (Eds.), *Reading disabilities: Diagnosis and component processes* (pp. 135–173). Dordrecht, Netherlands: Kluwer.

Tunmer, W. E., Nesdale, A. R., & Wright, A. D. (1987). Syntactic awareness and reading acquisition. *British Journal of Developmental Psychology, 5*, 25–34.

Turner, M. (2008). *Dyslexia portfolio assessment.* GL Assessment, NZ.CER.

Turvey, M. T., Feldman, L. B., & Lukatela, G. (1984). The Serbo-Croatian orthography constrains the reader to a phonologically analytic strategy. In L. Henderson (Ed.), *Orthographies and reading* (pp. 81–89). Mahwah, NJ: Lawrence Erlbaum.

Ullman, M. T., & Pierpont, E. I. (2005). Specific language impairment is not specific to language: The procedural deficit hypothesis. *Cortex, 41*, 399–433.

United Nations. (2006). *Convention on the rights of persons with disabilities* [Online]. Retrieved August 15, 2012 from http://www.un.org/disabilities/documents/convention/convopt prot-e.pdf.

Van Gelderen, A., Schoonen, R., De Glopper, K., Hulstijn, J., Simis, A., Snellings, P., & Stevenson, M. (2004). Linguistic knowledge, processing speed, and metacognitive knowledge in first- and second-language reading comprehension: A componential analysis. *Journal of Educational Psychology, 96*, 19–30.

Vellutino, F. R. (1979). *Dyslexia: Theory and research.* Cambridge, MA: MIT Press.

Vellutino, F. R., Scanlon, D. M., Small, S., & Fanuele, D. P. (2006). Response to intervention as a vehicle for distinguishing between children with and without reading disabilities: Evidence for the role of kindergarten and first-grade interventions. *Journal of Learning Disabilities, 39*, 157–169.

Vinegrad, M. (1994). A revised adult dyslexia check list. *Educare, 48*, 21–23.

Wagner, R. K., Torgesen, J. K., & Raschotte, C. A. (1999). *Comprehensive test of phonological processing.* Austin, TX: Pro-ed.

Wang, X., Georgiou, G. K., Das, J. P., & Li, Q. (2012). Cognitive processing skills and developmental dyslexia in Chinese. *Journal of Learning Disabilities, 45*, 526–537.

Washburn, E. K., Joshi, R. M., & Cantrell, E. B. (2011). Are preservice teachers prepared to teach struggling readers? *Annals of Dyslexia, 61*, 21–43.

Webb, S. (2007). The effect of repetition on vocabulary knowledge. *Applied Linguistics, 28*, 46–65.

Wechsler, D., & Stone, C. P. (2009). *Wechsler Memory Scale (WMS-IV)* (4th ed.). New York: Psychological Corporation.

White, L., Spada, N., Lightbown, P. M., & Ranta, L. (1991). Input enhancement and L2 question formation. *Applied Linguistics, 12,* 416–432.

Widdowson, H. G. (1993). *The ownership of English: IATEFL annual conference report, plenaries 1993.* Whitstable: IATEFL.

Wight, M. C. S. (2015). Students with learning disabilities in the foreign language environment and the practice of exemptions. *Foreign Language Annals, 48,* 39–55.

Willcutt, E. G., Doyle, A. E., Nigg, J. T., Faraone, S. V., & Pennington, B. F. (2005). Validity of the executive function theory of attention-deficit/hyperactivity disorder: A meta-analytic review. *Biological Psychiatry, 57,* 1336–1346.

Willcutt, E. G., Pennington, B. F., Chhabildas, N. A., Olson, R. K., & Hulslander, J. L. (2005). Neuropsychological analyses of comorbidity between RD and ADHD: In search of the common deficit. *Developmental Neuropsychology, 27,* 35–78.

Williams, J. N. (1999). Memory, attention, and inductive learning. *Studies in Second Language Acquisition, 21,* 1–48.

Willows, D. M., & Ryan, E. B. (1986). The development of grammatical sensitivity and its relationship to early reading achievement. *Reading Research Quarterly, 21,* 253–266.

Wimmer, H., & Goswami, U. (1994). The influence of orthographic consistency on reading development—Word recognition in English and German children. *Cognition, 51,* 91–103.

Wimmer, H., & Mayringer, H. (2002). Dysfluent reading in the absence of spelling difficulties: Aspecific disability in regular orthographies. *Journal of Educational Psychology, 94,* 272–277.

Wimmer, H., Mayringer, H., & Landerl, K. (2000). The double-deficit hypothesis and difficulties in learning to read a regular orthography. *Journal of Educational Psychology, 92,* 668–680.

Wing, L. (1981). Asperger's syndrome: A clinical account. *Psychological Medicine, 11,* 115–130.

Wire, V. (2005). Autistic Spectrum Disorders and learning foreign languages. *Support for Learning, 20,* 123–128.

Wolf, M. (1991). Naming speed and reading: The contribution of the cognitive neurosciences. *Reading Research Quarterly, 26,* 123–140.

Wolf, M., & Bowers, P. G. (1999). The double deficit hypothesis for the developmental dyslexias. *Journal of Educational Psychology, 91,* 1–24.

Xi, X. (2010). How do we go about investigating test fairness? *Language Testing, 27,* 147–170.

Yashima, T. (2002). Willingness to communicate in a second language: The Japanese EFL context. *Modern Language Journal, 86,* 54–66.

Yeung, S. S., Siegel, L. S., & Chan, C. K. (2013). Effects of a phonological awareness program on English reading and spelling among Hong Kong Chinese ESL children. *Reading and Writing, 26,* 681–704.

Zametkin, A. J., Nordahl, T. E., Gross, M., King, A. C., Semple, W. E., Rumsey, J., . . . Cohen, R. M. (1990). Cerebral glucose metabolism in adults with hyperactivity of childhood onset. *New England Journal of Medicine, 323,* 1361–1366.

Ziegler, J., & Goswami, U. (2005). Reading acquisition, developmental dyslexia and skilled reading across languages: A psycholinguistic grain size theory. *Psychological Bulletin, 31,* 3–29.

Ziegler, J., & Goswami, U. (2006). Becoming literate in different languages: Similar problems, different solutions. *Developmental Science, 9,* 426–453.

Ziegler, J. C., Bertrand, D., Tóth, D., Csépe, V., Reis, A., Faísca, L., . . . Blomert, L. (2010). Orthographic depth and its impact on universal predictors of reading: A cross-language investigation. *Psychological Science, 21,* 551–559.

Ziegler, J. C., Perry, C., Jacobs, A. M., & Braun, M. (2001). Identical words are read differently in different languages. *Psychological Science, 12,* 379–384.

Zimmerman, B. J. (1989). A social cognitive view of self-regulated academic learning. *Journal of Educational Psychology, 81,* 329–339.

Zuriff, G. E. (2000). Extra examination time for students with learning disabilities: An examination of the maximum potential thesis. *Applied Measurement in Education, 13,* 99–117.

INDEX

9 781138 911796